# A Path through Revelation

Bernard M. Woodland

E 38th St Press
Cary, NC

*A Path through Revelation*
© Copyright 2011 by Bernard M. Woodland
First printing, 2011   [1]

ISBN 978-1-936935-00-0

Library of Congress control number: 2011925647

Published by: E 38th St Press
Cary, NC
e38thstpress@hotmail.com

Permission granted to copy portions in accordance with sections 107-117 of title 17, U.S. code

Front cover photograph: *A Path in Bond Park* (Cary, NC)
© Copyright 2010 by Bernard Woodland

Back cover photograph: *Dad in Park* (thanks Nadya!)
© Copyright 2011 by Bernard Woodland

Scripture taken from the NEW AMERICAN STANDARD BIBLE®,
© Copyright 1960, 1962, 1963, 1968, 1971, 1972, 1973, 1975, 1977, 1995 by The Lockman Foundation
Used by permission. (www.Lockman.org)

*Cisco* is a trademark of Cisco Systems®

*Motorola* is a trademark of Motorola Mobility® and Motorola Solutions®

*PowerPoint*® is a trademark of Microsoft Corporation®

# Contents

Preface .................................................................... v

Part I    The Messages to the Churches ................ 1
1.  Background ........................................................ 2
2.  The Vision of Jesus (1:1–1:10) .............................................. 5
3.  Introducing the Seven Churches (1:11-1:20) ..................... 9
4.  The Seven Churches (2:1) .................................................. 14
5.  Ephesus (2:2–2:7) ............................................................. 16
6.  Smyrna (2:8–2:11) ............................................................ 18
7.  Pergamum (2:12–2:17) ..................................................... 21
8.  Thyatira (2:18–2:25) ........................................................ 29
9.  Sardis (3:1–3:6) ................................................................ 35
10. Philadelphia (3:7–3:13) ................................................... 39
11. Laodicea (3:14–3:22) ....................................................... 43
12. John's Next Vision (4:1–4:11) .......................................... 45

Part II   Modes of the Judgment of God ........... 52
1.  Introduction .................................................................... 53
2.  The Flood: Archetype of God's Judgment ....................... 53
3.  Predestined Judgment .................................................... 61
4.  Active and Passive Judgment .......................................... 68
5.  Associative and Proxy Judgment ..................................... 77
6.  Binary Judgment .............................................................. 81
7.  Judgment by Provoking God's Holiness .......................... 84
8.  Delegate Judgment .......................................................... 87
9.  Thwarted Judgment ......................................................... 90
10. Judgment in the New Testament .................................... 91

Part III  The Visions .......................................... 99
1.  The Lamb Receives the Book (5:1–5:14) ....................... 100
2.  Seeking the Time of the Seals ........................................ 110
3.  The First Seal: The Hunter (6:1–6:2) ............................. 112
4.  The Second Seal: War (6:3–6:4) ..................................... 115
5.  The Third Seal: Famine (6:5–6:6) ................................... 118
6.  The Fourth Seal: The Grim Reaper (6:7–6:8) ................ 120
7.  The Fifth Seal: A Pause for the Martyrs (6:9–6:11) ........ 122
8.  The Sixth Seal: All Is Shaken (6:12–6:17) ...................... 127
9.  The Bond-Servants Are Sealed (7:1–7:8) ....................... 131
10. The Multitude of the Righteous from the Great Tribulation (7:9–7:17) ............................................................... 133
11. The Seventh Seal (8:1–8:13) .......................................... 137
12. The Fifth Angel and the One Who Destroys (9:1–9:12) . 140
13. The Sixth Angel (9:13–9:21) .......................................... 144

14. The Strong Angel with the Little Book (10:1–10:11) ....... 147
15. Measuring the Temple (11:1–11:2a) ................................ 150
16. The Two Witnesses (11:2b–11:19) .................................. 155
17. The Woman and Child (12:1–12:6) ................................. 158
18. The Battle in the Spirit World (12:7–12:17) ................... 162
19. The Two Beasts (13:1–13:15) ......................................... 168
20. The Mark of the Beast System (13:16–13:18) ................ 173
21. The New Song, the Final Warning, and the Wine Press (14:1–14:20) ..................................................................... 177
22. Finishing the Wrath of God (15:1–16:21) ....................... 185
23. Babylon the Mother of Harlots (17:1–17:5) ................... 189
24. The Mystery of the Woman (17:6–17:18) ....................... 193
25. The End of Babylon (18:1–19:3) .................................... 195
26. Long-Awaited Endings (19:4–19:21) ............................. 200
27. First, the Abyss, then the Lake of Fire (20:1–20:15) ...... 205
28. The New Replaces the Old (21:1–22:5) .......................... 210
29. The Final Message (22:6–22:21) .................................... 215

## Part IV        Epilogue ............................................. 218

## Back Sections ....................................................... 220

Appendix A: The Third Horseman's Cost of Living Increase 221
Appendix B: Practical Difficulties of 6:13 ............................ 223
Appendix C: The 144 Thousand from the Twelve Tribes ...... 224
Appendix D: Electronic Banking System Technology ........... 226
Notes 230
Abbreviations ........................................................................ 230
References ............................................................................. 231
Scripture Index ...................................................................... 232
Index ...................................................................................... 236

# Preface

Knowing that a stack of books have already been written about Revelation, that the schools of opinion themselves, and not just the opinions, are cataloged in these books, yet another work on the topic must bring something to the table that the others don't. In the hope that the reader is not offended at the audacious presumption, *A Path through Revelation* is unique. Passages that others gloss over, it relishes dwelling on. For this reason (and because, quite frankly, I don't care for end-time prophecy) *A Path* complements and supplements other works, rather than replaces them. This is not the end-all commentary on Revelation—I have not an inkling of motivation for that.

In any event, if I might recommend a section of the book, I recommend section one, the seven churches. Like an archaeologist, who takes a pile of bones and draws profound conclusions from them, I've attempted to squeeze the last drop of juice out of a handful of verses in order to present to the reader what went on in these churches, the impression if one were to visit them. Since this is the most relevant portion of Revelation, it should garner the most attention.

The mystery aside of what motivates one writer to dwell on one subject, while another shuns the same, I delve into areas others do not. Any difficult or awkward passage that doesn't come across well in English, is ambiguous, or is just plain hard to understand, I go after like a chimpanzee trying to crack a nut. And this partly because I've come to the conclusion that NT Greek courses are taught the same way an old college buddy of mine liked to go fishing: his idea of fishing was to stop at a bar on the way there and sit and talk about it with the locals. Too many books on Greek claim this or that, but don't reflect the reality of what one might find in the text. Too many in academia read these books and forego reading Greek.

To begin to understand Revelation, a lot of material must be drawn together and brought to bear, and this I've attempted to do—not necessarily to explain the great mysteries of Revelation as to explain the little mysteries, in the hope that, in a small way, I can equip others to crack the large ones. In doing so, I bring to bear a life's experience. I am an engineer and am therefore prepared to contribute technical insights that most, if not all, have missed. At least I assume the duty to do so, and I'll be delighted if I can add but a pebble to the collective heap of understanding, but to do so I must explore what others have not. That's alright, I live to do so.

Now, there are some surprises locked away in Revelation that many are unaware of, one of which is the portrayal of the inter-working of the Trinity. Many Christians, in my experience, don't have a working-understanding of the Trinity, to the point where it becomes a deficiency in their prayer life. And speaking of surprises, I even surprised myself by wandering into an area like predestination vs. man's free will. Quite unexpected.

But to the die-hard end-time enthusiasts, I recommend they read the sections on the first horseman, on the technology for a mark-of-the-beast system, on putting 666 on one's forehead, and perhaps on the whore of Babylon. And they read the examination of the symbolism of the metals found in the statue in Daniel's interpretation of Nebuchadnezzar's dream. And add to this list the army that comes out of the east, plus Gog and Magog.

Like Super Bowl entertainment for those who don't like football, for the reader who has no interest in end-time prophecy, there're enough side-shows—too many, actually. And, a little secret, there's plenty for a pastor to steal, who might be stuck on some obscure passage in Revelation, and who can't find answers in any other book. This one just might have it. If not a question on Revelation, (if I might flatter myself) there's plenty of fresh biblical commentary throughout the book to make it worthwhile to sniff through, should one be in the habit of doing so. I touch on all kinds of topics—I even talk about sex. Hey, how many books on Revelation can you find both the true interpretation of Luke 10:17-19 and the true meaning of sex?

For what it's worth, the epilogue, which fills Part IV in its entirety, replaced a full Part IV, one consisting of a few chapters. That Part IV was a message to the church in contemporary America, and the scathing tone exhausted my fortitude. After a few rounds of editing, I axed it. I hope never to resurrect it.

*

Thanks to my sister Winnie, for patiently reading the manuscript, and listening to the drone of my voice, as I thought through many ideas over the phone with her.

> Bernie Woodland
> January, 2011
> e38thstpress@hotmail.com

# Part I

## The Messages to the Churches

Part I: The Messages to the Churches

# 1. Background

From the time it was written, Revelation has confounded many, but this has not dissuaded them from wandering into the forest. Can the book be comprehended in its entirety? No—we see through a mirror dimly. It can, however, be understood more clearly, and this measure of hope beckons to pursue.

Revelation is, for the most part, a vision in the spiritual world of things to come. The apparitions don't necessarily correspond to any single earthly counterpart. Plus the time sequence isn't always linear or sequential, and the visions can span large intervals. And it's bizarre—so much so that, in the ancient days of Christianity, it was almost excluded from the Bible. This obfuscation can only be mitigated, at least in this present era, and for this reason Revelation ducks undetected into the shadows of mystery.

But a few sources of the enigma, these originating from the reader's distance of perspective in time, in culture, and in comprehension of Scripture, can be redressed. Let us now highlight these differences of perspective.

\*

Scholars have categorized Revelation as a piece of Jewish apocryphal literature, which works were common in the first century A.D., the time of John's composition. Though Revelation stands out by virtue of its position in the Bible, it's better understood by queuing it alongside its peers, and noting the commonality in the genre. But can a book of the Bible be inspired by the Holy Spirit, but yet be neatly categorized alongside other non-inspired books? Yes—and if David were alive today, and still composing Psalms, the music could be R&B. Inspiration works through the minds of human beings, the wheels of which travel in the ruts formed by the wagons of others. When viewed in the light of apocryphal literature, Revelation's weirdness, such as the Jezebel-prophetess in the church of Thyatira who commits fornication with the members of the congregation, or the claim that the devil himself is about to cast some of the Smyrnans into prison, is expected. Perhaps categorizing the book makes it less egregious, and therefore more palatable. In any event, unlike our world, the book's audience, the early Church, needed the comfort and assurance that a Holy Spirit-breathed work of apocryphal literature delivered, the same comfort found in Paul's epistle, 1 Thessalonians. Paul's first epistle has more in common with Revelation than a first perusal might suggest.

But, to look at the differences in various books of the NT, the epistles of Paul, and with them Luke's writings, differ when com-

## Part I: The Messages to the Churches

pared to the writings of John, James, or Matthew, so much so that at times they appear to contradict each other, an example being the debate between faith as seen by Romans vs. faith as seen by James. John's style of writing is indicative of his Semitic, near-eastern bent, as much of Jesus' teaching is also a product of the Semitic mindset. Paul's is a product of the Greek mindset, which is Western—the American and European. The Semitic mind works differently than our own, introducing an extra layer of complications to understanding Scripture. Hence, several of the parables are difficult to comprehend, and appear not to jive with Paul's teaching. All Scripture is equally inspired by the Holy Spirit, but the orientation of each writer influences what he's inspired to write. The Bible is incomplete without Jesus' teachings balanced by Paul's epistles, and vice-versa.

Naturally, the Western mind gravitates towards the NT passages written by the Western authors, and cowers from the Semitic authors. A case in point illustrates this: Bible study groups invariably choose a book like Romans or Hebrews and never 1 John. Romans has logic, order, sequence—it progresses like a thesis. On the other hand, 1 John makes broad generalizations, not caring to enumerate exceptions for the benefit of the reader, and blatantly contradicts itself, according to the Western mind, as it meanders from subject to subject. To illustrate this further, read the below passages, then mentally summarize what John had to say concerning sin:

> 1 John 1:8-10 If we say that we have no sin, we are deceiving ourselves and the truth is not in us.
> [9]If we confess our sins, He is faithful and righteous to forgive us our sins and to cleanse us from all unrighteousness.
> [10]If we say that we have not sinned, we make Him a liar and His word is not in us.
>
> 1 John 3:4-9 Everyone who practices sin also practices lawlessness; and sin is lawlessness.
> [5]You know that He appeared in order to take away sins; and in Him there is no sin.
> [6]No one who abides in Him sins; no one who sins has seen Him or knows Him.
> [7]Little children, make sure no one deceives you; the one who practices righteousness is righteous, just as He is righteous;
> [8]the one who practices sin is of the devil; for the devil has sinned from the beginning. The Son of God appeared for this purpose, to destroy the works of the devil.

*Part I: The Messages to the Churches*

⁹No one who is born of God practices sin, because His seed abides in him; and he cannot sin, because he is born of God.

Does a Christian have sin or does he not? If 1 John 1:10 infers that all Christians have sinned, doesn't that contradict 1 John 3:6? Doesn't 3:6 disqualify Christians from knowing God? This is John's style, and the reader would do well to familiarize himself with his other books before plunging into Revelation.

Another example of the Western vs. Semitic mindsets is Paul's teaching on divorce in 1 Cor. 7 contrasted to Jesus' Semitic statement about divorce in Matt. 5:31,32. Paul's instructions appear to contradict Jesus'. Because he's Western, he lists rules and handles exceptions in a somewhat lengthy discourse. In response to those using an OT Scripture to justify divorce, Jesus the Semite makes this short statement: divorce, absent unfaithfulness, equals adultery—forget all the reasoning, wrangling, and loopholes. Who's correct, Paul or Jesus? They both are. But divorce can—and should—be viewed from both perspectives, the Western and the Semitic. Here's a challenge for the reader. Listen to a sermon or find a book on divorce and observe whether the following holds: copious exposition from 1 Cor. 7; little, if any, from Matt. 5:31,32. Why? The Western mind finds solace in 1 Cor. 7, not Matt. 5.

\*

Too many have attempted to decipher Revelation in isolation, neglecting to develop the background prerequisite to understanding this book. Revelation is tethered to the OT. John was influenced by the books of Genesis, Ezekiel, Daniel, and Zechariah, and by the Law of Moses. Revelation can, in fact, be viewed as a continuation of these books. Unlike us, John, like most in antiquity, had no library of books at hand, his cache consisting of a small collection of scrolls. These he poured his hours of study into, rereading passages out of Ezekiel and Daniel until the words spoke to him after he snuffed out the evening's last candle. We, on the other hand, who might've read Ezekiel once, maybe twice, in a lifetime, have never had the words saturate in our minds like John, and consequently live in ignorance of the extent that he draws upon these. Part of the shadow of mystery that hangs over Revelation recedes after one invests the time to comprehend the OT.

In this way, the symbols and figures of speech are first unraveled in the OT, and from there carried over to Revelation, as some verses in Revelation are only understood after one has gleaned the figures of speech from the OT (and, for that matter, NT), and then recognized their reappearance in Revelation. Though the listing for NT translations consumes pages, yet in the midst of these versions there remain unexplored nuances. At times, the English wording is awkward, the translation needing exposition or needing supplemental historical or cultural elaboration. One is unprepared to address the symbolic meaning of the Apocalypse if one is mired in the strangeness of language and culture.

Though one of the more extreme cases in Scripture, Revelation is not the only section of the Bible that employs symbols and metaphors. Parts of the Bible are literal, parts are figurative. The question arises, when does one know when to take a passage literally and when not to? Some say that the Bible can be interpreted any way—any way of one's choosing. Leaving its imprint on theology, this philosophy arose during the twentieth century, when the symbolism in literature became so ambiguous that the reader could assert his interpretation according to any whim. The Bible's use of symbolism has consistency, and the more one studies the Scriptures, the more one discerns the pattern. Difficult passages in Revelation can be gauged against this template of comprehension; ancient Jewish culture and ritual can be learned. What's left after pouring Revelation through the sieve of language, culture, and alternate viewpoints are the nuggets of enigma that are locked away—though in plain sight by virtue of the words.

*

Let us now embark on an exegesis of this book, and as the passersby who, on a cold, wet night is lured by the flickering lights in the window of a hospitable tavern, so we'll take the detours off the beaten trail as they bid us to come, while on a path through Revelation.

## 2. The Vision of Jesus (1:1–1:10)

The title *Revelation* comes from the opening verse, "The Revelation of Jesus Christ", where the Greek word for "Revelation" is *apokalupsis,* hence the connotation that *apocalypse* has acquired to impending destruction. Tracing through the NT the usage of *revelation* and the alternate form *to reveal*, the word means *something that God makes known to man that is beyond his human ability to come to know apart from God's intervention*. It's no surprise that supernatural events such as prophecies, those concerning the future, must be revealed to mankind, but even the widely circulated and readily available knowledge of God must be revealed to us, sometimes in spite of us already knowing it in our heads. When Paul referred to an earlier time in his life, here in Galatians…

*Part I: The Messages to the Churches*

> Gal. 1:15 But when God, who had set me apart even from my mother's womb and called me through His grace, was pleased <sup>16</sup>to **reveal** His Son in me

...At that time he already had a familiarity with the doctrines of Christianity, while persecuting those in the Way. But this knowledge hadn't registered on him, and he yet needed for it to be revealed to him, which happened on the road to Damascus. The Book of Revelation is concerned with the entire gamut of revelation—knowledge beyond the human senses or comprehension.

> Rev 1:1 The Revelation of Jesus Christ, which God gave Him to show to His bond-servants, the things which must soon take place; and He sent and communicated it by His angel to His bond-servant John,
> <sup>2</sup>who testified to the word of God and to the testimony of Jesus Christ, even to all that he saw.
> <sup>3</sup>Blessed is he who reads and those who hear the words of the prophecy, and heed the things which are written in it; for the time is near.

In 1:3, "the time is near" is an indication that what's delivered in the vision will at a minimum begin to come to pass in the near future: the time of the early Church.

> 1:4 John to the seven churches that are in Asia: Grace to you and peace, from Him who is and who was and who is to come, and from the seven Spirits who are before His throne,
> <sup>5</sup>and from Jesus Christ, the faithful witness, the firstborn of the dead, and the ruler of the kings of the earth. To Him who loves us and released us from our sins by His blood—
> <sup>6</sup>and He has made us to be a kingdom, priests to His God and Father—to Him be the glory and the dominion forever and ever. Amen.

Note in 1:4,5 the terse summation of Christian doctrine. First, the reference to the Trinity: the Father ("Him who is and who was and who is to come"), the Holy Spirit, then the Son, Jesus Christ. *Jesus* refers to his humanity; *Christ* to his deity. He was always Christ, the only begotten Son of God, but at a specific point in time became Jesus, whom God relegated to a life of trials for his time on earth, in which he was obedient and faithful—the faithful witness.

*Part I: The Messages to the Churches*

His work resulted in his death, but he was resurrected ("the firstborn of the dead"), and released his followers, the "kings of the earth" in 1:5, from sin. Now his disciples are "priests to His God". By definition a priest acts as an intermediary between man and God. But another definition is this: one who has access to and is an attendant to the holy presence of God. *Priest* as used in 1:6 draws on the latter, and the service of the priesthood of believers is actuated through prayer, as the prayer of a Christ follower is his or her spiritual service in the presence of God.

> 1:7 BEHOLD, HE IS COMING WITH THE CLOUDS, and every eye will see Him, even those who pierced Him; and all the tribes of the earth will mourn over Him. So it is to be. Amen.
> [8]"I am the Alpha and the Omega," says the Lord God, "who is and who was and who is to come, the Almighty."

Verse 1:7 begins with a quote from Daniel, and the quotation refers to Jesus' Second Coming, a central Christian doctrine, as codified in the Nicene Creed, "he will come again to judge the living and the dead". Verse 1:7 also indicates that Jesus' Second Coming will be visible by all persons, including those who're already dead, and those who did not believe in him. The word "mourn" in 1:7 means a deeply felt regret, disappointment, or loss that's similar to when a person mourns over a death. Here it applies to all the disobedient—present, past, and future—and the anguish of sorrow they'll have at his Second Coming. Certainly this includes "even those who pierced him"—those who crucified Jesus instead of receiving him. Revelation is a judgment against them, the wicked; the grace period ends. Payback time begins.

Examining another verse related to the Second Coming, Heb. 9:28, "...so Christ also, having been offered once to bear the sins of many, will appear a second time for salvation without reference to sin, to those who eagerly await Him." The phrase, "without reference to sin", means that Jesus' Second Coming won't be as the Lamb of God who takes away the sin of the world. That work is finished. The Jesus who laid down his life so that wicked men would crucify him is coming to judge what was done to him, and to rescue his disciples on the earth. Likewise, the phrase "for salvation" in the context of Heb. 9:28 does not refer to salvation from sin, but Jesus in his Second Coming rescuing the Faithful from the devices of the wicked.

Notice that in 1:8 God the Father and God the Son are combined into one person. Normally, Jesus is the one referred to as both the

## Part I: The Messages to the Churches

*Lord* and the *Alpha and Omega*, whereas God the Father is the Almighty; "who is and who was and who is to come" a couple verses before (1:4) referred to the Father. Although the Father, Son and Holy Spirit are three distinct persons, they are one God, not three.

> 1:9 I, John, your brother and fellow partaker in the tribulation and kingdom and perseverance which are in Jesus, was on the island called Patmos because of the word of God and the testimony of Jesus.

Verse 1:9 says that John was "on" the island of Patmos. The word *on* is an alternative translation to *in*, but the translators judiciously chose *on* over *in*. If one were to visit Patmos today and see the spot where John had his visions, one would be in a cave, and this is why a few argue that *in* should be used, not *on*.

Some assert that it was prophesied at the end of John's Gospel (John 21:18-23) that John would not suffer martyrdom. According to church history, he was the only one of the twelve apostles not martyred. Instead, he was exiled to Patmos. The church historian Tertullian wrote that John had been boiled in oil, but miraculously survived; hence all twelve experienced martyrdom of a sort. There's considerable doubt of the validity of this account, however, seeing that it has no confirmation.

> 1:10 I was in the Spirit on the Lord's day, and I heard behind me a loud voice like the sound of a trumpet,

The phrase "in the Spirit" refers to when the Holy Spirit comes upon a person in a powerful way, sometimes accompanied by prophecies or other miraculous works. This is not obvious in English, but in Greek the phrase "in the Spirit" (*en pneumati*) is the same as what's used in 1 Cor. 12:3, "no one speaking by the Spirit of God says, 'Jesus is accursed'; and no one can say, 'Jesus is Lord,' except by the Holy Spirit", which verbatim from the Greek reads, "*en pneumati* God while speaking he says". To understand *in the Spirit* from 1:10, one must first decipher 1 Cor. 12:3. There Paul literally said that no one "in the Spirit" can say Jesus is accursed. Any person can curse Jesus when not in the Spirit, but cannot while in the Spirit. Drawing from the entire twelfth chapter, the Holy Spirit comes upon a person, and in this condition he or she will prophesy, perform healings, etc. Being in the Spirit doesn't happen that often—certainly not enough, as believers must yield to the Spirit for it to occur. For this reason it says in Ephesians not to grieve the Holy Spirit and in 1 Thess. 5 not to "quench" (KJV) the Holy Spirit. But when Christians are in the Spirit, the supernatural power of God is in manifestation; 1 Cor. 12 indicates that being in the Spirit is prerequisite for God to perform miracles through a believer, or, in the case of John, to receive a vision.

John was in the Spirit on "the Lord's day", which is Sunday. Perhaps John was in the middle of Sunday morning worship. No one knows. Neither is it known if others were present. John heard a voice like a trumpet, which (supported by other NT references) is used to alert and direct, rather than produce music per se. Up until recent times trumpets were a means of broadcasting orders to troops in combat (1 Cor. 14:8). Think of a cavalry soldier in a Western sounding a charge on his bugle. The voice John heard jarred his attention, and caused him to snap to. But the trumpet here also reminds one of God's appearance to Moses on Mt. Sinai (Exod. 19:16), as the Israelites congregated around the base. Manifesting himself in might and holiness, God's visitation was accompanied by thunder, lighting, and the sound of a trumpet. Jesus' appearance to John smacks of that same awe.

## 3. Introducing the Seven Churches (1:11-1:20)

The first of multiple commands from an unseen voice for John to write what he sees is given. Later in the nineteenth chapter it's revealed that the unseen voice is not Jesus. It's fair to assume that the voice who speaks to John telling him to write what he sees is the same throughout the series of visions. Perhaps this is the angel of 1:1. The voice tells him to write in a "book"; the word here is actually *scroll*. Books didn't exist then.

> 1:11 saying, "Write in a book what you see, and send it to the seven churches: to Ephesus and to Smyrna and to Pergamum and to Thyatira and to Sardis and to Philadelphia and to Laodicea."

In the fourth verse of chapter 1, John refers to the churches "in Asia". This is the Roman province of Asia—western Turkey—not the continent of Asia as we know it today. There were seven churches, presumably spun off from Paul's original seed planted in Ephesus. They were in close proximity to one another, and, according to Metzger, are listed in the same order in Revelation in which one would travel by road in order to visit each of them. Seeing that the cost of copying a scroll was prohibitive, at that time scrolls contain-

## Part I: The Messages to the Churches

ing Scripture were shared amongst the churches, the epistles being no exception. John had intended the scroll to be shared in this manner, for he had oversight of these congregations. In 1:11 the command to John is to write this scroll, then have it circulated among all seven serially.

Ephesus had become one of the major centers of Christianity in the first century. Antioch had supplanted Jerusalem, as the Gentiles replaced the Jews, and Christianity, which was stronger in the eastern Roman Empire than the western, spread up the coast through Turkey and Greece.

Seven churches are listed, just like there's seven Spirits before the throne of God. Seven in the Bible is the number of completion. There's symbolism in these seven churches. Some say they represent eras in church history. Others say they symbolize seven categories of churches in general—that any church can be represented by one of the seven. Both are true; the messages to the seven are relevant beyond the seven. What's interesting about these seven churches is their diversity. And if churches in this day-and-age are diverse, how much more so the seven? One church is contending with the temptations of wealth, while down the road, their brethren are being persecuted.

> 1:12 Then I turned to see the voice that was speaking with me. And having turned I saw seven golden lampstands;
> [13] and in the middle of the lampstands I saw one like a son of man, clothed in a robe reaching to the feet, and girded across His chest with a golden sash.
> [14] His head and His hair were white like white wool, like snow; and His eyes were like a flame of fire.
> [15] His feet were like burnished bronze, when it has been made to glow in a furnace, and His voice was like the sound of many waters.

In 1:12 the Greek verb tenses might better render the verse this way: *I turned so I could be facing the voice while it was speaking to me.*

Verse 1:13 says, "I saw one like a son of man". John does not say, *I saw the Son of man*, although Jesus is repeatedly referred to as the Son of man in the Gospels. The term *son of man* has its origins in the OT, particularly Ezekiel. The Bible embeds family members into phrases, like *son of perdition, father of lies, call wisdom your sister*, etc. In the Bible the phrase *son of* means someone who's a perfect example, who faithfully personifies, or who's the epitome or

*Part I: The Messages to the Churches*

the total embodiment of a concept, ideal, or state of being. *Son of man* means several things. It means the perfect man; one who has the full spectrum of human qualities alive and fully functioning in himself; a sort of Renaissance man; a single specimen who's the most suitable representative for the human race; a person who stands in proxy for all human beings; a person of character and ability. All these describe Jesus. In 1:13 John didn't instantly recognize the man in the vision as the Christ, so he describes his first impression of the figure, and the impression is indicative of the charisma Jesus has. Certain angels surround the presence of God and become saturated with the glory and holiness that radiate from him, with the result that those on earth who see them are dazzled by their appearance, are afraid of them, or even mistakenly worship them. Although he can appear with the same dazzling splendor as God the Father, Jesus keeps the brilliant radiance at a minimum for the sake of the person with whom he's conversing. God the Son, the second person in the Trinity, is the one who's the gateway between God and man (1 Tim. 2:5). Moses wasn't permitted to look directly at Jehovah, but John can—and does—look directly at Jesus, that is, his post-resurrected bodily form. No man can look at the Almighty, because the brilliance of his glory would overwhelm and obliterate him. But anyone can gaze at Jesus instead, and that's his role in the Trinity.

Jesus described in 1:13-15 is wearing a robe with a golden sash; presumably the sash is for royalty. The luminance of his face and hair reflects the Almighty's glory. The white denotes purity. Looking in his eyes, one sees flames. The flames are his zeal, as was demonstrated when he cast the moneychangers out of the temple, and which gets passed through the Holy Spirit to his disciples. Folks who're filled with the Spirit are zealous.

The feet have the appearance of bronze—not bronze at room temperature, but when the metal is near its melting point and begins to glow. In that state it takes on a pretty orange hue. Those who work in steel mills say that watching a molten iron pour is a spectacular sight. Liquid bronze would have more color to it than iron. Just as one is mesmerized while gazing at the dying embers in the fireplace, or Christmas tree lights when they're covered with snow, so is the appearance of Jesus' feet (see also Rom. 10:15 and Isa. 52:7). In the OT feet symbolize the course a person's life takes, the trajectory of his practices. This is why his feet glow so beautifully.

Copied from Ezekiel 43:2, John says that his voice was like "many waters". Think of a waterfall, or white-water rapids, and the rumble it makes. Spread across the tonal spectrum, water like this

*Part I: The Messages to the Churches*

is loud and drowns out any other noise. This is the affect of Jesus' voice, just like his voice is also likened to a trumpet in 1:10. Both are loud and both will get your attention, but in a different way. Same voice, but multiple affects. The trumpet calls one to attention, whereas the water smothers one's hearing.

> 1:16 In His right hand He held seven stars, and out of His mouth came a sharp two-edged sword; and His face was like the sun shining in its strength.

The "right hand", an OT symbol, holds the object that a person has utmost concern and attention for. It's the greatest means a person has at his disposal to affect or accomplish an ends; the ready willingness and ease to do something. In this context it exemplifies the intimate attention he gives to the stars, which is explained later.

This and 19:15 refer to a "sharp sword". The Greek word here for *sword* is *rhomphaia* (pronounced *rom-fi'-a*). This is not the same as the Roman two-edged sword (*machaira*) referenced in the Full Armor of God (Eph. 6). It was the weapon-of-choice of the Thracians, a fierce, belligerent people who lived in the vicinity of present-day Bulgaria, not too far from, and all too familiar to, the churches in Asia, to whom Revelation was addressed. In spite of the paucity of archaeological discoveries about this weapon, it's known that a rhomphaia (one used for infantry, not cavalry, which was about 2 m [6 ft.]) is approximately 110-130 cm (4 ft.) long. The blade occupies half its length or more, depending on the variant: a typical blade was 60-80 cm and the tang (i.e. handle) was 50 cm. The blade was either straight or slightly curved, and was wielded with either one or with both hands. It could be used for thrusts like a spear—and was also a vicious chopping weapon in close-quarter combat. The Romans, having developed a partly-iron, partly-steel sword, enjoyed a technological advantage over their adversaries—but not up against the rhomphaia, which was also made of iron and steel. Steel is known for its strength, but it has another lesser-known quality: unlike bronze, a steel utensil can be sharpened keenly. All have learned the hard way the difference between a razor-sharp and a marginally sharp kitchen knife. In ancient combat a soldier with a sharp weapon need not apply nearly as much force against his opponent to inflict the same wound to exposed flesh. This was well-known in ancient times, as a couple verses in the NT include the adjective *sharp* in front of *sword* (Heb. 4:12 comes to mind). Contrary to popular belief, the Romans weren't bigger or stronger than their opponents—particularly with respect to the savage tribes to the north. They won wars by using technologically su-

## Part I: The Messages to the Churches

perior weapons, good training, and teamwork, and by having excellent administration and perseverance. But the Romans had a time with the Thracians. It's not hard to imagine a Roman legion squaring off against them, seeing their rhomphaias at a distance, and, with a groan, loathing the long day ahead. In fact, the rhomphaia was the only weapon for which the Romans were forced to make a modification to their armor. The modification was to strengthen the helmet, as the Thracians were swinging their weapons two-handed in overhead whacks to the head, getting around the big Roman shields this way. In addition, the rhomphaia had a pointy tip, so at times was held with one or two hands and thrust forward, no swinging involved. This is what John saw in his vision: a rhomphaia, like a long needle, poking straight out of Jesus' mouth—a poignant visualization of his words when he speaks.

Verse 1:14 already stated that Jesus' head, and therefore face, is white, but 1:16 describes not the color, but the intensity of it. His face has an intensity like the sun. All this had the following effect on John:

> 1:17 When I saw Him, I fell at His feet like a dead man. And He placed His right hand on me, saying, "Do not be afraid; I am the first and the last,
> [18]and the living One; and I was dead, and behold, I am alive forevermore, and I have the keys of death and of Hades.

The "keys" are the means of control which Jesus has over "death and Hades". Death in this context leans towards spiritual death—the fruition of the destruction caused by sin—more than towards physical death. The word "Hades" here is equivalent to what we call *the afterlife*. Over the years our concept of the afterlife has been modified by religion, philosophy, and even scientific advancement, but the ancient Jews lived in a world of little abstract thought, and they had scarce concern for life after death, hence the scarcity of OT references to it. Hades, though it encompasses hell, is not synonymous with hell. One may argue that Hades encompasses heaven (as a destination for departed souls) also. It's just a vague abstraction of the afterlife. This conception was held before and at the time of the writing of Revelation, but has been covered over by two thousand years of Christian hegemony.

> 1:19 "Therefore write the things which you have seen, and the things which are, and the things which will take place after these things.

*Part I: The Messages to the Churches*

<sup>20</sup>"As for the mystery of the seven stars which you saw in My right hand, and the seven golden lampstands: the seven stars are the angels of the seven churches, and the seven lampstands are the seven churches.

"Have seen" (or just "saw"), "are", and "will take place": the Revelation—*the Apocalypse*—is not just a vision of impending doom, as our present-day usage of *apocalypse* suggests. Not limited to that which is to come, the revelation spans past, present, and future. And it ends on a positive note.

In 1:20 the word for "angels" is *angelos*, which means *messenger*. A messenger's primary duty is the delivery of a message; the secondary duty is to interpret that message, and a tertiary is to act in proxy for the sender, i.e. to act as an agent. The angel in 1:20 is not an angel, a celestial being, but a person, namely the minister who delivers messages to the congregation or the spiritual leader of that congregation. Summers agrees with this interpretation. Jesus later tells John to direct what he's writing to the *angelos* of each church (2:1, 2:8, etc.). It doesn't make sense for this to be an angel—why would God send a message to a man, who must in turn relay it to an angel in the heavenlies? No, in this context the correct interpretation of *angelos* is *messenger*—a person. Jesus holds people in his right hand. He's intimately concerned with people. He died for them and not for angels.

The churches are referred to as "lampstands", a lampstand being the mount for a lamp but not the lamp itself. The light placed upon it is the spiritual life of the church, which is energized by the Holy Spirit, not by man. Often one feels the presence of the Holy Spirit in a church setting. Sometimes it just sweeps over the congregation during worship. It might be an atmosphere of love, or of peace, or of faith—but not something conjured by human means. All churches have, or at least should have, a spiritual lamp, the essence of it varying from church to church, a defining characteristic of the church.

## 4. The Seven Churches (2:1)

Chapters 2 and 3 address "the things which are" that Jesus spoke of in 1:19, namely, the seven churches of Revelation. Recall that Ephesus was the mother-church in the region and the rest her offspring. John was the bishop or overseer for this cluster of churches, probably assuming the position prior to his exile to Pat-

*Part I: The Messages to the Churches*

mos and continuing while he was on the island. As noted in Paul's epistles (Gal. 1:2 for example), it was common practice for a scroll of a NT book to be passed from congregation to congregation, where it was read aloud on Sunday gatherings, or any time the brethren got together. From this, the tradition of Scripture readings has passed to the present day, being preserved in the liturgy of the Roman Catholic Mass. Ephesus will receive the scroll first.

> 2:1 "To the angel of the church in Ephesus write: The One who holds the seven stars in His right hand, the One who walks among the seven golden lampstands, says this:

The "angel"—the messenger—is most likely an elder, bishop, or prophet. The NT and early Church writings like the Didache refer to these ecclesiastical offices, and these are not necessarily used in Christian denominations today (in spite of their claims of authenticity to the early Church). In any case, the messenger addresses the church, getting his instructions from Jesus, who, in this instance, is relaying them through John.

Jesus "walks among the seven golden lampstands", meaning that he regularly monitors and communes with them—not his physical presence, but through the third person of the Trinity. The apparition of Jesus in Revelation shows him giving the churches his undivided attention, affirmed by him saying later, "I know your deeds" or "I know your tribulation". This answers the question: how does Jesus occupy his time?

The messages to the churches follow a pattern. First, Jesus reminds the church who he is or what he's done. In fact, the two are the same: Jesus *is* what he's done. Or, put another way, what he's done here on earth defines who he is. Second, a commendation is given to the churches, recognizing first what they're doing right. This is introduced with the words, "I know your deeds". Next comes the rebuke for what they're doing wrong. The length of the commendation or rebuke varied from church to church. A church might receive all commendation or all rebuke; a short commendation followed by a long rebuke; no commendation and all rebuke. Next comes the prophecy for that church, a revelation of future events. If the church had received a substantial rebuke, the word of prophecy was a judgment. Finally is an exhortation to do good or to continue doing good.

*Part I: The Messages to the Churches*

## 5. Ephesus (2:2–2:7)

Ephesus was a wealthy, cosmopolitan city and became one of the early centers of Christianity. The tone of Paul's epistle to the Ephesians indicates a maturity in the congregation. By the time Revelation was written, the assembly in Ephesus was already thirty or so years old, and a second generation of members had grown up under the original disciples of Paul.

> 2:2 I know your deeds and your toil and perseverance, and that you cannot tolerate evil men, and you put to the test those who call themselves apostles, and they are not, and you found them to be false;
> 3and you have perseverance and have endured for My name's sake, and have not grown weary.

This second generation was developed in the precepts of their predecessors and, unlike some of the other churches of Revelation, their convictions weren't displaced by those who taught otherwise. To achieve this, they must've established a system of instruction. This is reinforced by the implication of the phrase in 2:2, "put to the test", the Greek *peirazo*, which applied here means *putting someone to the test to see if there's any evil to be found in them*. They were systematic in the testing of unfamiliar doctrines, so one deduces they were rigorous in the instruction of proper, established doctrine. By conjecture, the cosmopolitan nature of the city, being a major center of commerce, inculcated a sophistication that lent to the systematic means by which the Ephesians prosecuted their beliefs. Unlike many of their contemporary brethren, they had developed the intellectual side of the Christian faith.

Apostolic Christianity was still evolving in doctrine. The NT hadn't been accepted as canon—it hadn't been written yet. There was a problem with heresy not seen in modern Christianity. Nowadays the collated doctrines of the major Christian denominations are relatively homogenous and pristine. The heresy we have results from the influx of secular philosophies...humanism, feminism, liberal theology to name a few. But the problem they were having came from several sources, the wolves with hidden agendas who had infiltrated the churches. These were the so-called apostles, and they were propagating philosophies like Gnosticism, which denied that Jesus came in the flesh. The Christians back then were more susceptible, as Christianity was still a young movement.

*Part I: The Messages to the Churches*

But the Ephesians excelled where so many of their brethren failed, and Jesus commends them for this. They held fast to the original teaching of Paul, heeding his warnings about false doctrines, and, from the tone of 2:2, in their wisdom had established effective policies to detect and expel false teachers, as they loathed heresy. They held tenaciously to their beliefs. Nevertheless, Jesus finds fault with them:

> 2:4 'But I have this against you, that you have left your first love.
> [5]'Therefore remember from where you have fallen, and repent and do the deeds you did at first; or else I am coming to you and will remove your lampstand out of its place—unless you repent.

The word used for "left" in 2:5 (*aphiami*) is the same as is used in 1 Cor. 7, and as a Greek scholar pointed out, this Greek word has been found on ancient legal documents concerning divorce. In 1 Cor. 7 when applied to marriage, this word should be translated there *divorce,* and in 2:4 also, so that 2:4 would read, "...that you have divorced your first love." The severity of what the Ephesians had done is more apparent when *divorced* is used rather than *left,* as their actions were deliberate and not like two friends who for no concrete reason drift apart over time. Appearing more just in this light, the ensuing judgment in 2:5 is this: Jesus will remove their lampstand from its place. No lampstand means no lamp, which means no light. This means that the spiritual life of the church would vanish. It doesn't mean that God would cause a catastrophe that would destroy the church—although doing that would be another means of removing the lampstand! Over the course of Christianity many churches, and entire denominations for that matter, have been judged by God, and have had their lampstands removed. This happens on a spiritual level. The church continues to function in the natural, but becomes a dead church. Still, Jesus is torn in two over the Ephesians:

> 2:6 'Yet this you do have, that you hate the deeds of the Nicolaitans, which I also hate.
> [7]'He who has an ear, let him hear what the Spirit says to the churches. To him who overcomes, I will grant to eat of the tree of life which is in the Paradise of God.'

*Part I: The Messages to the Churches*

Such is the animosity that Jesus has towards heresy that a bond of fellowship with the Ephesians consists of their mutual hatred of the Nicolaitans (more on them later), perhaps the only redeemable quality of the Ephesians.

It's fitting that the last book of the Bible draws to a conclusion that which was opened in the first; the "tree of life" is mentioned a few times in Revelation, 2:7 being the first occasion. Recall the last act with respect to that tree:

> Gen. 3:24 So He drove the man out; and at the east of the garden of Eden He stationed the cherubim and the flaming sword which turned every direction to guard the way to the tree of life.

A cherub (*cherubim* is plural for *cherub*) is a type of angel surrounding the holiness of God, or things which God has made holy. As a principle in Scripture, holy and unholy cannot be mixed—the holy will destroy the unholy. The Garden of Eden is holy. This is why man had to be cast out of the Garden once he sinned. The sword here symbolizes the enforcement of spiritual law—the Law of Sin and of Death (Rom. 8). Sword-wielding cherubim blocking all portals into the Garden means that mankind cannot reclaim paradise by his own work. However, Revelation shows that access has been granted to reenter the garden. This access is the culmination of the progression from Genesis to Revelation. The atonement for sin has removed the dirt of unholiness. The tree is no longer inaccessible.

\*

Contemplating the church at Ephesus in retrospect, the mistake that they made was that their emphasis on the mental aspects of Christianity and on the institutions which they had created (Jesus commended them for both) crowded out a heart-felt devotion to the Lord. The love of correct doctrine, the development in it, and the prosecution of it had replaced the love of Christ. There're no specific sins which the Ephesians indulged in, and nothing on the surface appeared out of place. Their problem was in their hearts, not in their minds.

## 6. Smyrna (2:8–2:11)

> 2:8 "And to the angel of the church in Smyrna write: The first and the last, who was dead, and has come to life, says this:

## Part I: The Messages to the Churches

⁹"I know your tribulation and your poverty (but you are rich), and the blasphemy by those who say they are Jews and are not, but are a synagogue of Satan.

In the early days of Christianity, persecution was not as systematic as it would become. Persecution was localized so that in the same vicinity some congregations were persecuted, while others were not. The churches in Revelation were more diverse than the churches in today's America, if that can be imagined. One church was prospering financially, another was poor and afflicted. Persecution leads to poverty, as those being persecuted first lose their commercial rights, followed by a loss of property rights, legal rights, and finally a loss of personal liberty and the infliction of physical harm. Verse 2:9 implies that the Smyrnan's poverty was a result of their tribulation.

And in 2:9 Jesus commends the Smyrnans for their spiritual prosperity, which is in contradiction to their financial state. How often this is true—but how little this is understood. Simply being rich or poor doesn't make one nearer or farther from God. But, so often, a person of means will hold his wealth in higher esteem than his spiritual life (Prov. 10:15). It's only the trials in life that can truly ascertain that which occupies the upper echelon of a person's heart—Christ or money. In the account of the rich young ruler, who professed his adherence to the commandments, when forced to choose, he chose to worship the god named mammon, thus breaking the Second Commandment. A shortcoming of human nature is the wide dichotomy between what a person believes himself to be and what he actually is. Jesus exposes this hypocrisy to the Laodiceans, but the Smyrnans suffer from the opposite problem. Poverty is often mistaken for a lack of spirituality, as the folk who live on the bottom of the totem pole imbibe the image of what the world and their circumstances paint and not the image of their identity in Christ. Hence the encouragement by Jesus, "but you are rich".

> 2:10 'Do not fear what you are about to suffer. Behold, the devil is about to cast some of you into prison, so that you will be tested, and you will have tribulation for ten days. Be faithful until death, and I will give you the crown of life.

Persecution is caused by the devil, not by God. It's safe to say that Satan didn't come in the flesh and throw these Smyrnans into prison. Instead, he did it through men consumed by wickedness.

*Part I: The Messages to the Churches*

The puppeteer and not the puppets is identified in 2:10 as the doer of the deed. Sinners, to the extent of the darkness in their hearts, are susceptible to being manipulated by Satan, who animates them in his conflict against the Church. This satanic animation is insightful of the spiritual viewpoint of Revelation. Many events are portrayed not in their true physical sense, but by the behind-the-scenes actors in a drama taking place in the unseen spiritual world.

But this verse and others indicate that in a lot of cases God doesn't block persecution—in fact, he seldom does. Furthermore, there are a few occurrences in the NT, the Smyrnans included, where God prophesies to a Christian that he will endure persecution. Why is this so? Here's a proposition: God can't stop the wicked from persecuting the saints.

In any event, 2:10 says that the believers will be "tested". This is by the devil, and the word for *tested* in this context means that the devil is testing them to try to break them. The last part of the verse says that they'll be in prison for ten days—that's all—but implies that there'll be more persecutions in the years to come, and some of them will be killed. But in spite of it all, the Lord says not to fear this. Even in the midst of these ordeals, he is in control of the situation, and, above all, wants to be worshipped as God. How much more should we apply this to our every-day circumstances, and quit fearing the little, insignificant problems we face?

The "crown of life" is mentioned at the end of 2:10 as the reward for overcoming. Note that each of the seven churches is given a challenge to overcome, and a reward for achieving it. Each challenge is different, so is the reward. The crown here is the Greek word *stephanos*, and refers to the crowns awarded in contests like the Olympic Games, not a crown that a king wears. The laurel wreaths the Romans wore, those which were awarded in victory: this is what a stephanos is. This crown is given in this lifetime—not just in the lifetime to come. *Life* used in the NT is not just physical life, but spiritual life—the freshness and vigor with which one prosecutes his existence, and this regardless of circumstances. This is the life promised to the Smyrnans in their lifetimes—in the midst of persecution, and in the face of a prematurely terminated lifespan.

> 2:11 'He who has an ear, let him hear what the Spirit says to the churches. He who overcomes will not be hurt by the second death.'

Unlike the other churches, the Smyrnans are given two rewards for overcoming. Verse 2:11 lists the second, and echoes what's mentioned to the others, "He who has an ear, let him hear". The meaning is obvious, but the admonition the reader often misses by not stopping to meditate on the phrase, which is repeated for emphasis. By saying "to the churches", the audience is explicitly widened to all Christians of all time. There's a reward for overcoming. The reward in 2:11 refers to the "second death", later specified as the Lake of Fire, a place of punishment. It's not to be confused with spiritual death as seen throughout the NT, which is the spiritual condition of unbelievers while they're still alive on this earth (and afterwards).

Suffering persecution, life for the Smyrnans was difficult, but this had the benefit of purging them of heresy and indolence. Persecution and affliction stymie carnality, laziness, and the love of wealth over the love of Christ. If one were to have visited the Smyrnans, he or she would have found a genuine humility—one earned the hard way—and a pure and simple faith. And he or she would find that the Smyrnans had a poor self-image, the side-effect of the afflictions.

The prophecy Jesus gave would hold them over for one trial. When that trial ended, in all likelihood another would've begun, and Jesus would've given them a word for that next trial, continuing in this way for as many trials as were to come. This is the daily bread that comes out of heaven and is available to those who trust that Christ will walk with them in hard times. Like the Smyrnans, any who might suffer persecution should not fear what will come upon them, knowing that Jesus will manifest himself each step of the way.

## 7. Pergamum (2:12–2:17)

> 2:12 "And to the angel of the church in Pergamum write: The One who has the sharp two-edged sword says this:
> [13]"I know where you dwell, where Satan's throne is; and you hold fast My name, and did not deny My faith even in the days of Antipas, My witness, My faithful one, who was killed among you, where Satan dwells.

The "two-edged sword" is again the *rhomphaia*, as Jesus' words to the Pergamums jab and pierce in the same way as in 1:16. In contrast to Jesus the Lamb of God is Jesus the sword-wielder. Both images appear in this book, and although they're contrasting, they're not contradictory in spite of their dichotomy. The Lamb reminds us of what he *has* done, while the sword-wielder reminds of

*Part I: The Messages to the Churches*

what he *will* do. Our understanding of Jesus cannot be complete without considering both roles.

The messages to the churches always follow the same structure: complement what's being done well, rebuke what's being done wrong, specify a reward for staying the course. Mixed in somewhere is a reminder of who Jesus is, or what he's capable of, or what he intends to do. What the Pergamums were doing well was withstanding opposition from their ungodly neighbors.

According to church tradition, Antipas was appointed by John as bishop of Pergamum, and, alluded to by 2:13, killed by the locals who were in opposition to the truth. This may have happened long before John wrote Revelation. Furthermore, it appears that Antipas was the only one from Pergamum who was martyred. This is still prominent in Jesus' mind as he addresses this congregation. As is seen several times in Scripture, one very devoted person gets more of God's attention than a multitude of the lukewarm. In the OT, even after David's death, God still remembered him, and mentioned him repeatedly afterwards.

The specious affections of the Pergamum unbelievers were presumably attached to some pagan god. The Greek commentators Max Zerwick and Mary Grosvenor (Max & Mary for short) say that the "throne of Satan" refers to the Sanctuary of Aselepius. Under the surface of paganism, however, the city had yielded their hearts to Satan to such an extent that Satan is described as having a throne there. It's through philosophy or religion that the devil gets his best stranglehold over a person's heart, mind, and affections. It was religious folk who arranged to have Jesus killed and who persecuted Paul. In the NT there's an incident of a demon possessed man in a synagogue. And in Revelation, on a few occasions Satan's strongholds are pinpointed: strongholds in relation to a religion, philosophy, or false doctrine. Revelation gives us a glimpse in the spiritual domain, behind the curtain.

> 2:14 'But I have a few things against you, because you have there some who hold the teaching of Balaam, who kept teaching Balak to put a stumbling block before the sons of Israel, to eat things sacrificed to idols and to commit acts of immorality.

*Teaching* in the Greek has connotations of instruction to the listener of how her or she should conduct his or her life. The "teaching of Balaam" is the OT prototype of the *teaching of the Nicolaitans*; therefore, to understand the latter one must understand the former. Recall the account from the OT. Israel has spent forty years in the

*Part I: The Messages to the Churches*

desert, having shed the older, unbelieving generation, and emerges as a strong nation ready to take the Promised Land. Unlike the other inhabitants of Canaan, the nations of Moab and Midian are descendents of Abraham (Lot was practically Abraham's son). These two nations consult with the prophet Balaam, who, as a prophet, seems to have the spiritual authority to steer events, and this in spite of his own apostasy. Balaam has a knowledge of God, which knowledge was preserved in the nations of Midian and Moab, passed down to him from Abraham. The narrative suggests that Balaam was called as a prophet of the true God. In spite of his recalcitrance, God works with him and through him for the sake of Israel. But Balaam, although given ample opportunity to see the error of his ways—God even speaking to him through a donkey—will not repent. His deeds were not done out of ignorance, but out of knowledge, and that multiplies the wickedness of his sins.

The Moabites in their wisdom know they are militarily no match for the Israelites. The reason is that Israel has God's favor, and therefore cannot be defeated in battle. The Moabites recognize the hand of the Lord; their spiritual discernment is keen. Generations before, in their hearts they had abandoned Jehovah, and put Baal in his place. The names *Balaam* and *Balak* have an obvious connection with *Baal*, showing the bonds to that false god. So Balaam's advice is to tempt Israel to commit sin. Notice in 2:14 the word "kept" is inserted by the NASB, a more accurate translation of the imperfect tense of *to teach*; Balaam, not jut one time but persistently, was trying to persuade Balak down this path. The phrase "put a stumbling block before" in 2:14 means to tempt someone to sin. *Stumbling block* as used in the NT doesn't mean a sin of oversight, in spite of the literal meaning, but a sin caused by deliberate action. Once enticed, the sin is owned by the sinner. As the early Church recognized as Scripture the OT exclusively, they had their collection of favorite verses like any denomination does nowadays. Drawing on the same passages, certain sermons were repeated just as sermons circulate today. Apparently, this message of Balaam was one such popular sermon in the primitive church, as the problem of heresy was enormous. A NT reference to Balaam is found in Jude 11, where he's listed alongside Cain and Korah. What Balaam, Cain, and Korah have in common is apostasy: having known the truth and deliberately turning from it. This is the "unpardonable sin" mentioned in 1 John, the "sin against the Holy Spirit" in Mark's Gospel, and the sin that has no renewal in Heb. 6:4-8. This category of sinner differs from the category of ordinary heathen. The former has the knowledge of God, but turns from it. The latter sins in ignorance of God. The knowledge of right and wrong compounds the

*Part I: The Messages to the Churches*

actual wrongdoing. Were sin defined as a mathematical equation, it would be:

$$\text{sin} = (\text{sinful deeds}) \times (\text{knowledge of God})$$

Verse 2:14 ends by saying, "to eat things sacrificed to idols and to commit acts of immorality." The KJV minces no words; it ends, "to commit fornication". The Greek aorist infinitives *to eat* and *to commit fornication* leave no doubt that this phrase is used as an appositive, describing what Balaam was trying to get Balak to do. There's a single word in the Greek translated by "things sacrificed to idols": *eidoluthuta*. It's used in multiple places in the NT and has connotations of not just imbibing food but of participating in a ritual. Paul deals with the issue—there's more to it than just issuing a commandment.

Starting with the patriarch, sexual lewdness can be implanted in a tribe or nation at its inception, then, once established, propagated to subsequent generations. Moab, birthed by the incest of Lot with his daughter (Gen. 19:37), along with him Canaan, whom Noah condemned for an act of lewdness (Gen. 9:20-27), both fathered nations known for their shamelessness. Thus, as recounted in Numbers 25, the plan was to send Moabite women into the Israelite camp, so the women would commit fornication with the Israelites (see 1 Cor. 10:8 also). Once the sexual bond was formed, the Israelites could be lured into worshiping Baal. The notion of casual sex is a lie—sex is not casual, but is an act that emotionally and physically draws a couple together. The two become one flesh. Sexual infatuation is a binding agent. This is the reason the Bible—in fact, all societies—have mores that restrain it. Once a couple becomes sexually unified, the foundation is laid for one of the two to adopt the other's religion or philosophy. The one with the weaker convictions adopts those of the stronger. This destroyed Samson. And in Numbers 25, once Israel had committed fornication with the daughters of Moab, they then participated in the sacrifices to their gods (Num. 25:2). Numbers 25 expounds the *eidoluthuta* referred to in 2:14. Sacrifices to the gods involved the blessing, consecration, and consumption of food. Not only true in the time of Moses (Exod. 34:15), but true in NT times, *eidoluthuta* is sex, food, festivities, and pagan worship—all combined.

On a side note about the Balaam affair. Baal worship was prevalent in many nations and ages in that region. The reason is that Baal was the head god over other gods. This was significant because if one went to war against another nation, to insure victory one had better have the stronger god. But the Moabites and Midianites—as

## Part I: The Messages to the Churches

devoted as they were to him—recognized the superiority of Jehovah, and knew they had to break the Israelites to Baal, the obvious inferior of the two...although he was supposed to be the dominant god. In the OT the God Jehovah is demonstrated as having hegemony over all other gods. An example is when Moses turned his staff into a snake. The court magicians repeated the same trick, but Moses' snake consumed them. Israel, having the superior God and having seen his arm, his power on their behalf, abandoned Jehovah in lieu of a false surrogate. The logic is baffling. Would not the Israelites, having seen the power and superiority of their God, not stick to him in their time of need? Would not the Moabites, knowing the inferiority of Baal, reject him for Jehovah? Such is the reasoning of sin.

Eating food that had been sacrificed to idols (*eidoluthuta*) was a sticky issue for the early Church. The NT references seem at first ambiguous and somewhat contradictory. Addressed in Acts 15, 1 Cor. 8 and 10, Paul said all food was lawful to eat, including food sacrificed to idols—but then there's a prohibition against sacrificed food. What was going on? Back then, there was a lot of food sacrificed to idols, and it was dumped in the marketplace so that one couldn't tell what was what. In some places it was hard for Christians to buy produce that hadn't been sacrificed. Paul said it was alright to buy and eat this food, so long as it didn't cause another brother to stumble. In Paul's mind, food was food. You could chant over it all day, but it was still just a hunk of meat—the incantations were not to be taken seriously. But the risk here—the reason for the prohibition—was that Christians weren't just consuming the food, but were indulging in the festivities that accompanied eating it. Or at least thinking out of guilt due to misinformation that they were so implicated. Addressing the issue in 1 Cor., Paul says some don't have "knowledge" and that their conscience is weak. Paul's saying that there're certain Christians who when they eat such food become overwhelmed by guilt and condemnation, convinced they've committed some grave sin. They really haven't, but it's real in their minds anyways. They just can't break the mental association of the food with the sacrifice it was used in. Some Christians are like that. They feel guilty about things they ought not. Even after being told that it's alright, they still can't break the feeling. Paul says to respect these folk. Don't look down on them, and don't place them in a situation that's beyond their conscience's ability to handle. The commandment was for Christians to shun every vestige of idolatrous worship. Idolatry was tightly woven into the fabric and institutions of society; this made it difficult for a Christian to completely avoid it. But God's concerned whether a person is heartily engaged

*Part I: The Messages to the Churches*

in pagan worship—not actually what he or she is putting in his mouth, unless it's a reflection of what's in his or her heart. This is a basic philosophy of Christianity. When this tenet is applied to this issue, the confusion abates. But the problem with certain Christians was that while eating this food they were giving their hearts to idols.

Keep in mind that many obscene practices were an intricate part of idol worship. Temples were filled with temple prostitutes. The Greek word for *fornication* is almost the same for *prostitute*. Hence, just as eating was involved in idolatry, so was fornication. Pleasures of the flesh, pleasures of the mind—these made idolatry sumptuous. Numbers 25 makes this apparent. It was also pertinent to the times in which the Pergamums lived. Nothing had changed on that front.

The record of Balaam is a strong parallel to the Nicolaitan heresy: it's a metaphor. As Jewish apocryphal literature, Revelation is written thus: real people, things, and events are described through their metaphor, rather than directly. These examples early on in the book are unambiguous enough to aid in parsing the content later in the book, which becomes increasingly bizarre.

\*

According to the Church Fathers, the Nicolaitans were a heretical group founded by one Nicolas. Some have stated that this is the same Nicolas listed in Acts 6:5, who, along with Steven, was one of the first deacons. Although it's an intriguing theory, there's scant evidence to confirm it. But, according to the Church Fathers, the Nicolaitans lead "lives of unrestrained indulgence". After combining this evidence with the Pergamum passages, a clearer picture emerges. Nicolas was an early convert to Christianity, but turned from the truth to proclaim his message of carnal indulgence. Surely Nicolas knew the Scriptures well and was a zealous disciple before giving his heart over to Satan's heresy. The Nicolas from Acts fits the background perfectly: he was a proselyte from Antioch, a convert to Judaism, before becoming a Christian, and therefore had a foundation in the OT, back then the Bible for Christians. We'll never know if he was the same.

The two pieces—what's known from the Balaam narrative, and what little's been passed down about the Nicolaitans—mixed with a measure of deduction yield a myriad of understanding. It's doubtful that Nicolas actually taught Christians to participate in idol worship or to commit the physical act of fornication. The idolatry and fornication are components of the Balaam-metaphor. Had it been an actual part of the heresy, nobody would've been duped by it. Heretics weave clever, convincing arguments. But in the messages to

*Part I: The Messages to the Churches*

both Pergamum and Thyatira, the phrase, "eating things sacrificed to idols and committing fornication", appears. It looks more like this is a catch-phrase for heretical teachings, rather than for actual deeds.

By deduction the Nicolaitan heresy has the following traits:

1) The teaching of the Nicolaitans was started by one Nicolas
2) Nicolas had known the truth—had known it pretty well—and had turned from it
3) Nicolas, like Balaam, was persistent and persuasive
4) Nicolas went after Christians with his doctrine: a wolf in sheep's clothing
5) With clever arguments Nicolas taught that it's OK to indulge in licentious behavior
6) Just as the metaphorical sin of fornication (Num. 25) destroyed the Israelites who committed it, it would destroy the Christians who were drawn away by it
7) Believing this Nicolaitan heresy was a heinous sin, tantamount to idolatry

Owing to a few factors, the problem in the early Church of heresy (false prophets, the same thing) is not nearly as acute today. The reasons are as follow. First, the canonization of the NT as Scripture. This did not happen in the lifetime of the Apostles, but evolved over several decades. Second, the gradual hegemony of a single fellowship of believers, what evolved into the Catholic Church. The Catholic Church in the early centuries fought and won the battle against heresy, benefiting even denominations which later seceded. As the authority of the Church increased, so did its ability to suppress heresy, and therefore preserve the essentials of Christianity. The struggle against heresy is apparent in a casual reading of the Nicene Creed, by the specific enumeration of the Trinity. The Creed was created to communicate and enforce correct doctrine, and it was an effective deterrent to heresy, whose doctrines subverted the truth of the Trinity. In fact, the doctrine of the Trinity has been adopted by just about every spin-off to this day. For that matter, almost all of the Nicene Creed is adhered to by groups recognized as Christians.

What true heresy is has been lost through the centuries. Accusing their opposing disputants of heresy, Christians have magnified so many trivial arguments that the reality of true heresy has been lost. The NT contains an intact record of the monster of heresy, and it vehemently condemns it. This understanding needs to be revived

*Part I: The Messages to the Churches*

and relearned in its proper context. The modern-day heresy is liberal theology, and the growing consensus of this has caused somewhat of an ecumenical banding together of true Christians.

> 2:15 'So you also have some who in the same way hold the teaching of the Nicolaitans.
> [16]"Therefore repent; or else I am coming to you quickly, and I will make war against them with the sword of My mouth.

As the first part of 2:15 says "some", all this commotion is over a few, just as God slew the 23 thousand in Numbers 25, a small fraction of the Israelite assembly. Looking at the last part of 2:15, with the translation tweaked, Jesus said he would, *combat them using my mouth's rhomphaia*, i.e. the one that darts from his mouth. Jesus' spoken words are his weapons. Further along, in 2:16 he says he's "coming quickly", a phrase seen throughout the book, meaning *coming upon you all of a sudden* more so than *coming soon*, just like Jesus talked of the thief in the night. God is patient, and more patient, withholding judgment. But when it arrives, it comes on very quickly, is decisive, and is conclusive. This is the pattern of the judgment of God throughout the Bible. He's slow to anger. His judgment doesn't arrive gradually but arrives suddenly.

\*

For the Pergamums, it may have been a lack of single-mindedness that was responsible for their ambivalence towards the ravenous wolf of heresy. Or perhaps in their cerebral fascination with the far-fetched tenets of a new doctrine, they didn't recognize the danger of giving way to those who're opposed to the truth. But in either case, there're lessons to be learned from this church. While in general the church didn't indulge in heresy, the degree to which it tolerated it was reprehensible. To the modern ear the Nicolaitan heresy might sound strange, but does it vastly differ from, say, the ordination of gay bishops? There should be no compromise with liberal theology—to do so is sin. Mainline Protestant denominations that still have a substantial number of born-again Christians, who walk in the footsteps of the Pergamums, would do well to heed the warning. Jesus told Pergamum to get rid of the residual heresy. He held them responsible for it. He didn't tell them to try to work with those in error or to reach a compromise. The same message applies today. Although the modern schism was slow in the making, and Christians have been slow to recognize the sheep from the goats, this is all water under the bridge. These divided Protestant denominations must split. Their failure to act places them under the same condemnation as Pergamum.

*Part I: The Messages to the Churches*

2:17 'He who has an ear, let him hear what the Spirit says to the churches. To him who overcomes, to him I will give some of the hidden manna, and I will give him a white stone, and a new name written on the stone which no one knows but he who receives it.'

## 8. Thyatira (2:18–2:25)

2:18 "And to the angel of the church in Thyatira write: The Son of God, who has eyes like a flame of fire, and His feet are like burnished bronze, says this:
[19]'I know your deeds, and your love and faith and service and perseverance, and that your deeds of late are greater than at first.

Christians seldom emphasize perseverance, a crucial element of the Christian walk. Many get off to a good start but capitulate in the midst of trials. At times, in the flesh, by one's own ability, one can do right. But in the long run, when buffeted by trials, good works can't be sustained without faith, the grace of God, and the power of the Holy Spirit—combined with character and determination. The "deeds of late" are the fruit of perseverance, and are beyond the flesh's might. The "deeds of late" are more important "than first", insomuch as the Spirit is more important than the flesh.

The commendation was first. The rebuke follows:

2:20 'But I have this against you, that you tolerate the woman Jezebel, who calls herself a prophetess, and she teaches and leads My bond-servants astray so that they commit acts of immorality and eat things sacrificed to idols.

This is a metaphor, just as the "teaching of Balaam" was for the Pergamums. There was no woman named Jezebel in this church. Jezebel is a Phoenician name; even so, no one, not even sinners, name their children after villains. Revisiting 1 Kings 16, Ahab was the seventh and the most wicked in a succession of kings where each was worse than his predecessor. From 1 Kings 16:31: "He not only considered it trivial to commit the sins of Jeroboam son of Nebat, but he also married Jezebel daughter of Ethbaal king of the Sidonians, and began to serve Baal and worship him." Jezebel was a

*Part I: The Messages to the Churches*

daughter of a King of Tyre, and she was devoted to Baal. Whereas Ahab even in his wickedness might vacillate between good and evil, Jezebel—more wicked than Ahab—at these critical moments pushed him towards wickedness. Later on, after Ahab's demise, Jezebel went on to manipulate Ahaziah, then Jehoram. She was known for persecuting the servants of the Lord and supporting the prophets of Baal.

This "woman Jezebel" in Thyatira was a real woman, a prophetess. Like Jezebel, this Thyatiran prophetess was well-versed in the arts of manipulation, and these were impelled by a wicked heart. The role of a prophet in the early Church was to give messages of encouragement, often lengthy, to the congregation (Acts 15:30-33 as an example). They weren't involved in leadership positions, but nevertheless are ranked second in the list of ministries in Eph. 4 and 1 Cor. 12. They were known to itinerate, being supported by the churches they visited (as noted in the Didache). Their message was not primarily the *thus saith the Lord* variety, similarly a multitude of OT prophets were of little, if any, political consequence to Israel. A prophet in the NT, similar to the lesser-known ones in the OT, is a minister who gives spiritual encouragement and direction. But this "woman Jezebel" had gone awry and become a false prophet. Again, the same words, "commit acts of immorality [fornication] and eat things sacrificed to idols", that were given to the Pergamums. She was teaching heresy in the name of the Lord, but not actually teaching to commit fornication and participate in the *eidoluthuta* ("things sacrificed to idols"). The net result in Jesus' view is the same. Following Baal and following some strange doctrine are equivalent. The metaphors are fornication and *eidoluthuta*, but the act is heresy.

> 2:21 'I gave her time to repent, and she does not want to repent of her immorality.

The NASB, acknowledging the metaphorical use of this word, again changes the KJV word *fornication* to *immorality*, but the KJV is closer to the Greek text, leaving it to the reader to sort out the metaphors. Verse 2:21 is a key to previous and subsequent usages of "immorality" in Revelation. In a supporting thread, Heb. 12:16 says, "be ye not fornicators as Esau" (KJV), this verse in reference to Esau selling his birthright to Jacob in exchange for a bowl of stew to satisfy his hunger. Esau's was a metaphorical act of fornication. Recall from Genesis: Esau had returned from a long hunt, was hungry, and begged the stew from Jacob, who gave it in exchange for Esau's pledge to relinquish the birthright. Esau justified his actions by saying he was about to die. In reality he wouldn't have died had he skipped that meal—he just felt like he would and thus convinced himself that he would. How long can a person go without food? Forty days? Had Esau really been that close to starvation he wouldn't have had the strength to be out hunting. Or walking for that matter. To him, the food was more important than the spiritual blessing. This is the essence of fornication: the abandonment of a moral or holy commandment for momentary gratification. Used throughout Revelation, another definition of fornication that the reader might overlook is that it is a lewd, sexual act, often involving adultery and prostitution. Fornication in the biblical sense goes beyond pre-marital sex with one's fiancé. As Paul says in 1 Cor. 5, "It is actually reported that there is immorality [fornication] among you, and immorality of such a kind as does not exist even among the Gentiles, that someone has his father's wife." Paul's usage of *fornication* in this verse refers to the lewdness and immorality of the act. References in both Heb. 12 and 1 Cor. 5 should suffice to qualify the interpretation of *fornication* throughout Revelation, as this word appears several times, and it may be ambiguous absent the clarifying support from other verses.

Unlike the epistles, these messages to the churches are given in the words of Jesus himself and consequently give a different perspective than the epistles, although both are equally inspired. Here, Jesus himself speaks directly to the churches, and the insight yielded answers perplexing questions that aren't directly addressed in other parts of the Bible. One such question is this: how much can a Christian (or unbeliever in this case) sin before provoking the judgment or discipline of God? The answer is on display in 2:21: Jesus himself makes that decision on a case-by-case basis. As one might expect, there's a lot of factors that God considers if and when to judge someone—a person's history, attitudes of his or her heart, etc. As in the OT, so in the new. God gives a person a time span, in the Greek *kronos*, an appointed season, to put the sin away. In the same way, an employer might discipline an employee who's not doing what he or she is told. Having been informed by the employer, the employee is given time to clean up his or her act. Sometimes in the OT it appears that God loses his temper and sends a bolt of lighting screeching to earth. But this is not God's nature. The Bible doesn't always document the transgressions leading up to a judgment. Sometimes one only sees the judgment. But in the case of Israel having been brought out of Egypt, a full chronology is recorded, and it's evident that the patience and the forbearance of God precede his judgment. Rom. 3:5 says that God is just, meaning he applies justice, meaning he's fair. Throughout the years, religion

*Part I: The Messages to the Churches*

has taught that God is overly harsh (whereas liberal theology has taught that God is overly lenient). God is righteous in judgment, and this judgment will be perfect in its justice. Several OT Scriptures praise God's justice and judgment. The same method of justice that man in his wisdom applies God also applies. The difference is that God has access to hidden facts, and that he has perfect wisdom.

Her disciples, referred to as her "children" in 2:23, are committing "adultery" with her. They are not actually committing adultery with her, the act being a metaphor of the spiritual transgression.

> 2:22 'Behold, I will throw her on a bed of sickness, and those who commit adultery with her into great tribulation, unless they repent of her deeds.
> [23]'And I will kill her children with pestilence, and all the churches will know that I am He who searches the minds and hearts; and I will give to each one of you according to your deeds.

In the Greek, 2:22 omits the words "of sickness"; the original appears to be a phrase. Perhaps a more applicable translation would be, *Behold, I will lay you up in the hospital.* Sometimes God will judge one walking in sin with sickness. That's not taught much these days, but it's scriptural (see 1 Cor. 5:5, 11:30). Keep in mind, however, that the Thyatiran prophetess and her disciples were deep in apostasy—the sin was severe. God won't bring sickness on a person for a minor transgression.

It's interesting to note whom Jesus holds responsible for this sin. On the one hand, 2:20 blames the Jezebel-heretic for leading others astray. On the other hand, in 2:22, those who follow her are held accountable for their own actions. Psychologists have vacillated between contradictory theories that, on the one hand, fault society for the transgressions of its members, but, on the other hand, blame individuals solely, attributing behavior to a person's innate nature. Which is true? Both are, according to these verses.

The affliction of her and her disciples was to be a sign to the other churches that the sickness was from God. It would be obvious. In our current age, this type of thought is absent. But it happens: church-folk who fall deep into sin end up in the hospital, in prison, or even dead. What's difficult to comprehend is why Christians receive this judgment, and unbelievers don't. This has to do with the knowledge of God that such a person possesses, as sin is a function of knowledge; a Christian's potential for sin is greater than

*Part I: The Messages to the Churches*

the potential of a heathen. Committing sin out of knowledge is in a different category than committing it in ignorance. Children whose parents took them to church regularly while growing up, and who later backslide or never commit their lives to Christ, fall deep into sin that grows worse as they get older. Unlike the non-believer who acts wild in college, then settles down as he or she gets older, the kid who turns from the knowledge of God is unstable—he burns through marriages and engages in reckless behavior in his middle age.

In 2:23 Jesus is "he who searches the minds and hearts", similar to Rom. 8:27, also repeated in the Gospels. Jesus is intimately familiar with the deep thoughts of man because he's always sifting through the hearts...patiently but thoroughly. This occupies his time. That's what he was doing with the seven churches and the seven stars.

Apart from this prophetess and her coterie, the church was doing well. But it only took one sore spot to garner such condemnation. Yes, the Thyatirans were doing a lot of things right, but like most of the other churches, they had one glaring fault. Jesus spent more time talking about the fault than the positive points. In this instance the Thyatirans who weren't even following this heresy were rebuked for merely tolerating it. One or two discrepancies is all it takes to mar the good works, at least it appears that way on the surface. Underneath, these are the areas that people are living in rebellion to God, and such rebellion is a poison that spoils their entire spiritual life, preventing God from fulfilling his plans and destiny for them.

> 2:24 'But I say to you, the rest who are in Thyatira, who do not hold this teaching, who have not known the deep things of Satan, as they call them—I place no other burden on you.

This heresy is described here as "the deep things of Satan." All heresies—true heresies—are like that. The NT is consistent in its condemnation of them, an example being Gal. 1:8,9. Liberal theology, the modern-day heresy, must be treated as such. Would anyone dispute that Satan can be found in a prison? A brothel? How about a church or a seminary or a denomination?

> 2:25 'Nevertheless what you have, hold fast until I come.
> [26]"He who overcomes, and he who keeps My deeds until the end, TO HIM I WILL GIVE AUTHORITY OVER THE NATIONS;

*Part I: The Messages to the Churches*

²⁷AND HE SHALL RULE THEM WITH A ROD OF IRON, AS THE VESSELS OF THE POTTER ARE BROKEN TO PIECES, as I also have received authority from My Father; ²⁸and I will give him the morning star.
²⁹'He who has an ear, let him hear what the Spirit says to the churches.'

The condition for the prophecy for Thyatira starts in 2:26, as Jesus rewards "he who overcomes"—not the one off to a good start, nor the one who breaks under pressure, but the one who persists until the "end"—the word used in Greek means *the appropriate or obvious conclusion*.

But in spite of their sins, there's still a prophecy given to this church, a promise if they hold fast. This prophecy cannot be fulfilled in this age, but has fulfillment in an age to come. Christians who have remained faithful in this era of temptation will be rewarded by ruling over the nations, the peoples of the earth, instead of being ruled by them. From the beginning of time until now, nonbelievers have dominated and will continue to dominate the body politic. This will come to an end. Thus, the Book of Revelation is a promise, a message of hope to the brethren. In their pride some Christians see themselves in this age as the most suitable rulers. This view is held partly because Christians believe that they're wiser than non-Christians. While it's true that righteousness leads to wisdom and that unrighteousness is foolishness, merely being a Christian doesn't make one wise. The extent to which believers can lack wisdom is found in a quotation from the end of the parable of the unrighteous steward, "for the sons of this age are more shrewd in relation to their own kind than the sons of light" (Luke 16:8). But as is manifest in America's present political atmosphere, non-Christians—those who've rejected the truth—have substituted nonsensical, idealistic philosophies (such as *diversity* and *environmentalism*) in place of the truth, and these drive them to folly. Following Christian philosophy leads to wisdom.

In 2:28, "I will give him the morning star", is a bit of a paradox. Jesus himself spoke these words, and later in the book Jesus is said to be the Morning Star. Is Jesus saying he'll give himself to the Thyatirans (or anyone for that matter) if they overcome? A few problems with this. First, Jesus has *already* given himself to the Church—what more is there left for him to give than his life on the cross? Second, if Jesus were speaking of giving himself, why wasn't he explicit about it in this verse? And lastly, the context doesn't fit. The preceding verses are about the godly having authority over the world in a yet-to-be-revealed age. So either one of two logical outcomes remains: either the Morning Star in this verse does not refer to Jesus, or Jesus is not speaking in this verse. This invites the question, what exactly is the significance of the Morning Star? Unbeknownst to the ancients, the Morning Star is actually the planet Venus, which is only visible near the horizon shortly before dawn or after dusk. Actually, they didn't know that the orb that appeared at dawn and the one at dusk are the same. Venus is brilliant as it rises over the horizon, significantly brighter than any star, though thought to be one—planets per se were unknown then. In the Bible stars represent charismatic or influential leaders, or agents on a mission of some significance. Even today the word is used similarly, like in *movie star*. In the morning Venus appears as a *rising star*, one that's *on the way up* so to speak. By this reasoning, can the Morning Star in 2:28 be the most dominant nation, or an influential world leader, and not Jesus?

\*

Of the seven churches of Revelation, Pergamum and Thyatira had problems with heresy. Pergamum indulged in a widely-known heretical teaching, whereas Thyatira swallowed a lie propagated by one person. Like many heresies, the trap set by the Nicolaitans was an intellectual flirtation with the concepts put forth by a damnable doctrine. On the other hand, the Pergamums were spellbound by the charisma of a single lunatic, who probably through enchantment and intimidation was able to manipulate many in the congregation. This is what Jesus meant by, "a little leaven leavens the whole lump". Thyatira had a concentration of those susceptible to being ensnared by a cult—those who lack common sense, those who're sheepish, and those who're gullible while at the same time sensitive to spiritual things. A point of interest of Pergamum and Thyatira is that, the heresy aside, both had vigorous spiritual lives. Those who're the most fervent are the ones most vulnerable to deception. The solution for Thyatira was actually quite simple: get rid of the false prophetess, and the problem will disappear. The attachment those at Thyatira had with the Jezebel-woman was more emotional than intellectual; just as emotional attachment is easily formed, so it is easily severed. Not the case for Pergamum.

## 9. Sardis (3:1–3:6)

> 3:1 "To the angel of the church in Sardis write: He who has the seven Spirits of God and the seven stars, says this: 'I know

your deeds, that you have a name that you are alive, but you are dead.

The seven Spirits of God are mentioned a few times in Revelation. It's unspecified what exactly each Spirit is. Perhaps one is the "Spirit of truth" mentioned in John's Gospel. But one thing is known: the number seven in Scripture is the number of completion or perfection. *Spirit* in the Bible means two things. First, a celestial being, the obvious. Second, a prevailing attitude (spirit of fear [2 Tim. 1:7], spirit of faith [2 Cor. 4:13], etc.). It's conceivable that the word *Spirits* in "seven Spirits of God" are not directly referring to the Holy Spirit (Greek has no capitalization, so *spirit* is ambiguous), but are of the second meaning, i.e. they are the prevailing attitudes of God. In any case, in 5:6, it says, "the seven eyes on the Lamb, the seven Spirits of God, are sent out into all the earth". Jesus sent into all the earth the Holy Spirit on Pentecost, so the seven Spirits of 5:6 and the Holy Spirit of Acts 2 are both described as having been sent out. This agrees. But the seven spirits aren't mentioned in any other book besides Revelation, and furthermore aren't explained in Revelation. It's a mystery what these seven are.

The phrase, "that you have a name that you are alive, but you are dead", needs a bit of explaining. The word *name* in the Bible can mean a few things apart from the obvious. In several contexts it denotes a position of authority. But other times it means *reputation* or *character as recognized by others*. For example, in Gen. 6:4 the words "men of renown" is literally *men of a name*, meaning men having a reputation (in that case, a bad one). Similarly, in 3:1 the word "name" means *reputation* or *reputed character*. And the word "dead" in 3:1 refers to spiritual death, not literal death (this is common in the NT); the word "alive" would mean *spiritually alive*, not *physically alive*. So, rewording the latter half of 3:1, the following makes more sense:

> I know your deeds, that you have a reputation for being spiritually alive, but in fact you're spiritually dead.

Those outside this church believed the Christians in Sardis were spiritually lively. At one time that was true (3:3), but by the time of John's revelation, it was not. They were fixated by what others thought of them, believing the adulation; self-examination would've uncovered the things that had been progressively slipping, as indicated in the next verse:

## Part I: The Messages to the Churches

> 3:2 'Wake up, and strengthen the things that remain, which were about to die; for I have not found your deeds completed in the sight of My God.

Their spiritual life was going out like a candle under a glass jar. Jesus told them to strengthen what was left, lest it die out too. This is a dead church that was once alive. It's also described in 3:2 as a church that's asleep, akin to the sleep metaphor in Eph. 5:14.

> 3:3 'So remember what you have received and heard; and keep it, and repent. Therefore if you do not wake up, I will come like a thief, and you will not know at what hour I will come to you.

In 3:3 the "thief in the night" analogy is used once again. As a person falls deeper into sin, he or she is drawn into a state of spiritual desensitization. As the consequences of the sin wax, the sinner becomes less cognizant of the impending doom and more confident that he or she can elude it. The OT account of King Belshazzar illustrates this. Surrounded by the Persians, the King was confident that the city walls would keep the enemy out. He's holding a banquet in the middle of the siege, and has the audacity to bring in the Jerusalem temple goblets. This was the last straw, as the writing on the wall read, "you have been weighed in the scales and found wanting". Any objective view would have ascertained his dire predicament, namely that he was surrounded by the enemy and under siege. The last thing he should've done was to offend the God of Israel, whose might was in manifestation during his father Nebuchadnezzar's reign. Instead of paying homage—or even remaining indifferent—the king is so anesthetized by the hardness of his heart that he desecrates objects consecrated to the holy service of Jehovah. His doom comes like a thief in the night. Jesus reminds the church in Sardis that "you will not know at what hour I will come to you". Sinners think they know this hour—and always think it's a long way off. A person who truly believes that he himself doesn't know the hour will be vigilant, as the hour could manifest at any moment.

> 3:4 'But you have a few people in Sardis who have not soiled their garments; and they will walk with Me in white, for they are worthy.

## Part I: The Messages to the Churches

⁵'He who overcomes will thus be clothed in white garments; and I will not erase his name from the book of life, and I will confess his name before My Father and before His angels. ⁶'He who has an ear, let him hear what the Spirit says to the churches.'

Like in the entire Bible, in these verses the color and cleanliness of clothing represents the degree of righteousness. The ones who haven't "soiled their garments" are the few who haven't sunk into the lethargic sin the majority of the church was in. He who overcomes will be clothed in white, which implies that the clothes will be given to him: not a righteousness of one's own making, but a righteousness imputed by God. God rejected the fig leaves Adam and Eve tried to clothe themselves with, indicating that he rejects man's attempt to attain his own righteousness. The righteousness—the clothing—must be supplied by God, the same in Genesis as 3:5 here.

The prophecy also says that their names won't be erased from the Book of Life. To be erased from a book infers that an entry must've been there prior to erasure—a name was in the book, then removed. Given that an entry in the Book of Life is tantamount to a person being saved, this contradicts the once-saved-always-saved dogma. Names can be removed from the Book of Life. Christians can lose their salvation. Many at the church of Sardis had, or were running the risk of it.

\*

Of the seven churches, two were involved in heresies, two were healthy churches, and the remaining three had lost their spiritual zeal. These three are Ephesus, Sardis, and Laodicea. Their root causes for having slipped differ, however. Ephesus had come to believe that their adherence to church procedures qualified them spiritually. Meanwhile, their inner affections had turned from Jesus. The church at Sardis assessed their spiritual condition not from the affirmation of their heart, but by the praise of men. Most likely they continued in the external works of Christianity, while having a dead heart internally. Only Jesus can truly judge our heart; others judge us by our actions. A person can become self-deceived by maintaining a façade of works, causing him to be held in esteem by society. In the meantime his true spirituality slips—and he may not even recognize it until his sin grows to the point where it causes him to do something reckless, foolish, or immoral. But what these three churches have in common is deceit: dwelling in a state of deception. They believed themselves to be spiritual, but the reality was the opposite. This caused a state of slumber to creep over them. Their fervency in prayer slacked off; their quickness to put away sin diminished; they became comfortable, complacent, dull to the Holy Spirit. Often is asked how far a Christian can sink into sin before God will judge him or her. What's not considered is that the root-cause of sliding into sin is the failure to recognize the progressing problem and the resistance against any action that would pull oneself out. Knowing this, the question of how far a Christian can delve into sin is more like the following: once it's lost its brake and has begun to roll down the hill, how far can a car that was parked on a hilltop roll before it's too late to arrest it?

Both Sardis and Laodicea were self-deceived, and their deception drained their spiritual motivation. The reasons differed between the two. At one time the church at Sardis was spiritually vibrant. This is how they obtained their reputation, and they gloried in living in the past, boasting about what God had done in their midst in bygone years. Most likely, a handful of the old-timers were still around, complemented by a few younger, on-fire disciples; these were the ones God praised (3:4). In spite of their heart's slumber, as time went on their reputation persisted—with man but not with God. They esteemed the praise of man greater than the praise of God, and this was their bane.

## 10. Philadelphia (3:7–3:13)

It is asserted as fact, with no references submitted as validation, that the city of Philadelphia in the commonwealth of Pennsylvania is named after the city of Philadelphia in Revelation, and that this is because of the church in that ancient city—not because the name translated means *city of brotherly love*. No doubt the Quakers, who founded Pennsylvania, Philadelphia being their first city, were devout Christians dedicated to walking in love. Had the name come from the Greek roots and not from the Revelation church, they would've named it *Agapedelphia* instead. *Agape* is the Jesus-kind of love, not *phila*. A person concatenating two Greek words would know this. Agape-love is based on the object of the love; phila-love is a selfish love, love because of what the object does for oneself, namely companionship. Phila-love might love another because that person is witty or charismatic. But in the Quaker's study of the seven churches in Revelation, they ran across two that were praised by the Lord and received no rebuke: Smyrna and Philadelphia. The first was subject to persecution, and since there was no persecution

*Part I: The Messages to the Churches*

in the New World, they chose the second as the name for their city, in the hope that they might emulate the namesake. The translation *city of brotherly love* is but a fortuitous coincidence.

> 3:7 "And to the angel of the church in Philadelphia write: He who is holy, who is true, who has the key of David, who opens and no one will shut, and who shuts and no one opens, says this:
> [8]'I know your deeds Behold, I have put before you an open door which no one can shut, because you have a little power, and have kept My word, and have not denied My name.

Before delivering the prophesy which says that he has placed before them an open door, Jesus reminds them of his ability to open doors. A few times in the NT Paul wrote about an open or a shut door in reference to a ministry opportunity. Doors in the NT are typically associated with gaining or losing favor with people (1 Cor. 16:9; 2 Cor. 2:12; Col. 4:3). Man is the most remarkable of God's creation, as man has a free will and makes decisions autonomously, howbeit persuaded by external influences. It's one thing for God to use his power to change an inanimate object, but such a sheer use of power is unremarkable. It's another for God to dictate the path of a man, especially if the man's will is in opposition to his. To create a free-will being independent of oneself, then to induce him to follow a set path, all the while without violating the sovereignty of his free will, is an act that makes him God.

> 3:9 'Behold, I will cause those of the synagogue of Satan, who say that they are Jews and are not, but lie—I will make them come and bow down at your feet, and make them know that I have loved you.

Deductively, causing the Jews to bow at their feet is the open door from 3:7 and 3:8. It's doubtful that the Jews here would physically bow at the feet of these followers of Christ. This is symbolic. Revelation peers into the spiritual, as John's vision is of spiritual things, leaving it to the reader to make the connection to the natural. Examples like 3:9 contribute to the trail of evidence of this natural-physical parallelism. God was going to manipulate circumstances so that the unbelieving Jews—in the NT the most fierce opponents against the spread of Christianity—would pay homage to the Christians. There were a few Jews, ultra-religious (to quote Acts 23:12 from the KJV, "certain of the Jews"), who went out of their

*Part I: The Messages to the Churches*

way to hound Paul and persecute the early Christians at every bend in the road. They were in the thralls of Satan, as 3:9 says, "synagogue of Satan", and the origin of this was their zeal for the legalistic application of the Law of Moses. So much had they yielded their hearts to Satan that they became like marionettes manipulated by his evil hand. Similar to this, Paul's "thorn in the flesh", 2 Cor. 12:7, was a "messenger of Satan", a demon spirit that directed "certain of the Jews" to persecute him. In the spiritual-realm it was a demon sent against Paul. In the natural-realm it was a band of zealous, religious Jews who far exceeded the pagans in their animosity against Paul's message of the Gospel, freedom from the works of the Law.

To be clear, most of the Jews were not like this. Only a handful was, but a few made the early Christians' lives miserable. Even in this day there's a small group of Jews who're involved in egregious wickedness. Some have used this to justify anti-Semitism. But anti-Semitism itself has a satanic origin, as seen later in this book. These Jews "say that they are Jews and are not, but lie". One is Jewish by birth, of course, but a theme throughout the Bible is that faith makes one Jewish, not birth. This is how Gentiles—Rahab is an example—were injected into the lineage of Christ. Rom. 2:28,29 best sums this up.

But backtracking to 3:8, Jesus commends the Philadelphians for "having a little power". This could be interpreted a couple different ways, as the word for power (*dudamis*) has a few different meanings. It can mean *ability*, *might*, or *supernatural power*. Which one it means in this context is not entirely certain. They're commended for having a "little" power—an invitation to pursue even more.

> 3:10 'Because you have kept the word of My perseverance, I also will keep you from the hour of testing, that hour which is about to come upon the whole world, to test those who dwell on the earth.

The church in Philadelphia gets two prophecies and no rebukes. Had some of the other churches not been in sin, their prophecy could've been dispensed as a genuine prophetic word, and not squandered as a chastisement. This second prophecy is a foreshadowing for what comes next in the book: the promise is that the Philadelphians will be spared from the "hour of testing". But what is the hour of testing? Is it the opening of the seals John witnesses later? This does not occur (at least entirely) in the lifetime of the Philadelphian Christians.

*Part I: The Messages to the Churches*

> 3:11 'I am coming quickly; hold fast what you have, so that no one will take your crown.

The encouragement. Again, Jesus is coming quickly, and the believers are to be watchful, to be diligent, and to persevere. The crown in this verse, a *stephanos*, is a reward given to the victor. They had received their crown already—it wasn't to be given when they got to heaven. But they had to hold on to it, lest they lose it. Believers have crowns. They get them both on earth and in heaven. The ones on earth are earned—but as 3:11 indicates, they can be lost also.

> 3:12 'He who overcomes, I will make him a pillar in the temple of My God, and he will not go out from it anymore; and I will write on him the name of My God, and the name of the city of My God, the new Jerusalem, which comes down out of heaven from My God, and My new name.
> ¹³'He who has an ear, let him hear what the Spirit says to the churches.'

The promise to the overcomer of being made a "pillar in the temple of My God" is no mean reward. "...And he will not go out from it anymore": the position will be permanent. It's a mystery how such a short life can garner such long rewards, for good or for evil. Suffice to say, God is quite pleased by those who, in this lifetime, persevere in faith. The rewards are substantial and eternal.

Here also is the first reference to the new Jerusalem. This is Mt. Zion, mankind's existence without the corruption of sin, and the harm caused to the planet after the fall of man. It has to come down out of heaven from God; otherwise it would be polluted from man's touch. No matter how hard he tries, the Jerusalem which man has built—the ideal city, the utopian society—is corrupt. The Founding Fathers of the United States of America understood this, so in their quest to create a new government, they strove to create "a more perfect union". Societies and governments founded on humanistic idealism produce results which are the antithesis of the idealism they promise. Communism is the prime example. It's not until the reign of Jesus on the earth that a new Jerusalem can be sent down out of heaven, and such idealism in the form of the OT prophesies of men beating their swords into pruning hooks can be fulfilled.

There're a few references in Revelation of what's stated in 3:12, "I will write on him the name of My God". The significance of this phrase transcends the actual deed of writing a name on someone. "I will write on him" has its origins in the OT, and signifies the pronouncement, usually by God, of a person's accomplishments, character, or relationship to someone or something. Also in 3:12 is the first reference to the Great City. Cities are locales where people gather for a purpose, united in an undertaking, as was Babel in Genesis. The OT yearning for Jerusalem will be satiated by the end of Revelation.

\*

Of the seven, the church at Philadelphia (Smyrna notwithstanding) is in the best spiritual condition. But how did they gain favor with the Lord, whereas the others failed? The key was their "perseverance" (3:10). When describing them, Jesus twice uses the word *kept* (3:8, 3:10). Paul compares the Christian walk to a marathon and not a sprint. Marathons require perseverance; sprints do not. Like a soldier assigned the night watch, Christians must maintain a vigilance and alertness in their day-to-day lives. In this way they'll walk in the footsteps of the Philadelphians and will thus please the Lord.

## 11. Laodicea (3:14–3:22)

> 3:14 "To the angel of the church in Laodicea write: The Amen, the faithful and true Witness, the Beginning of the creation of God, says this:

Jesus is the "Amen", which in this context is the end of a matter, the final word spoken. And as Max & Mary say, the word "beginning" in this verse means the ultimate source of creation.

> 3:15 'I know your deeds, that you are neither cold nor hot; I wish that you were cold or hot.
> [16]"So because you are lukewarm, and neither hot nor cold, I will spit you out of My mouth.

The prophecy for this church is a warning to repent or get thrown out, and is frequently the text of sermons. The prior two verses must be interpreted in light of the next:

> 3:17 'Because you say, "I am rich, and have become wealthy, and have need of nothing," and you do not know that you are wretched and miserable and poor and blind and naked,

*Part I: The Messages to the Churches*

The root-cause of the Laodicean luke-warmness was their belief that they "have need of nothing". In actuality they did, but were far from recognizing it. Laodicea is the third in the set of churches to have lost its spiritual fervor. It's the only church where not even a hint of something positive is said about it. Their wealth in material goods lulled them into thinking they needed nothing more, including spiritual things. They saw no need to pursue good works, or a closer relationship with the Lord, as—in their mind—they had arrived already, so why the need? They're the polar opposite of Smyrna, as the Christians there had barely enough to live on—but had a rich spiritual life. In modern, developed countries, material prosperity in absolute terms has touched everyone, even those considered poor. The want for the basic needs in life—food, clothing, and shelter—is virtually non-existent. In these countries large portions of the Body of Christ have fallen into the same sin as the Laodiceans. How hard it is for a rich man to enter the kingdom of God. Those with abundance must be doubly-diligent to excel in zeal for the Lord, as they are handicapped by their prosperity. It's natural for a person of means to have a spiritual slumber overtake him or her. Most of those in the Gospels who sought after Jesus came to him because they had a pressing need. Of the ten lepers who were healed by Jesus, only one returned to thank him. Once they were no longer in need, their devotion to the Lord vanished almost immediately. This pitfall must be understood nowadays by Christians in the West.

> 3:18 I advise you to buy from Me gold refined by fire so that you may become rich, and white garments so that you may clothe yourself, and that the shame of your nakedness will not be revealed; and eye salve to anoint your eyes so that you may see.
> [19]"Those whom I love, I reprove and discipline; therefore be zealous and repent.

The "gold refined by fire" describes a real spirituality, a pure one, not an artificial one, but one derived from prayer from a contrite heart. The analogy is the purification of gold: the impurities inherent in gold are separated by heating the metal to a liquid, forcing the dross to the surface, to be removed. Any person can purify himself, rich or poor—it's just that the poor man has the stark realization that he must—he has no choice. The rich man lives in a world of deceit, where everything appears to be alright, but in fact the contrary is true. This is what Jesus meant by the eye salve.

*Part I: The Messages to the Churches*

In spite of the wrong, yet again Jesus extends a word of exhortation to do right:

> 3:20 'Behold, I stand at the door and knock; if anyone hears My voice and opens the door, I will come in to him and will dine with him, and he with Me.
> [21]'He who overcomes, I will grant to him to sit down with Me on My throne, as I also overcame and sat down with My Father on His throne.
> [22]'He who has an ear, let him hear what the Spirit says to the churches.'"

For this church, to "overcome" is to repent and to become zealous (3:19), and to stay that way. This needs to be taught in contemporary Western churches. The irony is that *Revelation 3:20* is often written on a sign and held by Christians at football games so the TV cameras will catch it while panning.

Though Laodicea has been the theme of many a sermon, the lesson bears repeating. The ability of wealth to produce a state of slumber and deception, to choke the Word like in the Parable of the Sower, is often beyond the imagination of those caught in its vortex. The complacency which ensues after one has through the abundance of material goods acquired physical comfort is nefarious by means of its deceitfulness. The perpetual warnings in the NT for vigilance address this audience.

## 12. John's Next Vision (4:1–4:11)

> 4:1 After these things I looked, and behold, a door standing open in heaven, and the first voice which I had heard, like the sound of a trumpet speaking with me, said, "Come up here, and I will show you what must take place after these things."
> [2]Immediately I was in the Spirit; and behold, a throne was standing in heaven, and One sitting on the throne.

"After these things" means that John's first vision stopped, then, after a short intermission, another began. The phrase "I looked, and behold" is a Hebrew idiom (see Max & Mary) indicating that what follows is a vision. In Greek the door "in heaven" includes the definite article to read *in the heavens*, and used in this way usually means *the sky* (see Acts 1:11), as the Greek word can mean either. In biblical times it was believed that heaven is up in the atmosphere and hell is under the earth. And for that matter, Satan and his demons inhabit the earth. There are several Scriptures supporting this concept, and it's not unreasonable to argue that heaven and hell are actually above and beneath. But in this physical world, being in outer space does not separate one from demons or make a person closer to the real heaven. In any event, from this passage, John looked up to see the open door. This suggests he was outside, at least at the inception of this second vision. John was seeing with his physical senses a door up in the sky. After he went up, however, he then became "in the Spirit", so his normal senses were suspended, and he was seeing into the spiritual realm—seeing heaven.

There're three types of visions: spiritual visions, trances, and open visions. A spiritual vision is a vision that one sees within his or her own spirit, while the physical senses remain active. It's the least spectacular of the three. A trance (Acts 10:10) is a vision in which one's physical senses are suspended, and in its place one sees the content from the vision. In an open vision, the physical senses are active while the vision occurs. The vision is superimposed upon what one already sees. John's vision of 4:1 is an open vision: he sees the sky as usual, but up in the sky a door appears. The door's accompanied by a voice, the voice telling him to come up, presumably to enter through the door. The other side of the door is heaven (4:2), and after passing through the door, John's vision changes from an open vision to a trance.

This is the second time in the book he's said to be *in the Spirit*, the same phrase used in 1 Cor. 12:3, in that passage speaking of someone who's prophesying. A person who's in the Spirit is visited, or moved upon, by the Holy Spirit in a special way to cause him or her to prophesy, to have a vision, or to have some other manifestation of the gifts of the Holy Spirit. With the Pentecostal movement's upsurge at the turn of the last century, people began to report having such experiences in the Holy Spirit. In spite of what many have said over the years, the supernatural working of the Holy Spirit hasn't ceased. While examining this phrase, however, one might recall 1 Cor. 12:2,3, (the wording for which has always been a mystery [Max & Mary offer two renditions of v. 2]):

> 1 Cor. 12:2 You know that when you were pagans, you were led astray to the mute idols, however you were led.
> [3] Therefore I make known to you that no one speaking by the Spirit of God says, "Jesus is accursed"; and no one can say, "Jesus is Lord," except by the Holy Spirit.

*Part I: The Messages to the Churches*

What's referred to in v. 2 above is that the pagans during their rituals would yield themselves to demon spirits, which would move upon them in a way which imitates (attempts to, at least) the Holy Spirit moving upon a servant of God. Verse 3 concerns a person who's been visited by a spirit—either a demonic spirit or the Holy Spirit, the source is uncertain—and provides a means to distinguish the source. So, in the case of someone "speaking by the Spirit of God", i.e. when he or she is moved upon by the Holy Spirit in a special way to prophesy, perform a miracle, etc., this person cannot say "Jesus is accursed". The converse applies to a person who's had a demon visit them for the purpose of an unclean prophecy. In this state, this one cannot say "Jesus is Lord"—although they could (and while not under the influence of a spirit frequently do) say it otherwise. In other words, 1 Cor. 12:2,3 doesn't apply to everyday-speech.

After John looks up and sees this door, his natural senses are suspended, and he sees into the spiritual realm. What he sees is a scene in heaven. The "one sitting on the throne" is God the Father, not Jesus. The two, the Father and the Son, are distinct persons having different roles, yet having the same nature, and coexisting in perfect harmony.

> 4:3 And He who was sitting was like a jasper stone and a sardius in appearance; and there was a rainbow around the throne, like an emerald in appearance.

There're two words for "jasper" in Greek, and both are found in 4:3: *sard* ("sardius" in 4:3), the red, more common jasper, and *iaspis* ("jasper" in 4:3), the rarer, green jasper. Jasper is usually polished to a smooth finish, producing a stone that has beauty and hardness, but is opaque, unlike diamonds or emeralds or sapphires. It can be a variety of colors, but the green and blue are rarer than the red. God's appearance here is like both the green and red forms, probably indicating a variety of colors. The rainbow surrounding the throne, however, was like an emerald—a brilliant green color, and translucent.

> 4:4 Around the throne were twenty-four thrones; and upon the thrones I saw twenty-four elders sitting, clothed in white garments, and golden crowns on their heads.

The twenty-four elders represent the best of mankind, the most righteous, the most worthy of God. Moses, at the behest of Jethro

*Part I: The Messages to the Churches*

(Exod. 18), established the precedence of elders, who were used to arbitrate civil and criminal cases in Israel. The elders in this way had authority over Israel. This tradition was passed down through many centuries (the Sanhedrin is derived from it), the form of government even being copied by the early Church. There've been a few theories put forth as to why there're twenty-four of them. Some say there're twelve from the OT, twelve from the NT—there were twelve tribes of Israel, and twelve apostles, therefore these twenty-four represent the chosen of God from both covenants. Who they are is a mystery that Revelation never answers. It's unlikely that twelve of them are in fact the Twelve Apostles for the simple reason that the apostle John views the twelve, therefore is not one of them, leaving the set incomplete.

The "seven spirits of God" is referenced for the second time in 4:5, and again without explanation. The prevalent wisdom is that these are the dominant characteristics of the Holy Spirit.

> 4:5 Out from the throne come flashes of lightning and sounds and peals of thunder. And there were seven lamps of fire burning before the throne, which are the seven Spirits of God;

The thunder and lightning is due to the holiness of God, terrible in its ferocity—one reason God must commune with mankind through a mediator (Jesus). Because of God's holiness, Moses, while receiving the Ten Commandments on Mt. Sinai, was unable to look at him directly, and in turn the Israelites were not able to look at Moses' face afterwards due to the brilliance of the glory of God which hadn't yet receded. The thunder and lighting represents the terror of the judgment of the Almighty. There are two aspects of God: his mercy and love, but also his holiness and judgment. The two are in harmony, but too infrequently does mankind consider both, preferring to see one at the expense of the other. In NT times the Lord's mercy prevails, but this mercy is but for a season. Revelation warns us that this season is about to end. Modern man, having been weaned on the mercy of God, and having shunned their predecessors who were overly consumed with the holiness of God, lacks the element of truth that the later brings to complement the former. Present thought is obsessed with God's mercy and ignores God's judgment.

*Part I: The Messages to the Churches*

> 4:6 and before the throne there was something like a sea of glass, like crystal; and in the center and around the throne, four living creatures full of eyes in front and behind.
> ⁷The first creature was like a lion, and the second creature like a calf, and the third creature had a face like that of a man, and the fourth creature was like a flying eagle.
> ⁸And the four living creatures, each one of them having six wings, are full of eyes around and within; and day and night they do not cease to say, "HOLY, HOLY, HOLY is THE LORD GOD, THE ALMIGHTY, WHO WAS AND WHO IS AND WHO IS TO COME."
> ⁹And when the living creatures give glory and honor and thanks to Him who sits on the throne, to Him who lives forever and ever...

Much of the symbolic imagery in John's visions can be traced back to the Book of Ezekiel. John studied this book—its influence is woven throughout Revelation. The four creatures are quite similar to what Ezekiel saw in his vision:

> Ezek. 1:4 As I looked, behold, a storm wind was coming from the north, a great cloud with fire flashing forth continually and a bright light around it, and in its midst something like glowing metal in the midst of the fire.
> ⁵Within it there were figures resembling four living beings. And this was their appearance: they had human form.
> ⁶Each of them had four faces and four wings.
> ⁷Their legs were straight and their feet were like a calf's hoof, and they gleamed like burnished bronze.
> ⁸Under their wings on their four sides were human hands. As for the faces and wings of the four of them,
> ⁹their wings touched one another; their faces did not turn when they moved, each went straight forward.
> ¹⁰As for the form of their faces, each had the face of a man; all four had the face of a lion on the right and the face of a bull on the left, and all four had the face of an eagle.
> ¹¹Such were their faces. Their wings were spread out above; each had two touching another being, and two covering their bodies.

Later in the tenth chapter of Ezekiel, these creatures are identified as cherubim, which are a spiritual being, similar to angels, but

## Part I: The Messages to the Churches

their role is to surround the Almighty's holiness. They have wings, and this is most likely the origination of the popular misconception that angels have wings. The wings are used to cover something or someone—not necessarily to fly.

> Isa. 1:2 Seraphim stood above Him, each having six wings: with two he covered his face, and with two he covered his feet, and with two he flew.
> ³And one called out to another and said, "Holy, Holy, Holy, is the LORD of hosts, The whole earth is full of His glory."

References to the cherubim appear a handful of times in the Bible; the seraphim only once (above). What defines the seraphim is that their purpose is to surround the throne of God, proclaiming his holiness. Perhaps seraphim are a type of cherubim. After Adam and Eve were kicked out of the Garden, cherubim were posted to prevent them from returning. Having sinned, they were ineligible to dwell in the same garden where God regularly visits.

According to Bullinger the four heads in Ezekiel "...are represented by the symbolic heads of the four great divisions of animate creation: the lion (of wild beasts), the ox (of tame beasts), the eagle (of birds), man (of humanity)." Bullinger further states that these four represent all of God's creation. Unlike Ezekiel's vision, where a single cherub has a set of these four animal faces, in John's vision four cherubim appear, each having one of the faces. These may be similar, yet different creatures—it's difficult to say.

To penetrate the mystery of the purpose of the seraphim eyes mentioned in 4:8 ("full of eyes around and within"), one draws on 5:7. In 5:7 Jesus has seven eyes, and the eyes are the Holy Spirit. In 4:8 no other details about the eyes are given. If the eyes represent spirits, then there're facets to a seraphim's spiritual nature.

But in John's vision the purpose of the cherubim and seraphim is to endlessly proclaim the holiness of God, and to prompt the elders to fall prostrate and worship him. Note that God is worshipped for his holiness, for simply being God, for having created all things:

> 4:10...the twenty-four elders will fall down before Him who sits on the throne, and will worship Him who lives forever and ever, and will cast their crowns before the throne, saying, ¹¹"Worthy are You, our Lord and our God, to receive glory and honor and power; for You created all things, and because of Your will they existed, and were created."

*Part I: The Messages to the Churches*

This is typical of the praise to God the Father. In contrast, Jesus is praised for what he accomplished here on earth. God is known for who he is; Jesus is known for what he's done. Because of Jesus' works, God the Father appointed him Lord. Both draw praise and worship, howbeit for different reasons. These reasons reflect the roles they play in the Trinity.

# Part II

# Modes of the Judgment of God

*Part II: Modes of the Judgment of God*

# 1. Introduction

A pause from this exegesis of Revelation is in order, as a more complete understanding of the judgment of God is prerequisite. From the fourth to the twentieth chapters, Revelation's primary theme is the judgment of God and his wrath poured out on the earth. All of Scripture must be drawn together to fully understand the judgment of God, a perplexing topic.

# 2. The Flood: Archetype of God's Judgment

The story of Noah and the flood is the archetype for how God's judgment works, and for this reason in Matt. 24 (also in Luke 17) Jesus remarked:

> Matt. 24:37 "For the coming of the Son of Man will be just like the days of Noah.
> [38]"For as in those days before the flood they were eating and drinking, marrying and giving in marriage, until the day that Noah entered the ark,
> [39]and they did not understand until the flood came and took them all away; so will the coming of the Son of Man be.

To fully appreciate the judgment in the time of Noah, all pertinent information must be gathered and scrutinized. There're some not so well-known details to this epic that can be gleaned by a careful reading of the text. The early genealogies in Genesis demonstrate that at that time God had selected a single lineage to be his people, and that Noah was the culmination. Prior to Noah was Enoch. Jude says the following about him:

> Jude 14 It was also about these men that Enoch, in the seventh generation from Adam, prophesied, saying, "Behold, the Lord came with many thousands of His holy ones,
> [15]to execute judgment upon all, and to convict all the ungodly of all their ungodly deeds which they have done in an ungodly way, and of all the harsh things which ungodly sinners have spoken against Him."

*Part II: Modes of the Judgment of God*

This prophecy is a quotation from the Book of Enoch, which explains why the early Church, when compiling the NT canon, refused to accept Jude (along with 2 Pet.) These two verses in Jude have a dual application: the time of Noah and the time of Jesus' Second Coming—two parallel events. They're just one of several verses in the Bible declaring that the ungodly are destined for a day of judgment for their wickedness. The references by Jude, and also 2 Pet. (see v. 5 below), call both Enoch and Noah preachers.

> 2 Pet. 2:4 For if God did not spare angels when they sinned, but cast them into hell and committed them to pits of darkness, reserved for judgment;
> [5] and did not spare the ancient world, but preserved Noah, a preacher of righteousness, with seven others, when He brought a flood upon the world of the ungodly;
> [6] and if He condemned the cities of Sodom and Gomorrah to destruction by reducing them to ashes, having made them an example to those who would live ungodly lives thereafter;
> [7] and if He rescued righteous Lot, oppressed by the sensual conduct of unprincipled men
> [8] (for by what he saw and heard that righteous man, while living among them, felt his righteous soul tormented day after day by their lawless deeds),
> [9] then the Lord knows how to rescue the godly from temptation, and to keep the unrighteous under punishment for the day of judgment,

Reading Jude and 2 Pet. is like getting wacked by the baseball bat of the certainty that God punishes the unrighteous for their wickedness. To magnify this certainty, Lot, not typically the hero in the Sunday sermon, receives more praises by Jude in vv. 7 and 8 than from all of the remainder of the Bible.

The judgment of Noah was slow in coming, though the wickedness had continued for a long while, as told below:

> 1 Pet. 3:18 For Christ also died for sins once for all, the just for the unjust, so that He might bring us to God, having been put to death in the flesh, but made alive in the spirit;
> [19] in which also He went and made proclamation to the spirits now in prison,
> [20] who once were disobedient, when the patience of God kept waiting in the days of Noah, during the construction of the

## Part II: Modes of the Judgment of God

ark, in which a few, that is, eight persons, were brought safely through the water.
[21]Corresponding to that, baptism now saves you—not the removal of dirt from the flesh, but an appeal to God for a good conscience—through the resurrection of Jesus Christ,

Verse 20 says, "when the patience of God kept waiting"—the NASB inserting the word "kept" to capture the Greek imperfect tense in "waiting", which tense justifies rewording the verse (in corporate vernacular) to say that it was the patience of God that caused him to *slip the schedule* or *push the date out* for the time of the flood. God hoped—in vain, but still hoped—that Noah's warning would be heeded and the flood averted. And because of the Lord's patience in this drama, Methuselah lived to be the oldest person, as recorded by the Bible. To quote Bullinger, the name Methuselah translated from Hebrew means, "when he is dead it shall be sent". A prophecy had been given when Methuselah was born that, when he died, judgment would fall. In fact, if one does a careful chronology of the genealogies, and correlates it to the date of the flood, one finds that Methuselah died the same year as the flood. By virtue of God's patience, the original date of the flood kept on getting postponed. God's judgment is not set in stone, but can change with the softening of man's heart, and by the mercy of God's patience. God creates dates for judgment, then, in his forbearance, overruns them. When he did this for the flood, he had to delay Methuselah's death as well, to preserve the promise of the prophecy. Methuselah's long life is a testimony to the patience of God while meting judgment.

A couple notes on the previous passage from 1 Pet. Verses 19 and 20 say that he "made a proclamation to the spirits now in prison, who once were disobedient". The "spirits now in prison" are referring to the ungodly men in Noah's time who perished in the flood. From the time of the flood to the time of his epistle, many centuries had elapsed, and these miscreants were still in "prison", i.e. hell. Jesus, on the morning of the third day, was himself released from prison. Before he left he preached to these wicked men who were still incarcerated there the message embedded in v. 18, namely that he died for the sins of the unjust. They could not act on this proclamation, however, as their opportunity to repent had expired the moment the flood came. God gives a window for man to repent. To man it seems long, too long. But to God it's not long enough, so he extends it, knowing the fate that awaits the unrepentant. These men whom Peter labels "disobedient" were not censured because of their everyday sin. Their rejection of the message, the one proclaimed over and over by Noah, was the source of their

## Part II: Modes of the Judgment of God

disobedience. Jesus' proclamation to them while in prison was not one of mercy, as it is for those who have the privilege of hearing it on this earth, but one of judgment.

The other note is v. 21, "corresponding to that, baptism now saves you—not the removal of dirt from the flesh...." The voyage of Noah through the water is symbolic of water baptism. Imported from the OT, in v. 21 the word *to save* is translated from its core meaning, namely *to be rescued from impending doom*. It has more than one application. Noah was *saved* from the flood. Christians are *saved* from sin. Thus, in this context baptism has two applications. The deluge of the flood baptized Noah. And Christians are saved from their sin by the rite of baptism. Or so the verse would indicate, and those who teach that a person cannot go to heaven without being baptized in water use verses such as these to buttress their arguments. But this verse goes on to say, "not the removal of dirt from the flesh, but an appeal to God for a good conscience". Peter is clarifying this controversial topic: the phrase means that it's not the actual washing with water during baptism that saves a person, but rather the decision of his or her heart—common sense to the Anabaptist posterity (and to the current Zeitgeist) in modern Christianity which professes that one becomes a Christian by his or her personal decision. Another cannot make that decision for you, nor will a ritual substitute for a confession. A person is a Christian by choice—not ceremony. This is all well and good, except that the NT has other verses (Mark 16:16; Rom. 6:4) which support the premise that water baptism saves a man. How do these jive? The answer is that neither side in the baptism debate is completely right and neither is completely wrong. Hence the bitterness of the dispute: both parties have a piece of truth; both ask the other to relinquish his. In NT times, unlike modern times, those who committed themselves to Christ were immediately baptized. The two events—committing your heart to Jesus and water baptism—came to be seen as one and the same because the one never occurred independent of the other. If one was water baptized, he or she must have professed Christ; a person who has confessed Christ as savior must have been baptized. Differentiating the two events has spawned this doctrinal barrier.

A parallel is the NT's usage of circumcision. Circumcision is the outward sign whereby a man accepts the Law, in an attempt to please God by the works thereof. A circumcised man is one who's attempting to be justified by the works of the Law. A person whose justification is based on the works of the Law is referred to as *circumcised*. The two are one and the same and therefore used interchangeably. Thus, Paul said in Gal. 5:2, "Behold I, Paul, say to you

## Part II: Modes of the Judgment of God

that if you receive circumcision, Christ will be of no benefit to you." It's not the physical act, the ritual, that displeases God but the man who chooses the works of the Law as a proxy for faith in Christ. Skipping to v. 4, "You have been severed from Christ, you who are seeking to be justified by law"—by this verse the connection between circumcision and one who seeks to be justified by the works of the Law is sealed. The connection between baptism and one who has professed faith in the Son of God works the same way; the two are inseparable.

\*

Tracking down the remaining NT comments on Noah, he's listed in the Faith Hall of Fame, Heb. 11:

> Heb. 11:7 By faith Noah, being warned by God about things not yet seen, in reverence prepared an ark for the salvation of his household, by which he condemned the world, and became an heir of the righteousness which is according to faith.

"Salvation" in the above verse's context means that Noah was rescued from the flood. It's not talking about his spiritual condition (primarily—the end of the verse refers to Noah's righteousness, his spiritual condition). What Peter meant when he said "condemned the world" is that Noah ensured that the world (i.e. those who are apart from God for whatever reason) would be destroyed by the flood. God could not send the flood until Noah could be safeguarded by the ark; by inverse logic, what Noah accomplished by having built the ark was the means of escaping the wrath of God that was universally dispensed on all living creatures. God did not intend, nor would allow, for Noah to suffer the fate of the disobedient.

In Matt. 24 Jesus not only compares the coming judgment to Noah, but gives us the poignant simile of the thief in the night, the vigilance that John so repetitiously admonishes the churches of Revelation. Mentioning this analogy in passing—even emphasizing it—does injustice to the repeated exhortations from Jesus in the Gospels and from John in Revelation. What does "come as a thief in the night" mean? When a burglar breaks into a house, he arrives suddenly and quickly concludes his larceny. To repel him one must maintain a heightened awareness at all times. To diligently sustain such an acute state of vigilance requires a special mindset, a serious demeanor, a single-minded purpose, a self-sacrifice. In the example of Noah's contemporaries, the godless were eating, drinking, marrying—living their everyday normal lives. And not a bad one, by the

*Part II: Modes of the Judgment of God*

sound of it. They were heedless to the calls for repentance. Their wickedness was piling up before God; all the while they had no self-awareness of it because of their negligence to monitor their spiritual condition. They had become so callous to sin that Noah appeared the fool, and they the wise. This is the opposite of being watchful; they stood no chance against the thief.

In the case of the early Church in the Roman Empire of the first and second centuries A.D., Roman historians have left a written record, which reveals similarities to Noah's time. What do the historians say of the Christians? According to Edwards in his classic *The History of the Decline and Fall of the Roman Empire*, they hardly mention them. The Romans became consumed by their everyday lives. A point Jesus was making in the Noah-lesson, which was also true with the Romans, is that there's a blindness that accompanies sin. This blindness is perpetuated by an immersion in the day-to-day affairs of life, and enables a callousness wherein sin foments. All God requires is a thankful heart. In an environment where a person's physical needs are met, with perhaps a bit extra to boot, an era of prosperity, the temptation to slide into a lifestyle where one neglects service to God is ever pressing and acute. As Genesis tells us of the wickedness being practiced in the time of Noah, Jesus on the other hand reminds us of the mundane things these people were involved in just before they fell off the precipice, so to speak. The flood came as a thief in the night, and they were caught off guard. But on the other hand, they had been warned repeatedly. In fact, the quotation from Jude, previously cited, has Enoch prophesying of impending judgment. Noah wasn't the only preacher in the family line. Generations before him Enoch was repeating the same message. But instead of repenting, their hearts became increasingly callous to the truth, and they shut their ears to it, living in a world of deceit, pursuing this, that, and the other—but not pursuing the knowledge of God. From their perspective, judgment appeared to come like a thief in the night. In fact, the opposite was true; judgment crept in at a turtle's pace.

\*

The saga of Noah and the flood has another aspect to it, having its origin in a theory that can be traced back to pre-Christian Jewish literature.

> Gen. 6:1 Now it came about, when men began to multiply on the face of the land, and daughters were born to them,
> ²that the sons of God saw that the daughters of men were beautiful; and they took wives for themselves, whomever they chose.

*Part II: Modes of the Judgment of God*

..........
⁴The Nephilim were on the earth in those days, and also afterward, when the sons of God came in to the daughters of men, and they bore children to them. Those were the mighty men who were of old, men of renown.
⁵Then the LORD saw that the wickedness of man was great on the earth, and that every intent of the thoughts of his heart was only evil continually.
..........
⁸But Noah found favor in the eyes of the LORD.
⁹These are the records of the generations of Noah. Noah was a righteous man, blameless in his time; Noah walked with God.
..........
¹²God looked on the earth, and behold, it was corrupt; for all flesh had corrupted their way upon the earth.
¹³Then God said to Noah, "The end of all flesh has come before Me; for the earth is filled with violence because of them; and behold, I am about to destroy them with the earth.

The theory is this: the giants (Hebrew *Nephilim* in v. 4) were the progeny of fallen angels who had had relations with women. This happened twice, in Noah's time and in David's. These giants were wicked. Verse 4 in Hebrew says they were "men of renown" or *men of a reputation*—a bad one. They had mixed their corrupt flesh with the entire human race except for Noah and his family. Verses 8 and 9 in Hebrew literally says that Noah was pure before God—meaning pure in flesh, not in spirit. He was the only descendant from Adam who hadn't been tainted by Nephilim flesh. The reason why God had to send the flood was to protect the last pure blood line, in order to repopulate the human race from this uncorrupted stock. Had God not taken action in Noah's time, there could have been no redemption for mankind. Jude subscribed to this theory, as he alludes to it in his epistle:

> Jude 6 And angels who did not keep their own domain, but abandoned their proper abode, He has kept in eternal bonds under darkness for the judgment of the great day,
> ⁷just as Sodom and Gomorrah and the cities around them, since they in the same way as these indulged in gross immorality and went after strange flesh, are exhibited as an example in undergoing the punishment of eternal fire.

*Part II: Modes of the Judgment of God*

The Lord had to destroy the world to prevent the corrupt flesh from inundating the pure, to prevent the irreversible destruction of his creation. Furthermore, since God had already prophesied the coming of Jesus (Gen. 3:15), the fulfillment of that prophecy could not be jeopardized. All of this was calculated in the wisdom and foreknowledge of God; the flood was the result. Consider this analogy: a person's working with a computer that has a recurring problem, and he has come to recognize when a crash is imminent. He's in the middle of writing a lengthy document—what will he do? First, he'll save the document to the hard drive, to prevent it from getting corrupted, then reboot the PC to restore it to a state of health (even if temporary). Once the computer's been rebooted, he can then reopen the document and continue to edit it. This is what God did in the days of Noah.

\*

As the Noah-epic is the standard for of God's judgment, all other biblical judgments contain one or more elements from this episode. These are the aspects of the flood-judgment:

1) God gave plenty of time and numerous warnings for those in sin to repent
2) The righteous (Noah and his family) were not included in the judgment, only sinners
3) The righteous endured hardship and travail until the end
4) It was by faith that Noah believed judgment was coming and thereby avoided it
5) When the judgment (the flood) arrived, the onslaught was swift, it achieved its objective quickly, and it was unavoidable by those for whom it was targeted
6) The flood was unexpected by those whom it destroyed, as they were headless to the warnings as they went about their day-to-day affairs
7) The results were permanent: those destroyed were never heard from again; the course of the world was altered
8) Though the flood was prophesied, God's mercy postponed the date
9) God had to bring judgment upon the wicked to prevent irreversible consequences

*Part II: Modes of the Judgment of God*

# 3. Predestined Judgment

Another narrative from the OT, one employing a mode of the judgment of God, is the Exodus. This saga, where God manifests himself to Pharaoh, is puzzling in some respects:

> Exod. 7:13 Yet **Pharaoh's heart was hardened**, and he did not listen to them, as the LORD had said.
>
> Exod. 7:22 But the magicians of Egypt did the same with their secret arts; and **Pharaoh's heart was hardened**, and he did not listen to them, as the LORD had said.
>
> Exod. 8:19 Then the magicians said to Pharaoh, "This is the finger of God." But **Pharaoh's heart was hardened**, and he did not listen to them, as the LORD had said.
>
> Exod.9:12 **And the LORD hardened Pharaoh's heart**, and he did not listen to them, just as the LORD had spoken to Moses.

The last quotation, Exod. 9:12, is the most baffling. It says that "the LORD hardened Pharaoh's heart", unlike the previous references which might insinuate that Pharaoh's heart was hardened as an act of his free will. How can this be? If man is a free-moral agent, independently choosing right or wrong, how is God the one who hardened Pharaoh's heart? This must be reconciled if one is to properly understand how God interacts with mankind. Here's a different instance which sheds light on the former:

> Rom. 9:10 And not only this, but there was Rebekah also, when she had conceived twins by one man, our father Isaac;
> ¹¹for though the twins were not yet born and had not done anything good or bad, so that God's purpose according to His choice would stand, not because of works but because of Him who calls,
> ¹²it was said to her, "THE OLDER WILL SERVE THE YOUNGER."
> ¹³Just as it is written, "JACOB I LOVED, BUT ESAU I HATED."
> ¹⁴What shall we say then? There is no injustice with God, is there? May it never be!

## Part II: Modes of the Judgment of God

¹⁵For He says to Moses, "I WILL HAVE MERCY ON WHOM I HAVE MERCY, AND I WILL HAVE COMPASSION ON WHOM I HAVE COMPASSION."
¹⁶So then it does not depend on the man who wills or the man who runs, but on God who has mercy.
¹⁷For the Scripture says to Pharaoh, "FOR THIS VERY PURPOSE I RAISED YOU UP, TO DEMONSTRATE MY POWER IN YOU, AND THAT MY NAME MIGHT BE PROCLAIMED THROUGHOUT THE WHOLE EARTH."
¹⁸So then He has mercy on whom He desires, and He hardens whom He desires.
¹⁹You will say to me then, "Why does He still find fault? For who resists His will?"
²⁰On the contrary, who are you, O man, who answers back to God? The thing molded will not say to the molder, "Why did you make me like this," will it?
²¹Or does not the potter have a right over the clay, to make from the same lump one vessel for honorable use and another for common use?

The above passage is a cornerstone to the doctrine of predestination as taught by Calvin. Actually, Calvin did not invent the doctrine himself, but acquired it from Augustine, who in turn adapted it from Greek philosophers. Predestination's memory acronym T.U.L.I.P.—the *T* standing for *total depravity*—teaches that a person's salvation is an act of God's sovereign will. Man has nothing to do with it, and in fact cannot since he is totally depraved. According to Calvin, God sees the past, present, and future at the same time. God knows the future before it happens, therefore it's predetermined, meaning it's predetermined that some be saved and others be damned. There's nothing a person can do to change his or her election. In modern times this doctrine has been assailed to the point where those who do teach it teach a modified, watered-down version of the original, to make it more palatable. It's taught mostly in seminaries—and not by tent-revival evangelists, who preach sermons from Acts 2:21 (KJV) "...whosoever shall call on the name of the Lord shall be saved", then ask, *Are you a whosoever?* They give altar calls for people to accept Christ as Lord and Savior—they never say, *Everyone who's predestined to be saved, come on down. For those of you who aren't, please don't clog the aisles.*

There are sets of Scriptures that declare that salvation is an act of one's free will, and others that confirm predestination. Too often, the faction on the one side of a doctrine dwells on those Scriptures

*Part II: Modes of the Judgment of God*

that support its position to the neglect of the ones that don't. The Bible, since it's inspired by God, has perfect harmony—but only when all Scriptures are taken into consideration. The dichotomy between free will and God's sovereignty is analogous to the theory of light that physicists had postulated by the early twentieth century. With the empirical evidence that light has wave properties, Maxwell developed a tidy set of equations called *Maxwell's Equations*. From these all the theoretical properties of light waves (electromagnetic radiation) were derived. Case closed...until physicists began to notice properties of light that could only be explained in terms of a particle model. This led to Planck's Quantum Theory, which states that matter, including light, has a dual nature. It's both wave and particle. Only after both theories were encompassed could the complete nature of light be understood. Either model—wave or particle—was incomplete by itself, and one used without the other could only explain a subset of the full properties observed by experiment. So it is with certain doctrines. A dispute will form two adversarial camps. Both parties become more entrenched in their positions, as both have a segment of the truth vindicated by Scripture that support their position. But a fragment cannot explain the whole puzzle while dismissing truth from the opposite camp.

What Paul said in v. 11 indicates that God chose Jacob over Esau out of the sovereign exercise of his will. He just did it. No explanation needed: "who are you, O man, who answers back to God?" (v. 20). That's one point of view. Not the last word from the Bible concerning Esau and Jacob, however:

> Heb. 12:16 that there be no immoral or godless person like Esau, who sold his own birthright for a single meal.
> [17]For you know that even afterwards, when he desired to inherit the blessing, he was rejected, for he found no place for repentance, though he sought for it with tears.

As mentioned in a previous chapter, Esau committed fornication metaphorically (the word "immoral" in v. 16 is literally *fornication*) by having such contempt for his birthright that, under pressure, he pawned it for a meal. This did not please God. Jacob, on the other hand, was the opposite. He wanted the birthright badly. Although, while in pursuit of it, he stooped to unethical measures for it, God was pleased by the hunger in his heart in spite of his wrong doings. Jacob, later on, paid for his underhandedness. That's another story. But the point is this: God's choice of Jacob over Esau wasn't arbitrary. He had reasons to reject Esau (v. 17 from before). The word "hated" (Rom. 9:13, "BUT ESAU I HATED") actually means *re-*

## Part II: Modes of the Judgment of God

*jected*. God didn't hate Esau—he rejected him when it came to awarding the birthright. One might point out that God chose Jacob over Esau before they were born, as in v. 11, "for though the twins were not yet born and had not done anything good or bad". This is true. But the prophecy given to Rebecca that Jacob would receive the birthright was given when she was pregnant, the same time that Esau and Jacob were struggling over who would be the firstborn. Esau was born while Jacob was holding onto his ankle. Being unborn babies, how on earth did Esau and Jacob know that the firstborn would inherit the birthright? How's it possible for an unborn child to know this, let alone act on it? It shows an understanding and a determination of heart, even while in the womb (a good case for pro-life). Based on the inclination of Jacob's and Esau's hearts before they were yet born, God awarded the birthright. Though it was predestined to be so, it was inextricably connected to the course chartered by their free wills.

The passage from Romans, however, highlights the sovereignty of God and discounts man's free will; in other words, God can do whatever he wants and is answerable to no one. In v. 15 Paul, quoting the Almighty speaking to Moses, writes, "I WILL HAVE MERCY ON WHOM I HAVE MERCY, AND I WILL HAVE COMPASSION ON WHOM I HAVE COMPASSION". Since all have sinned, no one is in the position to demand anything from God or to accuse God of doing anything unjust (hence earlier in Romans it says, "God has bound up all under sin"). Where is God's justice? God should show mercy to no one, but has chosen to show mercy to a few—according to his sovereign will, which is not arbitrary, though often hidden from man. God dispenses mercy to some, and the one he doesn't extend mercy to he extends justice, which is equivalent to judgment. Since man stands condemned when justice is preeminent, the justice of God becomes the judgment of God. Therefore, in order for man to have any relationship with God, God must extend mercy in place of justice. In the case of Esau, God extended justice. Esau forsook his birthright by his own doing, and God held him to it. God did not extend to Esau the mercy to undo what he'd done. As was quoted from Hebrews, "he found no place for repentance", which in modern vernacular means, *he couldn't turn the situation around*. Paul said rhetorically in v. 15, "There is no injustice with God, is there?" No, there is not, although at times it appears that way. Verse 16, "So then it does not depend on the man who wills or the man who runs, but on God who has mercy". Since man by his works cannot satisfy the requirements of God, the ability to fulfill a prophecy is not based on man's good works. This is what Paul meant in this verse. Only through the mercy of God are man's

## Part II: Modes of the Judgment of God

shortcomings overlooked so that man can win the prize—like Jacob. It was the mercy of God that ultimately allowed him to fulfill the prophecies laid before him. So the sovereignty of God is exercised by the extension or denial of his mercy. And God's mercy's granted if, after an examination of a man's heart, he's found worthy. Jesus, as was said to the church at Thyatira, "searches the hearts and minds". He finds a person worthy or unworthy and extends mercy to the worthy. In Revelation this mercy clothes believers in white—they obtain righteousness as an act of God's volition. Though a theme throughout the Bible, it's a stumbling block for those believing that by good works they can be right with God.

Not by coincidence, v. 17 refers to God's dealing with Pharaoh, where this study began. "FOR THIS VERY PURPOSE I RAISED YOU UP, TO DEMONSTRATE MY POWER IN YOU, AND THAT MY NAME MIGHT BE PROCLAIMED THROUGHOUT THE WHOLE EARTH." God raised up Pharaoh for the purpose of bringing judgment on Egypt. He hardened Pharaoh's heart. Is this fair? What kind of God does things like this?

The answer is that God didn't do it to Pharaoh, Pharaoh did it to himself. God just supplied him with enough rope for him to hang himself with. There're two aspects to this affair. Pharaoh, acting as a free-moral agent, brought destruction upon himself. His actions, viewed in and of themselves, warranted his receiving judgment. And it wasn't as though God looked for any small fault wherewith to chastise Pharaoh. Pharaoh had committed gross sin. God manifested himself in a mighty way to him, demonstrating his power on multiple occasions, so that Pharaoh knew whom he was dealing with—and in the darkness of his heart chose the path of evil. But the other view is that God raised up Pharaoh for this purpose, and hardened his heart to achieve his sovereign ends. Both views are true; neither contradicts the other; the complete truth encompasses both.

The Bible teaches predestination. Eph. 1:5 says, "having predestinated us unto the adoption of children" (KJV). According to the sovereignty of God, no one can come to Jesus unless the Father draws him (John 6:44). All disciples of Jesus were predestined to be so. Some have testified of the events preceding their decision for Christ, how all along God was leading them to that point. They were predestined to receive the Lord. This is one view. The other is that God so loved the world that he gave his only begotten Son. God gave his Son for anyone in the world, including those who would reject him.

Part of this dual-view dilemma stems from the foreknowledge of God. God knows the future, and man becomes philosophical while trying to fathom this. Actually, in the Bible God deals with man as though he does *not* know the future—with the exception of prophecies. It wouldn't be fair if God, knowing the future, would condemn us for something we hadn't done yet. In a sense, God knows the future but conceals it even from himself. According to another view, as free-moral agents, our future is not nor cannot be predetermined. If it were predetermined, man would not be a free-moral agent. But the means by which God knows man's future is that Jesus is intimately familiar with each person's heart. He knows a man's heart better than the man knows it himself. This familiarity enables God to predict what a person will do—to the point where God can project future events. And in the same way that God can predict the course of a single person, he can predict it for an aggregate (a people) also. God has foreseen the hearts of all of mankind years in advance, and therefore knows the future in totality—hence Revelation.

The lesson of judgment from the Bible's comments on Pharaoh is that there're two viewpoints to any such scenario. Since total understanding isn't obtained from a single view, but only when both views are taken into consideration, the Bible can be difficult to comprehend, because at times it only gives one view, and that view might make God appear harsh or having a short temper. But there're enough examples in Scripture where God's dealings with a single person or nation are laid out so that both views are on full display. In these cases the harmony is visible.

*

One of Jesus' favorite quotations, from Isaiah, illustrates a dual-viewpoint. (Embedded in Mark 4:12, the Parable of the Sower:)

> Mark 4:10 As soon as He was alone, His followers, along with the twelve, began asking Him about the parables.
> [11]And He was saying to them, "To you has been given the mystery of the kingdom of God, but those who are outside get everything in parables,
> [12]so that "WHILE SEEING, THEY MAY SEE AND NOT PERCEIVE, AND WHILE HEARING, THEY MAY HEAR AND NOT UNDERSTAND, OTHERWISE THEY MIGHT RETURN AND BE FORGIVEN."

Jesus divided the listeners into two groups: those who were predestined ("given" in v. 11) to hear and comprehend the Word and those who were not. Those who heard the Word, meaning those who received it into their hearts, are the good soil in the parable.

*Part II: Modes of the Judgment of God*

The hard soil, where the Word fell by the wayside and the birds then ate, Jesus in v. 11 equates with those on the "outside". They "get everything in parables", meaning that it's only a story to them—the Word was understood but was not received into their hearts, and thus had no affect on them. These God predestined to not hear the message. This, the predestination viewpoint, must be balanced by its complement, the free moral agent viewpoint. The union of these fragments of truth is the whole truth. The parable teaches that the Word is sown to all indiscriminately; what happens to it is determined by the receiver. The softness of a person's heart and the willingness of him or her to endure the afflictions and distractions that would kill the Word determine whether the Word comes to fruition in his or her life. Put another way, God only works in man's life through the Word. The receiver—not God—determines God's working.

When God predestines a person's fate, he has concluded that no circumstance or persuasion will ever change his or her heart's inclination, and thereafter their fate is sealed. In fact, a person's disposition can become so fixated that God will cease trying to convert him, seeing that it would be futile, thereby judging him unworthy.

The broader context from the passage in Isaiah that Jesus quotes from in the Sower takes this one step further. Not only does God conclude that a heart has become intransigently hardened, but he continues to extend his grace and mercy to them for the sole reason of satisfying his fairness in judgment. God knows they'll reject the subsequent offers, but does it anyways. On judgment day they are without excuse, and cannot accuse God of being unjust. As Jesus quotes Isaiah in v. 12, "seeing they may see and not perceive": this means God is sending his Word to them, but their rejection blinds them from the truth. Jesus continues quoting Isaiah, "otherwise they might return and be forgiven": God would forgive them, should they repent, but he knows that they won't.

> Isa. 6:8 Then I heard the voice of the Lord, saying, "Whom shall I send, and who will go for Us?" Then I said, "Here am I. Send me!"
> [9]He said, "Go, and tell this people: 'Keep on listening, but do not perceive; keep on looking, but do not understand.'
> [10]"Render the hearts of this people insensitive, their ears dull, and their eyes dim, otherwise they might see with their eyes, hear with their ears, understand with their hearts, and return and be healed."

*Part II: Modes of the Judgment of God*

[11]Then I said, "Lord, how long?" And He answered, "Until cities are devastated and without inhabitant, houses are without people and the land is utterly desolate..."

"Keep on listening, but do not perceive; keep on looking, but do not understand"—what does this mean? Isaiah's message is inverted; he's instructed to tell the people to continue along the same erroneous trajectory, and this because God's judgment is predetermined. Jehovah knows that Isaiah's vituperation only strengthens the hearers' resolve to disobey. The logic harmonizes the free moral viewpoint with the predestined viewpoint—although to the reader it makes little sense. God will not judge them if they repent. He's sending Isaiah with a message of impending judgment. This is only fair; he cannot judge them in righteousness if he hasn't given them ample warning. But God knows that the message will have the opposite effect—the more Israel hears the message, the greater their hearts will be hardened against it. This is their own doing, not God's. His intention is for Isaiah to continue with the message until their hearts have been calcified. At the same time, he will have on multiple occasions and over a sufficiently long time discharged his obligation to give them clear warnings, prerequisites for righteousness judgment. In fact, he intends Isaiah's preaching to continue until judgment actually falls, "until cities are devastated and without inhabitant." God in his righteousness directs Isaiah to continue to warn the Israelites until the end, knowing that all warnings will have been in vain.

\*

Although God's mercy overrides his judgment, this is not the case with predestined judgment, which occurs whenever a judgment is inescapable. Those judged don't merit the mercy of God; in fact, they merit the opposite. Predestined judgment is the foregone conclusion that those under scrutiny will continue on their path of disobedience, and for this reason God is justified in judging them ahead of time. Predestined judgment doesn't preempt man's free will, but anticipates it and encompasses it.

## 4. Active and Passive Judgment

God's judgments fall under one of the following categories: active judgment and passive judgment. Active judgment is when God through judgment causes something to happen. The destruction of Sodom and Gomorrah is a prime example. God actively destroyed

## Part II: Modes of the Judgment of God

those cities. The flood is another example. God actively caused the flood. Passive judgment is when God, in his judgment, removes his grace from a person or nation, or simply does nothing, leaving the recipient or recipients to their own devices, to suffer the consequences of their own doing.

As visited in the previous chapters, there're two viewpoints, a free will and a predestined, in God's judgment. Scripture occasionally—not always—chronicles both points of view. An example containing both is the judgment that God pronounced on Solomon because of his disobedience. This judgment prevents the succession of Rehoboam, Solomon's son, to the throne of Israel:

> 1 Kings 11:9 Now the LORD was angry with Solomon because his heart was turned away from the LORD...
> ..........
> [11]So the LORD said to Solomon, "Because you have done this, and you have not kept My covenant and My statutes, which I have commanded you, I will surely tear the kingdom from you, and will give it to your servant.

This is one view. The other view is made clear from the story of Rehoboam:

> 1 Kings 12:1 Then Rehoboam went to Shechem, for all Israel had come to Shechem to make him king.
> [2]Now when Jeroboam the son of Nebat heard of it, he was living in Egypt (for he was yet in Egypt, where he had fled from the presence of King Solomon).
> [3]Then they sent and called him, and Jeroboam and all the assembly of Israel came and spoke to Rehoboam, saying,
> [4]"Your father made our yoke hard; now therefore lighten the hard service of your father and his heavy yoke which he put on us, and we will serve you."
> [5]Then he said to them, "Depart for three days, then return to me." So the people departed.
> [6]King Rehoboam consulted with the elders who had served his father Solomon while he was still alive, saying, "How do you counsel me to answer this people?"
> [7]Then they spoke to him, saying, "If you will be a servant to this people today, and will serve them and grant them their petition, and speak good words to them, then they will be your servants forever."

## Part II: Modes of the Judgment of God

⁸But he forsook the counsel of the elders which they had given him, and consulted with the young men who grew up with him and served him.

⁹So he said to them, "What counsel do you give that we may answer this people who have spoken to me, saying, 'Lighten the yoke which your father put on us'?"

¹⁰The young men who grew up with him spoke to him, saying, "Thus you shall say to this people who spoke to you, saying, 'Your father made our yoke heavy, now you make it lighter for us!' But you shall speak to them, 'My little finger is thicker than my father's loins!

¹¹'Whereas my father loaded you with a heavy yoke, I will add to your yoke; my father disciplined you with whips, but I will discipline you with scorpions.'"

¹²Then Jeroboam and all the people came to Rehoboam on the third day as the king had directed, saying, "Return to me on the third day."

¹³The king answered the people harshly, for he forsook the advice of the elders which they had given him,

¹⁴and he spoke to them according to the advice of the young men, saying, "My father made your yoke heavy, but I will add to your yoke; my father disciplined you with whips, but I will discipline you with scorpions."

¹⁵So the king did not listen to the people; for it was a turn of events from the LORD, that He might establish His word, which the LORD spoke through Ahijah the Shilonite to Jeroboam the son of Nebat.

¹⁶When all Israel saw that the king did not listen to them, the people answered the king, saying,

"What portion do we have in David? We have no inheritance in the son of Jesse; To your tents, O Israel! Now look after your own house, David!" So Israel departed to their tents.

¹⁷But as for the sons of Israel who lived in the cities of Judah, Rehoboam reigned over them.

¹⁸Then King Rehoboam sent Adoram, who was over the forced labor, and all Israel stoned him to death. And King Rehoboam made haste to mount his chariot to flee to Jerusalem.

¹⁹So Israel has been in rebellion against the house of David to this day.

. . . . . . . . . .

*Part II: Modes of the Judgment of God*

²²But the word of God came to Shemaiah the man of God, saying,
²³"Speak to Rehoboam the son of Solomon, king of Judah, and to all the house of Judah and Benjamin and to the rest of the people, saying,
²⁴'Thus says the LORD, "You must not go up and fight against your relatives the sons of Israel; return every man to his house, for this thing has come from Me."' So they listened to the word of the LORD, and returned and went their way according to the word of the LORD.

"To your tents, O Israel! Now look after your own house, David!"—passages like these make the Bible a masterpiece of literature. Rehoboam, through his own arrogance and foolishness, loses the throne. According to the narrative, God had nothing to do with it. In fact, that's exactly what caused Rehoboam to succumb to the prophecy: God *didn't* do anything to stop the sequence from unfolding, which led to the schism between the northern and southern kingdoms. It's what God didn't do that caused the fulfillment of the prophecy. Rehoboam had consulted counselors who had advised him of the prudent course of action. And he had plenty of time to think things over. There was every opportunity to avert this calamity; the consequences were entirely of his making.

Several times in the Bible, when characters are judged by God, the judgment encompasses their children or their nation. This isn't fair at first glance, but upon closer inspection, there's more to the story than what the words uttered in judgment might suggest. God doesn't punish people for the transgressions of others—in spite of instances in Scripture where God appears to do just that. In the case of Solomon, when the prophecy was given, one might conclude that God was being unfair to Solomon's son—after all, what had Rehoboam to do with Solomon's sin? But as the history reveals, God's dealings with Rehoboam are just. He's given a clean sheet of paper at the start of his reign, and he blows it. When giving the prophecy to Solomon, God in his wisdom knew that his justness demands that he deal fairly with Rehoboam. This he did, and the disparate viewpoints are wrapped up tidily.

But again, the judgment of Solomon visited upon Rehoboam is merely a withholding of God's mercy. Man in his sinful state is not only wicked but foolish as well. And man, left to his foolishness, is capable of his own spectacular destruction. All God has to do is sit back and watch. It's the grace of God, prompted by the prayers of

*Part II: Modes of the Judgment of God*

the righteous, which, intervening, negates the self-destructive tendencies that are the nature of fallen man.

\*

Another example of passive judgment is God's appointed trials for Job. It appears that God acted unfairly towards Job's sons and daughters.

> Job 1:9 Then Satan answered the LORD, "Does Job fear God for nothing?
> [10]"Have You not made a hedge about him and his house and all that he has, on every side? You have blessed the work of his hands, and his possessions have increased in the land.
> [11]"But put forth Your hand now and touch all that he has; he will surely curse You to Your face."
> [12]Then the LORD said to Satan, "Behold, all that he has is in your power, only do not put forth your hand on him." So Satan departed from the presence of the LORD.

The Lord tests Job, but his family is killed off in the process. How is this fair? A closer look at the family: Job's wife said, "Curse God and die!" (Job 2:9). Not a woman of faith. Job was in the habit of offering sacrifices on behalf of his sons and daughters in case they had sinned (Job 1:4,5). Why the concern? He knew them well—they probably had sinned. God weighed these considerations before Satan was turned loose on Job. The kin came up short in God's estimation. It had been the favor of Jehovah on Job, which included his entire household, that had been protecting them all along. Standing on their own individual relationship with the Lord apart from Job, their failure to walk in obedience, prerequisite for the OT "hedge" (Job 1:10) of God's protection around the Faithful, caused their annihilation at the hands of the devil. The Bible only gives a glimpse of this, as the book centers around Job. But God was fair to all, even to Job—his trials were temporary. Bible scholars believe they lasted from a few months to a couple years at the most. James 5:11 puts this in perspective: "You have heard of the endurance of Job and have seen the outcome of the Lord's dealings, that the Lord is full of compassion and is merciful." James's summarization is in order, as the length of the chapters might obscure the bottom line: Job led a good life, had an interlude of intense trials, but afterwards lived 140 years to a ripe old age.

\*

In studying the judgment of God, one cannot avoid the question of whether in NT times God judges nations or empires like he did in

## Part II: Modes of the Judgment of God

the OT. The broader question is whether God blesses a nation, causing it to rise, or judges it, causing it to decline. And if God does indeed intervene in the course of nations, how does he do so? In the church age, God's covenant is with individuals, not nations (his final dealings with Israel notwithstanding). This is a departure from the OT, and for this reason one cannot find in the NT where God is actively judging a nation (except for Israel). However, God does bestow his blessings and does judge nations in a passive manner. This can be difficult to distinguish from the natural vicissitudes of human affairs, however. It's through wisdom, integrity, willpower, and unity that nations are built; the depletion of these causes a nation to collapse. God's blessing causes justice and the like to prevail, and in the long run these result in prosperity.

But behind the scenes, in the spiritual realm, forces are at work to drive a nation in one direction or the other. The Holy Spirit and evil spirits work on the minds and hearts of people, singularly and collectively. Thus, a great nation can be built up or torn down. Of course, a nation can ascend above its neighbors by its own doing, without the impetus of spiritual persuasion and apart from the application of spiritual law. Man is an autonomous creature. But the indirect consequences of sin put spiritual laws into motion which cause the nation to succumb to a decay of corruption from within. This is presently at work in the United States and other countries.

Because of the blessing of the Lord, nations have been exalted beyond their stature. An example is the Dutch Republic at the tail end of the Reformation. For a season this tiny country came to be numbered among the dominant nations of the world. As the Netherlands embraced the Reformation, a spiritual revival spread throughout the land, augmented by an infusion of French Protestants called Huguenots. And Holland at this time became a haven for Jews. In the spiritual domain, God blessed the nation and caused it to prosper above its neighbors. In the natural, the influx of peoples of vigor and moral character produced an efficacy that propagated throughout Dutch industry, bringing success to their pursuits. Up until recent times the U.S. enjoyed this kind of blessing.

\*

Rom. 1 is the most complete NT discourse on passive judgment. Notice the three occurrences of the calling-card, "God gave them over":

> Rom. 1:18 For the wrath of God is revealed from heaven against all ungodliness and unrighteousness of men who suppress the truth in unrighteousness,

## Part II: Modes of the Judgment of God

¹⁹because that which is known about God is evident within them; for God made it evident to them.
²⁰For since the creation of the world His invisible attributes, His eternal power and divine nature, have been clearly seen, being understood through what has been made, so that they are without excuse.
²¹For even though they knew God, they did not honor Him as God or give thanks, but they became futile in their speculations, and their foolish heart was darkened.
²²Professing to be wise, they became fools,
²³and exchanged the glory of the incorruptible God for an image in the form of corruptible man and of birds and four-footed animals and crawling creatures.
²⁴Therefore **God gave them over** in the lusts of their hearts to impurity, so that their bodies would be dishonored among them.
²⁵For they exchanged the truth of God for a lie, and worshiped and served the creature rather than the Creator, who is blessed forever. Amen.
²⁶For this reason **God gave them over** to degrading passions; for their women exchanged the natural function for that which is unnatural,
. . . . . . . . . .
²⁸And just as they did not see fit to acknowledge God any longer, **God gave them over** to a depraved mind, to do those things which are not proper,
. . . . . . . . . .
³²and although they know the ordinance of God, that those who practice such things are worthy of death, they not only do the same, but also give hearty approval to those who practice them.

    Apparently, according to this passage, there is some sort of inherent restraint that limits the extent of fallen man's depravity. The ungodly referred to by Rom. 1 are not the run-of-the-mill heathen, but have multiplied their iniquities by resisting the true knowledge of God, illustrating that sin equals transgression multiplied by knowledge. The rejection of this knowledge invokes the wrath of God. The judgment is passive—God allows them to be consumed by their own passions and depravity. Does God cause this? No, they cause it themselves. God releases them from any semblance of his grace, however.

*Part II: Modes of the Judgment of God*

In fact, the Rom. 1 judgment is in progress in the West. Rampant homosexuality is an indicator (vv. 26, 27). The countries where true Christian revival had once been profuse acquired the knowledge of the Father as their heritage. Subsequent generations, having rejected this knowledge, have received God's judgment, even as Romans states. In fact, the stark veracity of these verses is manifestly apparent. Paul states that homosexuality is a perverted passion. But society, as each rubs shoulders with gays, has come to believe that God made them so, that they have no choice in the matter, that they are what they are. That's partially true. The passive judgment of God, having lifted the floodgates to this consuming infatuation, created an environment where some—randomly it would appear—are smitten by reprobate desires, and, apart from Christ, are unable by their own ability to resist them (nor are Christians immune to this temptation). According to Rom. 1, the unleashing of this lust is reserved for the nations who have parted with the Gospel. Nations where the truth of the Gospel has never been exalted have a significantly lower percentage of homosexuals. This is not to say that these nations' deeds are less sinful than those of the West. They are not (the knowledge multiplier notwithstanding). But God doesn't afflict them with the passive judgment laid out in Rom. 1.

As gays think they're made that way, that there's no way they can change, there's no hope for them in their own mind. Christians believe that it's a behavior—a lust—one that can be altered. The world rails against them for claiming such. But there's hope in God's Word—hope that the bondage of sexual sin can be broken. In spite of the politically correct veneer, the world will never accept the gay lifestyle as normal since it goes against the "natural function" (v. 27), "natural" referring to precepts held by all of mankind, and not just Christians. The media is fond of portraying gays as having a sexual disposition identical to straights—howbeit with a simple swap of gender in their partners. But unlike the average heterosexual, the mind of the homosexual man is overwhelmed with thoughts of sex, which thoughts he blurts out in casual conversation. The media won't report the extent of gay promiscuity. The world, de-coupled from Christian morals, teaches that it's alright to be gay—but it's morally wrong to be sexually promiscuous, straight or gay. Nowadays, people are not shocked at the revelation that one is gay, but the revelation that he is promiscuously gay. But by nature a homosexual man is promiscuous. The spread of hepatitis and AIDS is proof: those diseases are propagated by promiscuity. Verse 27 says that the men "burned in their desire toward one another". What does the remainder of this verse mean, "and receiving in their

## Part II: Modes of the Judgment of God

own persons the due penalty of their error"? What is the penalty? Some have proclaimed that AIDS is God's judgment (active judgment) against gays. It's not. His judgment can only be averted by repentance—and sometimes not even that. If AIDS was a judgment of the Almighty, safe-sex could not thwart it. But the disease has touched the innocent as well; it would not be fair for God to afflict them along with the unjust. But, to address the question, the penalty is this: homosexuals are psychologically and emotional subverted by their putrid indulgence, to the extent that it affects their personality, their demeanor—even the way they walk and the way they talk. Of course, the "penalty of their error" doesn't means that gays aren't as smart or are less talented or less capable than straights, but it does mean that gay men can be singled out by their effeminate nature.

The variations from one individual to another mean that sexual temptation will vex one person, but another is immune. Considering it easy to resist the temptation, those who are immune judge those who are not. The truth is that most Christians don't have the spiritual sinew to repulse a temptation the likes of homosexuality. Neither do most churches teach the forthright truth of the Word that would build the fortitude to overcome such monsters. In general this is true of most serious tests a Christian might face. About all the Church can do is shuttle the weak into a support group with those who will sympathize with them. The redemption which was purchased by Jesus' sacrifice cannot be realized without a total commitment to Christ, namely a dedication to the Word of God and the working of the Holy Spirit, and this is absent from must congregations.

\*

Identifying whether judgment occurs in the Bible is simple—God will judge someone or some nation, and the means by which it occurs determines if it's active or passive. In this age it's difficult to tell whether God's judgment is in play or not—let alone if it's active or passive. One cannot tell by circumstances if judgment has occurred since misfortunes can be coincidental. And the difference between a passive judgment and the consequence of man's natural pride and folly is difficult to ascertain without God having revealed it. The only way to conclusively tell if God is judging is if he reveals it to mankind. This can happen in two ways: it's written in Scripture or the Father reveals it prophetically. The judgments noted in the Bible are either histories, are prophecies yet to be fulfilled, or are generalities as to how God judges (Rom. 1 for example). Judgment in the NT is different than the OT. This is true if for no other reason than the difference in the prophet's ministry between OT and NT.

*Part II: Modes of the Judgment of God*

But in spite of this, there've been an abundance of ministers saying with certitude that God will judge so-and-so or this nation or that nation. They follow little logic, reasoning, or NT precepts. Proving from the Bible how judgment transpires is one thing; applying it to this day and age is another. But staying within the guidelines of the knowledge of the judgment of God, when God judges mankind he always communicates to him what he will do. It makes no more sense for God to judge man without first warning him than it does for a nation to stockpile nuclear weapons as a means of mutual-assured destruction and not inform their adversaries of such a stockpile and of the determination to use it.

## 5. Associative and Proxy Judgment

At times, in the Bible the leader of a nation is judged, and along with him the entire nation. Pharaoh and the Exodus is one example. It was Pharaoh whose heart was hardened...but what about the rest of the Egyptians? The plagues visited all of Egypt, as though all were partakers in Pharaoh's sin.

Likewise, all of Israel was judged for the actions of a few. The parable of the vineyard keepers in Luke 20:9-18 confirms that God judged Israel because of their rejection of the Messiah. The fig tree that Jesus cursed in Mark 11 is symbolic of Israel's impending judgment. The Romans destroyed Jerusalem in 70 A.D. and dispersed the remainder in 135 A.D. This was the inception of anti-Semitism, persisting to the present day. On the one hand, the wicked are the source of anti-Semitism. On the other hand, God has held the Jews principally responsible for crucifying Jesus. This assertion is proven by Peter's speech on Pentecost:

> Acts 2:22 "Men of Israel, listen to these words: Jesus the Nazarene, a man attested to you by God with miracles and wonders and signs which God performed through Him in your midst, just as you yourselves know—
> [23]this Man, delivered over by the predetermined plan and foreknowledge of God, **you nailed to a cross** by the hands of godless men and put Him to death.

These words say that, though the Romans were involved, it was the Jews primarily who were responsible for putting Jesus to death. Yes, it was the will of God for Jesus to die, as these verses affirm. But God held the Jews responsible. Not a popular message, nor one

*Part II: Modes of the Judgment of God*

that seems fair. How can this be? The Scribes and Pharisees hated him indeed, but what about all the folks Christ healed and taught during his earthly ministry? Were they not greater in number? Why hold them guilty for the actions of a few? The answer is found in Matt. 27:25: the entire nation condemned itself with the oath, "His blood shall be on us and on our children!" God held them to it. Jesus' popularity reached an apex during his second year of ministry, only to wane in his third and final year. Just as nine of the ten lepers forgot to thank Jesus after he had healed them, the crowd turned on him at his trial, following the instigation of their leaders.

God in his wisdom brings disjointed threads of a plot together to a single point, to fulfill a single end. In the passion of Christ, these three threads were working in tandem: God's predetermined plan that Jesus' sacrifice would be payment for our sins; Israel's crucifixion of the Christ; the Romans as the agents who carried out the crucifixion. How God deals with each thread, both dependent and independent of the others, demonstrates his wisdom. God judged the Jews, but, on the other hand, Jesus had to be crucified as a propitiation for sin, and someone had to be held accountable. But, as in the parable of the vineyard keepers, the judgment of the Jews was something that had been gaining momentum for a long time; Jesus' slaughter was the straw that broke the camel's back. And the final thread is this: without the Roman's involvement, several prophesies specifying Jesus' crucifixion could not have been fulfilled (or they were given knowing that the Romans were to crucify the Christ).

\*

As a nation tethers its will to that of its leaders, both the blessing and the curse that fall upon the leaders are inherited by the followers. Associative judgment is judging the followers, those who walk in the steps of the leader. Blindly following in this way is difficult for the Western mind to comprehend, as independent thought is cherished. In the modern age there's an abundance of disseminated media to abet the formation of independent and contrary opinions. Other cultures are not so. But the operative action is to bind one's heart and will to another. When the latter is judged, the former is also.

Both associative and proxy judgment convict those who're not directly implicated in the transgressions of others. This is contrary to justice in human terms, and as a result of running across such occurrences in the Bible, some register unanswered questions in the back of their mind, while others reject the inspiration of Scripture, concluding that the God of the Bible isn't fair. But he is fair. God never judges in unrighteousness. Those who're the recipients of

*Part II: Modes of the Judgment of God*

associative judgment, though they haven't personally committed the transgression, are passive accomplices to those who have.

\*

Proxy judgment is defined by Luke 11:50:

> Luke 11:47 "Woe to you! For you build the tombs of the prophets, and it was your fathers who killed them.
> [48]"So you are witnesses and approve the deeds of your fathers; because it was they who killed them, and you build their tombs.
> [49]"For this reason also the wisdom of God said, 'I will send to them prophets and apostles, and some of them they will kill and some they will persecute,
> [50]so that the blood of all the prophets, shed since the foundation of the world, may be charged against this generation
> [51]from the blood of Abel to the blood of Zechariah, who was killed between the altar and the house of God; yes, I tell you, it shall be charged against this generation.'

Jesus held the Judean leaders of that day guilty of martyring the prophets. This is proxy judgment: God judges those who live in a later time for deeds formerly committed; God heaps the penalty for past transgressions on a singular, present transgression. In this passage from Luke, the singular transgression is the crucifixion of Jesus, and the past transgressions were the martyrdom of the prophets.

Jesus, in v. 51, identifies Abel as the first martyr, numbering him with the prophets who were slain. A closer look at what the Bible says about Abel:

> Heb. 11:4 By faith Abel offered to God a better sacrifice than Cain, through which he obtained the testimony that he was righteous, God testifying about his gifts, and through faith, though he is dead, he still speaks.

Abel's sacrifice was done in faith—Cain's was not. The difference between their sacrifices was not in quality or in quantity—in spite of what many have supposed—but it was that Abel's sacrifice was a blood sacrifice. A theme throughout the Bible is that without the shedding of blood there is no forgiveness for sin (Heb. 9:22). God initiated blood sacrifices when he found Adam and Eve naked and clothed them with animal skins. God sacrificed the animals' lives to provide the skins, setting the example of a blood sacrifice for sin. Having established the precedence, he subsequently expected such sacrifices. Though Genesis does not say this explicitly, it had been communicated. Abel chose to follow; Cain chose to disobey. Perhaps Cain thought he could compensate for his lack of obedience with a more lavish offering. Or at least an equivalent. Whatever his thoughts, the result was an evil deed. Both 1 John 3:12 and Jude 11 say that Cain was evil. In 1 John it infers that his evil existed *before* he killed Abel, not just as a result. The evil referred to by these references by John and Jude is his sacrifice. This is a picture of man seeking salvation by his works, intentionally apart from the redeeming blood of Christ. It's evil in God's eyes. It was also the same road the Pharisees traveled on. The verse 1 John 3:12 says that Cain "slew" Abel, the Greek word insinuating slaying with a knife, as opposed to a bludgeoning. Cain invented murder; he dreamed it up when he saw Abel slit the throat of the lamb. Cain, having been admonished by God over his sacrifice, thought to himself, "I'll give God a sacrifice he'll never forget!" With this, he took a knife and slit Abel's throat, imitating the sacrificial slaughter of an animal. One surmises that he used a knife because God said that Abel's blood was crying out from the ground (Gen. 4:10). In a metaphorical sense, Abel was a sacrifice, a type who has his fulfillment in Jesus the anti-type, as noted in the NT. And, ironically, God has never forgotten the blood of Abel either...

> Heb. 12:24 ...and to Jesus, the mediator of a new covenant, and to the sprinkled blood, which speaks better than the blood of Abel.

The Pharisees walked in the footsteps of Cain, and, having partaken of the knowledge of Abel and the subsequent trail of OT martyrs, became culpable of the guilt of them all. Therefore, it's just to charge them with the blood of these saints. This is proxy judgment: the one judged is held accountable for deeds he didn't actually commit but participated in in spirit.

There're a few puzzling verses, such as this one from Exodus, that are explained by proxy judgment.

> Exod. 20:5 "You shall not worship them [other gods] or serve them; for I, the LORD your God, am a jealous God, visiting the iniquity of the fathers on the children, on the third and the fourth generations of those who hate Me,

*Part II: Modes of the Judgment of God*

Certainly it's not fair for God to punish the offspring of a man for the father's sins. If God is a just God, then why is this in the Bible? What's not explained here is that God judges the children and grandchildren for the sins of their father or grandfather because these descendants knowingly walk in the same sin, in spite of the negative example that should dissuade them. They, who have seen the fruits firsthand and who know up close the iniquities of their parents, that much more ought to turn from these ways and do good. But for this reason, God is unwilling to extend them patience and mercy, which virtues he owes to no man. Just as a righteous man or woman can intercede, and God will head their prayers, and intervene to another's benefit, so God shuns those who out of choice are implicated with a wicked man or woman. Because sin equals transgression multiplied by knowledge, proxy judgment is compounded by the knowledge component instead of by the actual deed. The immense comprehension of the sin incurs proxy judgment.

## 6. Binary Judgment

> Matt. 13:47 "Again, the kingdom of heaven is like a dragnet cast into the sea, and gathering fish of every kind;
> [48] and when it was filled, they drew it up on the beach; and they sat down and gathered the good fish into containers, but the bad they threw away.
> [49] "So it will be at the end of the age; the angels will come forth and take out the wicked from among the righteous,
> [50] and will throw them into the furnace of fire; in that place there will be weeping and gnashing of teeth.

After a haul, when fishermen separate the fish as Jesus described, they sort them rapidly, scanning for a couple characteristics. Experienced fishermen can quickly—in a second or less—tell if a fish is worth keeping or not based on the type of the fish, the size of the fish, and the fish's condition. But they don't need to gaze at any one fish, as fisherman look for easily recognizable characteristics to sort them. Wouldn't it be odd to find a fisherman holding a fish, staring at it, wondering if he should keep it or not? Maybe he wants to keep it, maybe he doesn't, he's undecided—no, the decision is made quickly and is final: the fish is either kept or not kept, no in-between.

## Part II: Modes of the Judgment of God

This illustrates the principle of binary judgment. A person is either of one camp or the other. God judges him or her based on whether he or she is one or the other, but never in-between. God tarries in his judgment, taking every aspect into consideration—not a detail escapes his eyes, and not a piece is overlooked. As a result, those who believe in a salvation based on works presuppose a judgment based on works. Unlike the parable of the fishermen, which exemplifies binary judgment, a meticulous scrutiny of works would be lengthy, pitting a man's sins against his good deeds, successes against failures, strengths against shortcomings. This is contrary to the principle of binary judgment; one is either in or out, pass or fail, no sliding scale, no grading on a curve. Because mankind is so mentally predisposed to a judgment based on works, binary judgment is foreign.

Another example of binary judgment is the parable of the sheep and the goats:

> Matt. 25:32 "All the nations will be gathered before Him; and He will separate them from one another, as the shepherd separates the sheep from the goats;
> [33]and He will put the sheep on His right, and the goats on the left.

The sheep are good; the goats are bad; there is no half-sheep, half-goat category. This might question whether God is fair. Although some unbelievers are decent, moral people, and some Christians are immoral, no one is good in God's eyes. His standards are too high for anyone to reach; even a so-called good man falls short. This enables God to choose the means for salvation—not for man to choose. And when a man rejects the means, like when Cain rejected God's requirements for a pleasing sacrifice, then God rejects that man. The rejection comes in the form of a judgment based on works, only the standard is not lowered, making a guilty verdict inevitable.

The parable of the sheep and the goats does not end in v. 33, but continues:

> Matt. 25:34 "Then the King will say to those on His right, 'Come, you who are blessed of My Father, inherit the kingdom prepared for you from the foundation of the world.
> [35]'For I was hungry, and you gave Me something to eat; I was thirsty, and you gave Me something to drink; I was a stranger, and you invited Me in;

## Part II: Modes of the Judgment of God

³⁶naked, and you clothed Me; I was sick, and you visited Me; I was in prison, and you came to Me.'
³⁷"Then the righteous will answer Him, 'Lord, when did we see You hungry, and feed You, or thirsty, and give You something to drink?
³⁸'And when did we see You a stranger, and invite You in, or naked, and clothe You?
³⁹'When did we see You sick, or in prison, and come to You?'
⁴⁰"The King will answer and say to them, 'Truly I say to you, to the extent that you did it to one of these brothers of Mine, even the least of them, you did it to Me.'
⁴¹"Then He will also say to those on His left, 'Depart from Me, accursed ones, into the eternal fire which has been prepared for the devil and his angels;
⁴²for I was hungry, and you gave Me nothing to eat; I was thirsty, and you gave Me nothing to drink;
⁴³I was a stranger, and you did not invite Me in; naked, and you did not clothe Me; sick, and in prison, and you did not visit Me.'
⁴⁴"Then they themselves also will answer, 'Lord, when did we see You hungry, or thirsty, or a stranger, or naked, or sick, or in prison, and did not take care of You?'
⁴⁵"Then He will answer them, 'Truly I say to you, to the extent that you did not do it to one of the least of these, you did not do it to Me.'
⁴⁶"These will go away into eternal punishment, but the righteous into eternal life."

When did we see you a stranger?—When did we see you sick?—Both the righteous and unrighteous asked...but why? Could they not remember their own doings? No, because these deeds were done out of habit, and what's done out of habit isn't remembered—makes no difference whether it's handing a few dollars to one in need or it's brushing one's teeth. Those who're mindful of themselves when doing a kind act can't help but to remember it. Their hearts are self-congratulatory. These are not the good deeds that Jesus rewards. When one does good from habit, it's because he or she has a good heart. Jesus remembers this and rewards it. On the opposite side, the bad deeds that one remembers are the ones that produce guilt and inner anxiety. Such pangs of regret come from a tender heart. The wicked do evil out of habit, and these acts are quickly forgotten. Jesus remembers those also. Come judgment day, all will be brought to light.

These two adjacent passages (Matt. 25:32-33; 25:34-46) are meant to be interpreted together, as they're in the same context. Jesus separates the sheep from the goats, the righteous from the unrighteous, a binary judgment. But then he affirms that the decision was based on their works. How can this be? If salvation is by works, then there must be a sliding scale to judge the works—this is not binary. But in Matthew, Jesus distinguishes the sheep from the goats based on their works—but only the ones they do from habit, i.e. the forgotten ones. A person who knows the Father is spiritually renewed on the inside as a result. One's true inner nature determines one's works of habit; conversely, one's works of habit are indicative of one's true nature. True, that even the wicked do good works. But these are a veneer obscuring what's on the inside; this veneer cannot be sustained over time and under pressure. All that is hidden shall be revealed. In time it's by fire that one's works are vetted.

In the never-ending debate over salvation, there've been two schools of thought. The first is that one is essentially born into a Christian family, and is therefore Christian. The second is that one makes a decision for Christ at some point in his life, and thereby becomes a Christian. Jesus in this passage from Matthew agrees with neither; one is a Christian if one does good works; one cannot be a Christian and do evil works. You will know them by their fruit, in other words. How can this be? The debate itself is not wrong, but the nature of the debate forces a Western viewpoint on this issue. The Semitic viewpoint, namely Jesus', counterbalances the issue. There appear to be contradictions, but there are not—just differing viewpoints.

## 7. Judgment by Provoking God's Holiness

In 1 Samuel 4 and 5 the Israelites bore the ark of the covenant before them in battle, but it was seized by the Philistines, who brought it into the temple of their god Dagon, seating it next to the statue. God smote the Philistines with tumors, after which they returned the ark to Israel. Years later, David brings the ark to Jerusalem. While being drawn on a cart, the ark begins to topple:

## Part II: Modes of the Judgment of God

> 2 Sam. 6:6 But when they came to the threshing floor of Nacon, Uzzah reached out toward the ark of God and took hold of it, for the oxen nearly upset it.
> ⁷And the anger of the LORD burned against Uzzah, and God struck him down there for his irreverence; and he died there by the ark of God.
> ⁸David became angry because of the LORD'S outburst against Uzzah, and that place is called Perez-uzzah to this day.

God judged Uzzah. David didn't understand. Bullinger inserted this explanation in his commentary:

> This was contrary to the divinely prescribed law (Num. 4:15, 7:9, 10:21; Deut 10, etc.) When the Philistines did it in ignorance no judgment fell on them, because the Law of Moses was not delivered to them. But David should have known: hence judgment came. The solemn lesson is that anything introduced into the worship of God contrary to His requirements is deserving of His judgments.

No problem next time David had to move the ark, as he had learned his lesson from the first episode. He follows the protocol prescribed by the Law:

> 1 Chron. 15:1 Now David built houses for himself in the city of David; and he prepared a place for the ark of God and pitched a tent for it.
> ²Then David said, "No one is to carry the ark of God but the Levites; for the LORD chose them to carry the ark of God and to minister to Him forever."

Uzzah trespassed on the holiness of God, which cannot come in direct contact with man, else it will destroy him. God must screen man from the intensity of his holiness. After Moses' visitation with the LORD, he had to have his face shielded to protect the Israelites from the fading glory still radiating from his countenance. God's holiness cannot coexist with sinful man—it will destroy man if it comes in direct contact with him. Only the blood of Jesus slakes the fury of his holiness.

Uzzah's judgment was compounded by the knowledge of God; another proof of the quasi-mathematical formula, sin equals transgression multiplied by knowledge. The Philistines differed vastly from the Israelites in their knowledge of God. This caused God's

*Part II: Modes of the Judgment of God*

wrath to fall on Uzzah for momentarily touching the ark, but not to fall on the Philistines, who had their hands all over it.

\*

A breach in the barrier that restrains God's holiness caused judgment to fall on Ananias and Sapphira. Recall in Acts 5 that Ananias (in the presence of the Holy Spirit) lied about how much he sold his house for. He sold it for a certain amount, then held back part of the proceeds for himself. As Luke records, he was not under compulsion to sell the property in the first place; he did it for appearance's sake. Was it anyone's business how much he had sold the property for? Neither a big nor a vicious lie, but nevertheless a lie. Not the first one ever told, nor the last—but how many people, Christian or not, are struck dead for lying? Why Ananias? The answer is this: direct contact with God's holiness absent any sort of shield will kill a person who's tainted with even a residue of sin. It's like touching a high-voltage line. Jesus isolates his chosen from the deadly affects of God's holiness. God's holiness and sin cannot coexist. Jesus, having become the substitute for sin, enabled God to vent his holiness on him rather than on us. This is the only thing that prevents us from being obliterated in the presence of God. It also explains why, on a few occasions in the OT, after God spoke to a person, he would tell them to offer a sacrifice afterwards, even if they hadn't explicitly sinned. Like a sedative, the sacrifice appeased his wrath. It was a symbol of the ultimate sacrifice to come, and this reminder placated God. God wants to commune with man, but is prevented from direct communion with him because of the wrath that would result from the exposure of his holiness. Even if man's sin were slight, God's holiness, being infinitely large, would still overwhelm. For this reason God must use an intermediary to communicate with man—this is the role of the Son. The righteous and the sinner both interact with Jesus, and did so in the Gospels. A bolt of lightning carries a tremendous burst of energy. When it passes through a medium, it'll either destroy it or leave it intact. Whether lightning, while passing through, destroys an object or not depends on the object's purity. Likewise, Jesus, because he's sinless, can stand in the holy presence of God unscathed. There he intercedes for us (Heb. 7:25); that is, since we can't stand in God's presence, he relays our prayers for us.

Wherever God's holy presence resides, the tolerance for sin is minimal. Such is the case for the OT priests' service in the Tabernacle. Not a place where sin is tolerated. Two of Aaron's sons, also priests, violated a commandment while on the premises. One surmises that the sin was rooted either in an intention to tempt the Lord or in a stupor of negligence. The proximity to God's holiness

*Part II: Modes of the Judgment of God*

compounded and amplified the severity of the sin and the resulting judgment:

> Lev. 10:1 Now Nadab and Abihu, the sons of Aaron, took their respective firepans, and after putting fire in them, placed incense on it and offered strange fire before the LORD, which He had not commanded them.
> ²And fire came out from the presence of the LORD and consumed them, and they died before the LORD.
> ³Then Moses said to Aaron, "It is what the LORD spoke, saying, 'By those who come near Me I will be treated as holy, And before all the people I will be honored.'" So Aaron, therefore, kept silent.

Though aggravating the punishment for sin, being surrounded by God's holiness has its advantages. When Israel adhered to God's commandments, the Lord's holiness pervaded the assembly. The Book of Joshua begins with a new, young generation of Israelites, having been purged of the old, unbelieving generation, the older ones having died in the desert because of their sin, poised to take the Promised Land. The book recounts them racking up a series of victories. Not a foe could withstand them, as the holiness of God saturated their assembly, the Lord going out before them in battle—until the seventh chapter, when Joshua suffered his first setback at Ai. He, unaccustomed to defeat, knew there must've been a reason. The sin of one man Achan had caused the presence of the Lord to be lifted from the nation. Not a major transgression, but God's holiness could not cohabit with even a trifling sin. One or the other had to go. To purge the nation of iniquity, and thus enable the return of God's presence, Achan had to be killed. The Law had severe penalties for sin, often death, for what nowadays are considered trivial offences. According to the biblical record, these harsh sentences were seldom enforced. But enforcement of the Law was prerequisite for God's holiness to dwell in the midst of the nation, for his holiness is exacting by nature—to the point of requiring the blood of his only begotten.

## 8. Delegate Judgment

A person in authority will delegate limited powers to a surrogate. This has been done since ancient times. One of the first instances of this in the Bible is Pharaoh delegating all the kingdom's

## Part II: Modes of the Judgment of God

administrative powers to Joseph after he had interpreted his dream. Pharaoh saw the obvious, that Joseph was used of God to interpret dreams. But he also surmised Joseph's other outstanding traits, that he had integrity and had a knack for administration. Jacob also knew this—that's why he sent him on errands to keep an eye on his brothers. Potiphar knew it too, so did the jailer. All quickly promoted Joseph to positions of authority and delegated to him responsibilities. Pharaoh, having heard of the coming famine, realized that he needed to find a competent manager to entrust the well-being of the empire, and having shrewdly recognized this ability in Joseph, designated him second in the kingdom—a prime minister. That's why when his brothers met him in Egypt they feared him so—had he wanted to, he needn't have asked permission to put them to death, the power had already been delegated to him. Pharaoh didn't fear that Joseph might usurp the throne, though Joseph was reverenced like himself.

Delegated authority is actuated when one confers part or all his powers on another. The deputy receives the authority of the one delegating, for the purpose of acting in his place. There're advantages of vesting subordinates with authority to act in one's absence, especially in the ancient world where travelling great distances was arduous and time consuming. Armed with a sealed letter, or appointed to a position of authority, an emissary so dispatched could on behalf of the sender conduct business in the sender's stead. Or perhaps a person of capability or specific skills, in extraordinary circumstances, like in Joseph's case, might need to be empowered with control over peoples and resources in order to solve a difficult task. Armies do this regularly. Having witnessed this in the service, the centurion in Matt. 8 knew how authority worked, and recognized that Jesus had the power to delegate the same in spiritual matters. Upon hearing this, Jesus commended him for his great faith—for indeed he does delegate authority to others.

Take the example from the ending of Matt. 9, proceeding into Matt. 10 (there were no chapter breaks in the original text):

> Matt. 9:36 Seeing the people, He felt compassion for them, because they were distressed and dispirited like sheep without a shepherd.
> [37] Then He said to His disciples, "The harvest is plentiful, but the workers are few.
> [38] "Therefore beseech the Lord of the harvest to send out workers into His harvest."

## Part II: Modes of the Judgment of God

Matt. 10:1 Jesus summoned His twelve disciples and gave them authority over unclean spirits, to cast them out, and to heal every kind of disease and every kind of sickness.

. . . . . . . . . .

[14]"Whoever does not receive you, nor heed your words, as you go out of that house or that city, shake the dust off your feet. [15]"Truly I say to you, it will be more tolerable for the land of Sodom and Gomorrah in the day of judgment than for that city.

During his ministry, Jesus' body limited him. He couldn't be in more than one place at one time, and there were more people to teach and heal than he had time to visit. His only alternative was to give to his disciples the authority to do the same works he did and to send them out. This is one reason why the Holy Spirit was given at Pentecost. Jesus, since he was soon to depart the earth, sent the Holy Spirit to dwell in Christians so they would continue to do the works he did. That's why he said in John's Gospel that it was more advantageous for him to leave and to send the Holy Spirit. With delegated authority comes multiplied effectiveness.

The point of this discourse is this: rejection of the one whom God invests authority in is equivalent to rejecting him. The resulting judgment is named *delegate judgment*. Those who resist or refuse the lieutenants (Matt. 10:14,15) are actually resisting Jesus, who considers it thus, v. 15 confirms it. Jesus knows, had he been there personally, that he would've received the same treatment, because he would've done the same things his disciples did.

On a side note, the severity of the condemnation spoken in v. 15 is great because the miracles they saw were greater than what Sodom and Gomorrah saw. This is what's meant by the blasphemy of the Holy Spirit (Matt. 12:31,32; Mark 3:28-30): a person commits this when, after having been given undeniable proof through a miracle testifying to the existence and will of God, he opposes God. This is also the unpardonable sin mentioned in 1 John. It's unpardonable because there's nothing more God can do to win the guilty person. His heart is thoroughly hardened against the Gospel. It's a heinous sin, worse than the sin of Sodom and Gomorrah, according to Jesus.

*Part II: Modes of the Judgment of God*

## 9. **Thwarted Judgment**

Visiting Abraham to inform him that he will soon have a son, the three celestial visitors pause before departing.

> Gen. 18:16 Then the men rose up from there, and looked down toward Sodom; and Abraham was walking with them to send them off.
> [17]The LORD said, "Shall I hide from Abraham what I am about to do,
> [18]since Abraham will surely become a great and mighty nation, and in him all the nations of the earth will be blessed?
> [19]"For I have chosen him, so that he may command his children and his household after him to keep the way of the LORD by doing righteousness and justice, so that the LORD may bring upon Abraham what He has spoken about him."
> [20]And the LORD said, "The outcry of Sodom and Gomorrah is indeed great, and their sin is exceedingly grave.
> [21]"I will go down now, and see if they have done entirely according to its outcry, which has come to Me; and if not, I will know.

Though the sin of Sodom and Gomorrah warrants judgment, the Lord counsels with Abraham the friend of God (2 Chron. 20:7; Isa. 41:8) beforehand. Abraham entreats him and almost dissuades him from venting his wrath on the cities. Had Abraham asked one more time, one wonders if God would've granted his request, and spared the cities for the sake of one righteous man. Most think so. It's a wonder that a man can intercede with God to obviate his judgment.

But this is not the only instance. The Israelites command Aaron to build the golden calf (Exod. 32:1). This provokes God's wrath. Moses the servant of God intercedes (like Abraham), and judgment is again rescinded.

> Exod. 32:9 The LORD said to Moses, "I have seen this people, and behold, they are an obstinate people.
> [10]"Now then let Me alone, that My anger may burn against them and that I may destroy them; and I will make of you a great nation."

In another incident God permits the reversal of a prophecy at the behest of the recipient:

*Part II: Modes of the Judgment of God*

> Isa. 38:1 In those days Hezekiah became mortally ill. And Isaiah the prophet the son of Amoz came to him and said to him, "Thus says the LORD, 'Set your house in order, for you shall die and not live.'"
> ²Then Hezekiah turned his face to the wall and prayed to the LORD,
> ³and said, "Remember now, O LORD, I beseech You, how I have walked before You in truth and with a whole heart, and have done what is good in Your sight." And Hezekiah wept bitterly.
> ⁴Then the word of the LORD came to Isaiah, saying,
> ⁵"Go and say to Hezekiah, 'Thus says the LORD, the God of your father David, "I have heard your prayer, I have seen your tears; behold, I will add fifteen years to your life.

These examples illustrate thwarted judgment. The principle is the same: God's plans are changed by the intercession of man, usually a single man. This privilege God does not grant lightly—Abraham, Noah, and Hezekiah are extraordinary characters. But the privilege is, on occasion, granted. Thwarted judgment exemplifies how God accommodates man's free will. The marvel of God's will is the extent to which it's subservient to a righteous man's yearnings. The opposite is true in the case of those who oppose him (*predestined judgment*). With respect to the wicked, God's judgments are foreordained and intransigent. But with respect to the righteous, his plans become malleable.

## 10. Judgment in the New Testament

Occasionally one hears an evangelist or pastor proclaim that God is going to judge so-and-so, this group, that group, this nation or that nation. The preacher issues rebukes like the prophets of old, saying that as surely as God judged in the past (Sodom and Gomorrah is a favorite), he will judge now. Or perhaps a prayer warrior will cry out that the Holy Spirit has pronounced judgment over someone in the church. Is this biblically sound?

OT judgments were enacted in the lifetime of the offender or offenders, rather than enacted in the afterlife as an imprisonment in the fires of hell—a notable difference between the OT and NT. Does God judge in the NT the same as the OT, where the sentence is car-

## Part II: Modes of the Judgment of God

ried out while on earth (or both in this life and the next)? By insinuation Jesus addresses this:

> Luke 10:12 "I say to you, it will be more tolerable in that day for Sodom than for that city.
> [13]"Woe to you, Chorazin! Woe to you, Bethsaida! For if the miracles had been performed in Tyre and Sidon which occurred in you, they would have repented long ago, sitting in sackcloth and ashes.
> [14]"But it will be more tolerable for Tyre and Sidon in the judgment than for you.
> [15]"And you, Capernaum, will not be exalted to heaven, will you? You will be brought down to Hades!

Unlike the prototype cities Sodom and Gomorrah, Chorazin and Bethsaida receive the wrath of God in the life to come. This demonstrates the NT principle that judgment is primarily dispensed in the afterlife. Apart from Revelation, the NT has no specific prophecy of doom against a nation (with the exception of Israel).

Likewise, there're few pronouncements against individuals. Christians are occasionally judged for walking in sin (1 Cor. 5:4,5; 1 Cor. 10:1-11; 1 Cor. 11:29-32; 1 Thess. 4:6); the ungodly even less so. Alexander the coppersmith (2 Tim. 4:14) and Herod (Acts. 12:20-25) are exceptions to NT judgments against unbelievers. Both were hindering the propagation of the Gospel, and this might be the only circumstance for which God in NT times judges sinners prior to their demise.

Why does God judge by one standard in the OT and by another in the NT? Why not continue dispensing earthly punishments in this age? Plenty deserve it. A few reasons for the change. First, in the hope that heathens will repent and be saved, "who desires all men to be saved and to come to the knowledge of the truth" (1 Tim. 2:4). In the NT salvation is readily available to all through faith from a contrite heart. Jesus' death and resurrection made it available to Jew and Gentile alike. Likewise, in the OT any could come to God—but with difficulty, as the knowledge of God was not proclaimed outside of Israel, nor was faith in Christ explicitly available. One of the purposes of Jesus' death was to make salvation readily accessible by all mankind, not just a select few. Since the choice of accepting Christ's sacrifice is only available while one is still living, a premature death due to an active judgment truncates the window wherein one can make an affirmative decision. Even if this were not the case, the abundance of grace in the NT supersedes the OT mode

## Part II: Modes of the Judgment of God

of judgment—but only in this lifetime. Second, the OT has, across the board, little mention of the afterlife. Hence a reason for the controversy in Jesus' day over the resurrection, i.e. if there is life after death. To the Semitic mind judgment would have been ineffective had it been relegated to the life after. Third, God no longer deals with nations like he did in the OT; all nations are now comprised of believers and unbelievers. To judge a nation is to affect the Christians in that nation as well as the non-Christians. That the percentage of saints varies from nation to nation is of no consequence. Is a percentage the ultimate deciding factor for God, or is he moved by devotion and fervency, and not by numbers? God will spare the city for the sake of ten righteous, so to speak. Fourth, any earthly loss, whether a loss in health, prosperity, or a shortened life, pales in comparison, in both duration and in magnitude, to an eternity in hell, which is the ultimate NT judgment.

*

Apart from the question of whether in the NT era God judges or not, and how judgment is dispensed, is gauging the severity of judgment in this age. The question of severity has been obfuscated by passages such as this:

> Matt. 5:38 "You have heard that it was said, 'AN EYE FOR AN EYE, AND A TOOTH FOR A TOOTH.'
> [39]"But I say to you, do not resist an evil person; but whoever slaps you on your right cheek, turn the other to him also."
> . . . . . . . . . .
> [43]"You have heard that it was said, 'YOU SHALL LOVE YOUR NEIGHBOR and hate your enemy.'
> [44]"But I say to you, love your enemies and pray for those who persecute you..."

Many have heard these verses in church while growing up and were left with the impression that Christians are, without complaint, supposed to allow anyone to step on them and should not stand up for their own rights. The world, on the other hand, oppresses the weak, and won't hesitate to take advantage of anyone who won't defend himself. Thus acquired, the understanding is that God was the God of retribution in the OT, but in the NT things have changed. Peter reinforces much of the same:

> 1 Pet. 3:8 To sum up, all of you be harmonious, sympathetic, brotherly, kindhearted, and humble in spirit;

## Part II: Modes of the Judgment of God

> ⁹not returning evil for evil or insult for insult, but giving a blessing instead;

Verses such as these have ingrained this one-sided impression. The other side of the coin has not been as well published:

> Acts 23:2 The high priest Ananias commanded those standing beside him to strike him on the mouth.
> ³Then Paul said to him, "God is going to strike you, you whitewashed wall! Do you sit to try me according to the Law, and in violation of the Law order me to be struck?"
> . . . . . . . . . .
> ⁶But perceiving that one group were Sadducees and the other Pharisees, Paul began crying out in the Council, "Brethren, I am a Pharisee, a son of Pharisees; I am on trial for the hope and resurrection of the dead!"
> ⁷As he said this, there occurred a dissension between the Pharisees and Sadducees, and the assembly was divided.

Here Paul is literally slapped on the cheek (mouth actually, but close enough). What does he do, does he let his persecutors walk all over him? No, he stands up for his rights, telling them that what they did was illegal and reminding them that God will pay them back. Not the only time Paul said the Lord would punish those who persecuted him:

> 2 Tim. 4:14 Alexander the coppersmith did me much harm; the Lord will repay him according to his deeds.
>
> 2 Thess. 1:6 For after all it is only just for God to repay with affliction those who afflict you...

Not the religious picture of turning the other cheek. And lest one thinks this is just Paul, Peter echoes the same:

> 1 Pet. 4:4 In all this, they are surprised that you do not run with them into the same excesses of dissipation, and they malign you;
> ⁵but they will give account to Him who is ready to judge the living and the dead.

## Part II: Modes of the Judgment of God

In order to ascertain the whole truth, the prior passage from Matthew must be interpreted in its context, then the other Scriptures considered. Matt. 5:38-44 is extracted from the Sermon on the Mount, where Jesus follows this format: he quotes from the Law of Moses then appends to it a new commandment. The new commandment is the same as the old except that it's tougher: it addresses the attitude of the heart that caused the transgression in the first place. The Law in this case, is "an eye for an eye, tooth for a tooth". This was part of Israel's civil and criminal code. An assault was redressed by retribution; the victim had the right to get even. Jesus is saying that Christians don't have to retaliate; let the score be uneven. But this doesn't mean that a Christ follower shouldn't take prudent steps to avoid being abused. In Acts 23 Paul did everything in his power to avoid persecution. Jesus' remark and Peter's remark apply to those who cannot evade harm, who have become victims, instructing them how to bear up in the midst of it. And at times Paul almost revels in knowing that those who persecute him will receive just recompense—not from himself but from God. Together, these form a balanced synopsis of how a Christian should endure persecution, and is best summarized thus:

> Rom. 12:19 Never take your own revenge, beloved, but leave room for the wrath of God, for it is written, "VENGEANCE IS MINE, I WILL REPAY," says the Lord.
>20"BUT IF YOUR ENEMY IS HUNGRY, FEED HIM, AND IF HE IS THIRSTY, GIVE HIM A DRINK; FOR IN SO DOING YOU WILL HEAP BURNING COALS ON HIS HEAD."
> 21Do not be overcome by evil, but overcome evil with good.

It's justice for God to judge those who afflict Christians. Since Revelation is centered around God's judgment, it's naturally skewed towards God's vengeance, and away from turning the other cheek. In the second chapter Jesus would not forget Antipas's martyrdom. There were not as many first century Christians martyred as the number killed since then. Confirmed by Paul Johnson, Gibbon's history (in its dry scorn) estimates that the Catholic Church killed several times more Protestants than the sum of all martyred at the hands of the Romans. The histories from the Church Fathers are filled with details of persecutions. As the early Church evolved, and the spiritual propensities of Christendom shifted, the Church magnified and exaggerated the extent of the former persecutions. This impression has been handed down to the present age. Keep in

## Part II: Modes of the Judgment of God

mind that it was not until the third century that Christian suppression became a uniform government policy. As confirmed by the NT, early persecutions were sporadic and local. Most of the martyrs were church leaders, as the Romans tried to disperse the movement by annihilating the leadership. But, on the other hand, though relatively small in number God was displeased by the death of the likes of Antipas (2:13). It was not simply the number of saints killed, but that his best servants were massacred. Justice demands retribution for these iniquities.

But Revelation is not alone in prophesying the judgment of the ungodly, as exemplified by the following verse. Note that "SAVED" here means *rescued from impending doom*.

> 1 Pet. 5:18 AND IF IT IS WITH DIFFICULTY THAT THE RIGHTEOUS IS SAVED, WHAT WILL BECOME OF THE GODLESS MAN AND THE SINNER?

> 2 Pet. 2:9 ..then the Lord knows how to rescue the godly from temptation, and to keep the unrighteous under punishment for the day of judgment...

\*

Quoted a few pages ago, Matt. 9:15 demonstrates that, in spite of misconceptions, NT judgments are harsher than those of the OT. With the extra measure of grace and of the knowledge of God comes an extra measure of accountability, and hence judgment. Hebrews describes this in detail:

> Heb. 12:18 For you have not come to a mountain that can be touched and to a blazing fire, and to darkness and gloom and whirlwind,
> [19]and to the blast of a trumpet and the sound of words which sound was such that those who heard begged that no further word be spoken to them.
> [20]For they could not bear the command, "IF EVEN A BEAST TOUCHES THE MOUNTAIN, IT WILL BE STONED."
> [21]And so terrible was the sight, that Moses said, "I AM FULL OF FEAR and trembling."
> [22]But you have come to Mount Zion and to the city of the living God, the heavenly Jerusalem, and to myriads of angels,
> [23]to the general assembly and church of the firstborn who are enrolled in heaven, and to God, the Judge of all, and to the spirits of the righteous made perfect,

## Part II: Modes of the Judgment of God

²⁴and to Jesus, the mediator of a new covenant, and to the sprinkled blood, which speaks better than the blood of Abel.
²⁵See to it that you do not refuse Him who is speaking. For if those did not escape when they refused him who warned them on earth, much less will we escape who turn away from Him who warns from heaven.
²⁶And His voice shook the earth then, but now He has promised, saying, "YET ONCE MORE I WILL SHAKE NOT ONLY THE EARTH, BUT ALSO THE HEAVEN."
²⁷This expression, "Yet once more," denotes the removing of those things which can be shaken, as of created things, so that those things which cannot be shaken may remain.
²⁸Therefore, since we receive a kingdom which cannot be shaken, let us show gratitude, by which we may offer to God an acceptable service with reverence and awe;
²⁹for our God is a consuming fire.

The author of Hebrews is comparing two mountains, Mt. Sinai and Mt. Zion. These two are the two covenants between God and man (see Gal. 4:21-31 also). Mt. Sinai is the Law of Moses; Mt. Zion is faith in Jesus Christ. Sinai is where God appeared to Moses and gave him the Law. Although Mt. Zion is an actual mountain, through the Bible Zion takes on a symbolic meaning, no longer referring to the earthly mountain but to an idealistic state of being. In this way Zion in the OT represents the fulfillment of God's plans, the correction of shortcomings. Zion in the NT is freedom from the bondage of the Law, the life in the Spirit. The passage from Hebrews begins by saying, "you have not come to a mountain that can be touched", signifying Zion.

Next, vv. 18 to 21 are a recap of Moses' ascent of Sinai to receive the Law (Exod. 19 and onwards). All Israel is commanded to gather around the mountain. A line of demarcation is drawn around the base. If any person or animal crosses the line, that being must be stoned. The scene is one of terror and fright. The symbolism points to the ruthlessly exacting nature of the Law, to the fear of transgressing it, and to the punishment for those who do. There's a clear separation between the holy God above, up on the mountain, and man below, down around the base. Accompanied by thunder and lightning, there's enough of the presence of the Almighty to terrify, a reminder of the wrath of Jehovah against those who don't obey his commandments. In v. 19, the words spoken terrify the hearers, to the extent that they "begged that no further word be spoken", the natural human reflex to the commandments of the Law. The Word

## Part II: Modes of the Judgment of God

of God in that form yields guilt, sin, and condemnation. The holiness of God, absent mercy, exposes the sheer sinfulness of man; man cowers from this. As it says, the letter kills but the Spirit gives life (2 Cor. 3:6).

But further still in the passage, the comparison to the new covenant begins, the covenant of grace and mercy (John 1:16). The admonition in v. 25, "See to it that you do not refuse Him who is speaking", refers to God speaking in the NT, not OT. The comparison, of course, is the Lord speaking from Mt. Sinai vs. the Lord speaking through the Gospel. The second half of v. 25, however, is a warning: just as the Almighty on Mt. Sinai warned the Israelites in the wilderness, so he warns all mankind in NT times. "...Much less will we escape who turn away from Him who warns from heaven." If there was judgment to those who refused God under the old covenant, how much more judgment to those who refuse him under the new covenant? The Gospel has greater mercy and grace. But it's a two-edged sword: along with the increase in grace is an increase in judgment. This is what the passage in Hebrews is saying.

And yet further. In v. 26 God promises to shake the earth again, like he did on Mt. Sinai. This prophecy has been fulfilled in the preaching of the Gospel, as v. 28 alludes. Those receiving it should offer up an acceptable service (v. 28), believers' worship being an anti-type of OT sacrifice, with "reverence and awe; for our God is a consuming fire." God appeared on Mt. Sinai as a consuming fire. And in the NT he has not ceased to manifest himself as a consuming fire, in spite of the forbearance of Christ. It's the nature of fire to consume; the more fuel heaped on a conflagration, the greater it consumes. Thus, judgment appears this way in Revelation.

# Part III

# The Visions

*Part III: The Visions*

## 1. The Lamb Receives the Book (5:1–5:14)

> 5:1 I saw in the right hand of Him who sat on the throne a book written inside and on the back, sealed up with seven seals.

The word "book" from the Greek is *scroll*. The writing was on the "inside and on the back"; the word *back* must refer to its back when unfurled. Therefore, a more understandable translation for "inside and on the back" is *front and back*. Expounding on the verb tense, the word "written" could read, "reached a state where the writing has been completed". The word for "sealed up" uses the prefix *kata* joined to the ordinary word for *sealed*, finely adjusting the meaning from *sealed* to *sealed up*. With the addition of the prefix, the slight change means it was sealed as completely as it could be. An analogy is the difference between the phrases *filling a bucket with water* and *filling up a bucket with water*. Putting all the pieces together, the following is a more precise translation:

> I saw in the right hand of Him who sat on the throne a scroll that reached a state where the writing had been completed. It was written on the front and back and completely sealed over by seven seals.

From the description, every last word of what was intended or necessary to be put in the book was there. Not a detail omitted. It's written on both sides, front and back, as the writer had to use the back side to include everything that needed to be there. It's like a woman on a vacation who writes a postcard about all the things she's done, and crams details into every available space, and must print in tiny letters because she has run out of room. This is the idea conveyed by 5:1—except that the scroll contains God's wrath.

The book lists the entire record of God's predestined judgments against mankind for the rejection of the Gospel and persecution of the saints. Just as judgment had been building up until the time of Noah, so it accumulates in the church age. Judgments are queued up, so to speak, prepared to be poured out on mankind once God's patience has been exhausted. The seals are intact when John first sees them, so one would assume God's patience had not yet run its course.

In use until recent times, seals were used for two purposes. First, to verify the authenticity of a document. Second, to prove that

*Part III: The Visions*

the document had not yet been read. To seal a paper letter in an envelope, one might use a lighted candle to drip melted wax over the back of the envelope, where the flap closes. While the wax was not yet cooled, the wax would be stamped. The wax, once cooled, would adhere to the paper in such a way that it would be impossible to open the envelope without breaking the wax. The stamp forms a contoured image in the wax, which, like a signature, an expert could differentiate a forgery from the genuine article.

The breaking of the seals implies that the book's contents will be read; reading the book implies the invocation of the judgments therein.

> 5:2 And I saw a strong angel proclaiming with a loud voice, "Who is worthy to open the book and to break its seals?"
> ³And no one in heaven or on the earth or under the earth was able to open the book or to look into it.

Two questions come to mind. First, the time correlation. Second, the impetus to break the seals. To address the time issue, some basic assumptions must be made. It's assumed that time exists in heaven, that events happen in time, and that time there progresses forward. This is called *real-time* (a computer science term). An additional assumption is that there's a correlation between heaven's real-time (or *heaven-time*) and earth's real-time (*earth-time*). Both move forward, but not necessarily at the same rate, one with respect to the other. Events happen at distinct points in time, be it earth-time or heaven-time. An event that happens in heaven will occur at a distinct point in time on earth, and vice-versa. However, earth-time and heaven-time do not progress forward at the same rate. Furthermore, the relationship between earth-time and heaven-time fluctuates.

For example, an observer in heaven might witness a scene that feels like twenty minutes (of heaven-time) to him or her, but has spanned two weeks on the earth (of earth-time). And vice-versa—in fact this is how God created the earth in six days. The time span in earth-time was actually millions of years, but to the Lord nothing interesting happened, so God fast-forwarded earth-time like one would fast-forward a tiresome scene in a DVD. The relationship between earth and heaven-times is a lot like time dilation and contraction according to Einstein's Theory of Special Relativity.

The Theory of Special Relativity is often misunderstood. According to Special Relativity, it's possible for a space traveler, travelling at a high speed, to spend a month on a space craft, and discover, upon returning to earth, that ten years have transpired while he

*Part III: The Visions*

was gone. Both the astronaut and the inhabitants of earth went forward in time, but the astronaut went forward at a slower rate. In spite of what some have said about Special Relativity, it's not possible to go backwards in time. It's only possible for two parties to go forward in time at different rates, so that one ages more slowly or more quickly with respect to the other.

Likewise, in parts of Revelation heaven-time moves forward quicker than earth-time. Some visions span centuries. Furthermore, a large portion of John's visions are of things that have not yet occurred in heaven—let alone on earth. After all, a prophecy foretells of what the future holds. But a disputed question is whether John's vision is of things that have happened, are happening, or will happen. There are different schools of thought as to when the visions will occur or have occurred with respect to earth-time. In other words, were the horsemen loosed in the first century A.D.? Or one in the first century, one in the second, etc?

The second question is the impetus to break the seals. God is pictured holding the scroll, indefinitely it would seem, until one is found worthy to open it. This implies that God has no intention of opening it on his own; it will stay closed until one is found who's worthy to open it. And no one in heaven, on the earth, or under the earth is found.

The three places human spirits dwell are in heaven (which is the same as in the sky), on earth, and under the earth. Spirits of the deceased go either up or down. Up is heaven, down is hell: the norm, not only in Revelation, but for all the writers of the Bible.

> Rom. 10:6 But the righteousness based on faith speaks as follows: "DO NOT SAY IN YOUR HEART, 'WHO WILL ASCEND INTO HEAVEN?' (that is, to bring Christ down), [7]or 'WHO WILL DESCEND INTO THE ABYSS?' (that is, to bring Christ up from the dead)."

According to the above verse (and this quoted from the OT), Christ, who's not on the earth, must be either above it or beneath it. In Dante's *Inferno*, hell is depicted as nine circles of suffering within the earth. In other words, Dante, representing the contemporary consensus, believed that hell was in the center of the earth, a conception that originated from the Bible, Revelation included. Perhaps hell actually is in the earth's core. That would be difficult to ascertain.

Later on in Revelation there're references to the earth being flat and references to it having four corners. This was the popular perception at the time (although the Greeks knew that the earth was

*Part III: The Visions*

actually round). God has chosen to reveal to man spiritual matters only, that concerning man's relationship with God. God has not chosen to reveal many—if any—scientific facts. Man is constrained by the knowledge of the time: John describes what he sees in terms of his understanding. The revelation is correct, but John's scientific reasoning is erroneous, he and the society in which he lived.

But all three—above, on, and beneath—are searched for one worthy to open the book. Why one would search under the earth is anyone's guess. Probably for the sake of completeness. Like trying the glass slipper on all the maidens in the kingdom in search of Cinderella, all souls who are alive or who have once lived are auditioned to see if one might be found who's worthy. The Father has determined not to open the book until such is found. The question is, why would God look for someone worthy enough to break the seals? He doesn't need approval from anyone. But he defers the commencement of judgment until such a one approaches the thrown and breaks the seals. God, and with him all of heaven, wait.

Looking at the transfer of the scroll from another perspective, it's a pageant within the Trinity: God the Father holds the scroll, God the Son must open it. Both play a role, both roles differ, and absent either player judgment will not take place. Yet another confirmation of the authenticity of Revelation—the proper relationship between the Father and Son. The Father originates the scroll, the Son is worthy to open it, the worthiness derived from his obedience on earth.

John apparently believed that God was looking for a person other than Jesus to come forward to open the book. Or he forgot that Jesus enjoys the same privileges of any human being. Or he thought that it would be below Jesus' dignity to approach the throne. It's difficult to tell, but he appears to have forgotten the humanity of Jesus, because in 5:5 he's reminded by the elder that there's an Israelite, a descendent of David, who's worthy.

> 5:4 Then I began to weep greatly because no one was found worthy to open the book or to look into it;
> ⁵and one of the elders said to me, "Stop weeping; behold, the Lion that is from the tribe of Judah, the Root of David, has overcome so as to open the book and its seven seals."

The translation of 5:4 begins, "I began to weep", the phrase originating from one Greek word. Since the pronoun is not explicitly specified, it could be translated *I* or *they*. The translators chose "I". In the flow of events, this sounds right. However, in 5:5, the elder says, *mā klaie* (translated "stop weeping") to John, instead of

## Part III: The Visions

*ou klaie, mā* denoting hypothetical action. The use of this word, and the omission of the pronoun, means that there's a remote possibility of an alternative translation:

> Then they began to weep greatly...and one of the elders said to me, "don't you start weeping now..."

"They" would be the twenty-four elders and the four living creatures, as opposed to the "I", referring to John, a dispassionate spectator. The elders and living beings, the participants, are passionate. Later on, the elders sing.

To John, it's a tragedy that no one is found worthy to open the book. Does he realize that the book is one of judgment of the wicked? Had he known the wrath to be unleashed upon the earth, would he have wept still? Certainly—Revelation longs for judgment, no turning the other cheek. Recompense is past due, and it's just a matter of cracking open what God has already stored up. Jesus is found worthy for the primary reason that he, more than any other, has suffered persecution unjustly at the hands of sinners. Jesus knows what's in the scroll and desires to open it. The judgment of God won't be unfurled until he decides to approach the throne. It's true that by the will of God the Father all things are directed. But it's equally true that God has put all things in the hands of his Son. The worthiness of Christ through his obedience to death is on an equal par with the will of God the Father. These two members of the Godhead are equal; they obtain equality by each exalting the other.

> 5:6 And I saw between the throne (with the four living creatures) and the elders a Lamb standing, as if slain, having seven horns and seven eyes, which are the seven Spirits of God, sent out into all the earth.
> ⁷And He came and took the book out of the right hand of Him who sat on the throne.

The lamb, the well-known symbol of Jesus' sacrifice, represents what he has done, and this has made him worthy to approach the throne. Simply being God's only begotten Son was not qualification enough; his works earned him his worthiness.

\*

Creatures with horns first appear in Revelation in 5:6. These symbols are familiar, as they're used in the eighth and ninth chapters of Daniel, and also in Zechariah:

*Part III: The Visions*

> Zech. 1:18 Then I lifted up my eyes and looked, and behold, there were four horns.
> [19]So I said to the angel who was speaking with me, "What are these?" And he answered me, "These are the horns which have scattered Judah, Israel and Jerusalem."
> [20]Then the LORD showed me four craftsmen.
> [21]I said, "What are these coming to do?" And he said, "These are the horns which have scattered Judah so that no man lifts up his head; but these craftsmen have come to terrify them, to throw down the horns of the nations who have lifted up their horns against the land of Judah in order to scatter it."

Although horns enable an animal of prey to defend itself against predators, this is not their primary function. During the mating season, two males contest for dominance against one another using their horns. The ancients observed this in nature; horns therefore became symbols of dominance. Jesus has seven horns, seven the number of completion. His dominance is complete, as the Father has made him Lord over all in heaven, on earth, and under the earth. The irony is that a Lamb, a small, gentle creature, should have horns.

And finally 5:6 states that Jesus has seven eyes. Like the seven lamps before the throne of God, these are the seven Spirits of God. The Holy Spirit's appearance in the scene of 5:6 completes the Trinity's trio.

> 5:8 When He had taken the book, the four living creatures and the twenty-four elders fell down before the Lamb, each one holding a harp and golden bowls full of incense, which are the prayers of the saints.

If Paul called the Corinthians, not known for their good behavior, "saints" (1 Cor. 1:2), then any believer is a saint. Saints, the *holy ones*, are so named not because of their great works but because of Jesus' great work. The Bible, Revelation included, says (in the passive voice) that Christians have been clothed or washed. Jesus did it; they did not earn it; their only participation in the work was to receive it.

Used in the ministry in the Tabernacle, according to 5:8 incense is also used in heaven, but is comprised of the prayers of the saints. Heaven stores up prayers in bowls. Prayer can only be offered by those still on earth. There're different types of prayers, but the

*Part III: The Visions*

prayers in these bowls are worship, praise, and thanksgiving—not prayers of faith, which asks God for something. This is certain because prayer appears here as incense, and incense was burned in the Holy Place of the temple, signifying its use in worship. According to 5:8 worship offered up by the Faithful on earth is collected and stored by the twenty-four elders for later use, as the aroma that permeates the presence of God. This is how God receives the worship of his people.

> 5:9 And they sang a new song, saying, "Worthy are You to take the book and to break its seals; for You were slain, and purchased for God with Your blood men from every tribe and tongue and people and nation.

In the Bible a *song* means a few things, but fundamentally it's a deep stirring of the heart—but not necessarily a hymn or actual melody. Of the instances where David wrote of a *new song*, not all were set to music (Ps. 40:3 for example). Words put to music play the chords of the heart—it's only natural for a tune to accompany stirring words. Consider *The Song of Solomon*: it's not a song at all, but rather a theme story, one that touches the heart. The book begins thus: "The Song of Songs, which is Solomon's", or as the alternative found in the NASB footnote, "The best of the songs, which is Solomon's". This prelude infers that Solomon collected true stories, and this one was his best. Though without music, it is a song nevertheless. But a *song* in the biblical sense is not simply words put to music. It stirs, it touches, it reminisces the pondering of the heart.

Psalms, hymns, and spiritual songs (Eph. 5:19) should be on the lips of every believer, as his or her devotion to the Lord should be a deep, stirring passion. Music is the natural companion of any passion, but in the Scriptures it's the message conveyed by the song's words that are the important part of the song—not the music. Too often contemporary worship ministries have gone astray in this regard—the music takes ascendancy over the lyrics, and not vice-versa.

But John didn't write *song*, but "new song", a phrase from the OT (Ps. 33:3, 40:3, 96:1, etc.). A new song is not necessarily one that's original, but one that comes from a refreshed heart, when bitter defeat has been replaced with victory. Having reached a favorable end, the joy of the Lord sparks a new song. The song John heard in this vision was one of joy.

This song praises Jesus, saying that he's worthy, but not because he's the Son of God but because of his death in obedience to God. The Father's glory is intrinsic; Jesus' glory comes as a result of what

## Part III: The Visions

he's done. Thus, by his deeds he attained his lordship, and not by his sonship—whereas God the Father is glorified for who he is. This is why Jesus appears as a lamb here—this is what qualifies him to take the scroll out of God's hands. By this action, Jesus specifies and determines God's timing. All things have been prepared by the Father, but it's the Son who pulls the trigger, so to speak. The Father's sovereignty is surrendered to the whims of the one who gave his life for mankind. There is no conflict, as the Father and Son are in perfect harmony. It would be safe to assume that this incident of Jesus exercising the prerogative to receive the scroll and break the seals is not atypical. He regularly acts in this fashion in the affairs of each Christian's life. God has things prepared for those who love him, but it's the other persons of the Godhead who draw it out of his hands.

\*

In spite of the duration that the doctrine of the Trinity has been universally accepted as dogma, it's still not well understood. The Bible instructs Christians to pray to God the Father, not to Jesus. Jesus does receive worship and thanksgiving—but that's the extent of the prayer he receives. His role is an intermediary to the Father. The problem in prayer is one of accessing the Father, as John says,

> 1 John 5:14 This is the confidence which we have before Him, that, if we ask anything according to His will, He hears us.
> [15]And if we know that He hears us in whatever we ask, we know that we have the requests which we have asked from Him.

All it takes is for God to hear a prayer, and he will grant it. The difficult part is *hearing* the request. God only hears requests that are brought through his Son and are in line with his will. Of course, hearing in the context of these verses in 1 John implies not just that God hears but that he takes to heart. If God knows and takes to his heart any prayer from one of his chosen, it will be granted. Prayers that are not answered were not heard (with the heart) in the first place. The difficulty in getting one's prayers answered is equivalent to the difficulty in getting God to hear one's prayers. Jesus is the liaison, the intercessor, the intermediary, the gateway, the interface between God and man. He's also the lord, or supervisor, over a Christian's spiritual life, and for this reason "searches the hearts" (v. 27 below) so that he might know how to rightly dispense encouragement, discipline, and guidance.

*Part III: The Visions*

> Rom 8:26 In the same way the Spirit also helps our weakness; for we do not know how to pray as we should, but the Spirit Himself intercedes for us with groanings too deep for words; [27]and He who searches the hearts knows what the mind of the Spirit is, because He intercedes for the saints according to the will of God.
> [28]And we know that God causes all things to work together for good to those who love God, to those who are called according to His purpose.
> [29]For those whom He foreknew, He also predestined to become conformed to the image of His Son, so that He would be the firstborn among many brethren;

The Spirit searches the "depths of God" (v. 10 below), while the Son searches the hearts, or inner thoughts, of man.

> 1 Cor. 2:9 but just as it is written, "THINGS WHICH EYE HAS NOT SEEN AND EAR HAS NOT HEARD, AND which HAVE NOT ENTERED THE HEART OF MAN, ALL THAT GOD HAS PREPARED FOR THOSE WHO LOVE HIM."
> [10] For to us God revealed them through the Spirit; for the Spirit searches all things, even the depths of God.

While the Spirit (Rom. 8:26) and the Son (Rom. 8:27) intercede on behalf of the child of God, their roles in intercession differ. Christ is the gateway to the Father, but the Spirit is the helper in the utilization of the gateway. The Holy Spirit enables and amplifies the prayer life of the one praying; without him, in "our weakness" (Rom. 8:26) we could never express ourselves adequately in prayer. Simple prayers are conveyed in words, but deep prayers are "too deep for words" and can only be uttered in "groanings" (Rom. 8:26). These groanings come from the Spirit; speaking in tongues facilitates them. The depths of the sorrow of repentance, the agony over sin, the yearning to walk in the light of the Word, the longing on behalf of another who's in need—these are the groanings of the Holy Spirit that are woven into prayers, and Jesus, who "knows the mind of the Spirit" (v. 27), carries these to the Father who, when he hears them, "causes all things to work together for good". The fulfillment of that which is "predestined" (v. 29) is contingent upon a prayer life that correctly employs the Son and the Spirit. Just because God predestined something is no guarantee that it will come to pass. Verse 28 says that "God causes all things to work together

## Part III: The Visions

for good". This is God's response to a prayer received by his Son and by the help of the Spirit. The truth of v. 28 contradicts years to traditional teaching; it's absurd to believe that God is the cause of all events (like car accidents or drive-by shootings) in a Christian's life.

In 1 Cor. 2:10 it says that God revealed that which he's prepared through the Spirit. The Father prepares things and intends for them to be delivered to mankind. That's his role in the Trinity. The Son and the Spirit take these things and open them. It is by God's Word that the Father works in a believer's life. This is the same as Jesus taking something out of God's hands, just as the lamb takes the scroll in 5:8. But the Holy Spirit is also involved in revealing and in manifesting these things, not just the Father and Son. Only when all three are engaged does a Christian receive what God has prepared for him or her. It's a popular misconception that God intervenes randomly in the affairs of man. He does not. God acts through his Word. He won't do anything apart from it. If one chosen of God expects help from the Father in an aspect of life, he or she must find relevant Scriptures that address the issue, and put them into practice. It's not enough to believe in God—one must believe in his Word. Lots of folks believe in God. Satan does not resist this kind of belief. The world loves to hear prayers offered up to God, but objects when a prayer is offered in the name of Jesus.

But still, this is not enough. Leave the Spirit out and nothing will work. It's analogous to an airplane taking off, when it races down the runway, and then rotates, expecting to leave the ground—and it does. Like a miracle, some invisible force causes it to become airborne. So the Holy Spirit, when a Christian acts on Scripture, makes it all work. The dry words of the Bible cannot do this, but must be transformed into a spiritual experience. Man is a spiritual being, and it's by man's spirit that he has communion with the Holy Spirit. Man is constantly trying to use his mind in matters that only his spirit can grasp. The intellectual side of Christianity constantly pulls the Church into an extreme of intellectualism, legalism, and silly, trifling religiosity. Those in the West are not taught to be spirit-conscious. They have the other pieces of the puzzle, but are missing one critical piece, one person of the Godhead. Their Christian walk is dry, difficult, and void of spiritual dynamics. Sin lurks one step behind them. Only by giving proper place to the operation of the Holy Spirit can they get the monkey of carnality and intellectualism off their backs.

*

At the end of the next verse is another prophecy (like 1 Cor. 6:2) that, one day, the Faithful will reign upon the earth:

> 5:10 "You have made them to be a kingdom and priests to our God; and they will reign upon the earth."

Every cross-reference Bible should link this to 1 Pet. 2:9, and vice-versa. Both these verses say that all believers are priests, a reference to OT priests. As noted before, a priest performs two duties. First, he's a representative, a necessary buffer, between the people and God. This is needed because access to God is restricted because of his holiness. Second, he's a minister designated to offer worship, in one form or another, to God, like the sacrifices and incense of the Mosaic covenant, which symbolize the praise and worship offered up by believers in the Spirit (Heb. 13:15; Eph. 5:2). Both 5:10 and 1 Pet. 2:9 allude to this second priestly duty, and not the first.

> 5:11 Then I looked, and I heard the voice of many angels around the throne and the living creatures and the elders; and the number of them was myriads of myriads, and thousands of thousands,
> [12] saying with a loud voice, "Worthy is the Lamb that was slain to receive power and riches and wisdom and might and honor and glory and blessing."
> [13] And every created thing which is in heaven and on the earth and under the earth and on the sea, and all things in them, I heard saying, "To Him who sits on the throne, and to the Lamb, be blessing and honor and glory and dominion forever and ever."
> [14] And the four living creatures kept saying, "Amen." And the elders fell down and worshiped.

In 5:13, the creatures praise both God the Father and Jesus equally, confirming that Jesus, not just God the Father, receives praise and worship. The two are peers.

## 2. Seeking the Time of the Seals

Since the scroll contains the predestined judgment of God, as the seals are broken, it's unleashed on the earth. This is the moment when God's patience has run out, like when the flood broke in the days of Noah. The duration of God's patience is longer than man's, but his fury, once unleashed, is more severe. And God's al-

## Part III: The Visions

ways righteous in judgment, meaning that he's fair by man's standard of fairness. In the dispensation of the NT, with the increase in grace and in a greater knowledge of God, man is held to a higher level of accountability. Judgment is harsher under the new covenant than under the old.

Revelation was written for Christians suffering at the hands of the ungodly, but it was also written to all the Faithful. The stench of corrupt man's heart has not gone unnoticed by Jehovah; assuredly judgment will come upon the sinner. God has not forgotten that his only Son, sent to earth to heal mankind, was crucified by the same. Neither has the Son. God has prepared retribution, and Jesus unleashes it.

Since the time of the OT prophecies, all of Israel and all of the Church has longed to peer into that scroll, figuratively speaking—in other words, to put an end to the misery that sinners inflict on the world. Even the apostles yearned to know the time when the ungodly will cease and desist:

> Acts 1:6 So when they had come together, they were asking Him, saying, "Lord, is it at this time You are restoring the kingdom to Israel?"
> ⁷He said to them, "It is not for you to know times or epochs which the Father has fixed by His own authority;
> ⁸but you will receive power when the Holy Spirit has come upon you; and you shall be My witnesses both in Jerusalem, and in all Judea and Samaria, and even to the remotest part of the earth."

In v. 6, the words, "they were asking him", are more verbosely translated, *they kept on asking him over and over again.* Finally Jesus answered—but not the answer they wanted to hear. Christians still ask this question, except they ask it of Revelation. The answer in both cases is the same: "It is not for you to know the times". Jesus redirected them to the works that the Father was planning to do through them, and these were not hidden. Jesus in v. 8 tells them to wait for the baptism in the Holy Spirit. Once baptized in the Spirit, they would be effective witnesses to the world. The baptism is the initiation into the signs and wonders, and these get unbelievers' attention. This, the "power" received in v. 8, would equip them to evangelize the Gospel and launch a world-wide revolution. This was God's plan. Getting caught up in end-time predictions would've been a distraction. It's still a distraction.

*Part III: The Visions*

There're a handful (invariably Evangelicals) who're obsessed with end-time prophecy. Any time topics are solicited for the next Bible study, they're quick to suggest end-time prophecy. Their thirst for studying this topic is unquenchable. Charismatics and Pentecostals are mostly immune from this disease. Why? Because their preoccupation with the baptism in the Holy Spirit and the working of miracles leaves no end-time prophecy vacuum. They're pursuing what Jesus told the Church in Acts 1:8. Science has taught modern man that miracles do not exist, that man is not a spiritual being. This has trickled into the Church, producing a Christianity dominated by intellectualism. Nothing wrong with using one's mind; to fully understand the Scriptures takes much study. Paul and Luke were known for their intellectual prowess. But the Western suppression of belief in the supernatural, which began in the Renaissance as a reaction against an oppressive religion, has distorted the Gospel. In spite of their excesses, the Pentecostal and Charismatic movements' contribution to Christianity is to balance the mind with the spirit. Since Evangelicals have rejected the Spirit (i.e. the baptism in the Holy Spirit subsequent to salvation), an unfulfilled void drives them to study Revelation. This isn't what God intended the book to be used for.

## 3. The First Seal: The Hunter (6:1–6:2)

> 6:1 Then I saw when the Lamb broke one of the seven seals, and I heard one of the four living creatures saying as with a voice of thunder, "Come."
> ²I looked, and behold, a white horse, and he who sat on it had a bow; and a crown was given to him, and he went out conquering and to conquer.

Repeating the Hebrew idiom, "I looked, and behold", which first appeared in 4:1 and connotes that a vision will ensue, John's attention is jarred the moment the first seal is opened. The scene changes radically from the throng gathered around the throne to the apparition of the first horse and rider. As there're four cherubim and four horsemen, each cherub takes a turn heralding the next rider. The portents conveyed by the four progress from bad to worse, as the judgments become increasingly severe.

Of the four horsemen, the first is the only one whose identity is unspecified. A theory held by Metzger and others is that he's a Parthian warrior and that white was a sacred color to the Parthians.

*Part III: The Visions*

The Parthians often utilized archers on horseback, waging harassing attacks against their enemies, advancing and retreating. Viewed from the time Revelation was written, the Parthians, descended from the Persians, were an extant enemy of the Roman Empire. The first horseman, according to this theory, signifies them going to war against the Romans.

Gazing back in history, ancient Rome constituted the pinnacle of the deployment of heavy infantry. The sword, having replaced the spear, was the primary weapon, as exemplified in the next horseman. The Romans were harassed by Parthian archers on horseback, but these archers were never much of a threat, as the Romans later developed tactics to counter them. In most every army they were ever used, archers were auxiliary units used to supplement heavy troops or cavalry. The Greeks developed the phalanx, which entailed arranging armored soldiers in organized lines, rather than as a mob, and training them to maneuver on the battlefield in unison, as one coordinated body. These infantry troops used their shields to deflect the arrows of the enemy, as noted in the Armor of God (Eph. 6:16). The Romans, in close formation, could, if necessary, enclose themselves in a wall of shields, as a remedy against a barrage of arrows. As archers were by virtue of their service usually placed at a safe distance from the melee of battle, they had no need for heavy armor, as those in the vanguard had to don armor consisting of bronze or iron, customized to fit the wearer in a mesh or plate covering. The cost of equipping archers was less, and the need for training them was small (they could practice target shooting in their spare time)—hence the ability to draft them en masse from the common folk, mobilizing them only in times of war. The point is this: an archer is not the expected symbol for a warrior from that period. One should look elsewhere for the meaning of the first horseman, the archer.

Another theory, advanced here, is that the first horseman is symbolic of a monarch going on a lion hunt. Back in ancient times, lions inhabited the Middle East, and the king was praised for ridding the countryside of them. Prov. 22:13: "The sluggard says, 'There is a lion outside; I will be killed in the streets!'" At the time Proverbs was written, this danger was not implausible, although lions in that region have long since become extinct. The preferred weapon used to hunt lions would be a bow. And the hunter would be on horseback, in all likelihood. Of course, the fact that the horsemen in Revelation were mounted is independent of their purpose. The horses signify their going forth into all the earth. The fact that the Parthians had mounted archers does not contribute to the

*Part III: The Visions*

proposition that the first rider symbolizes a Parthian mounted archer (nor does the coincidence of the hunter on a horse).

And what of the crown? The crown, Revelation says, was given to the horseman. Picture a laurel wreath being awarded to a winner in a Roman contest, as this is the meaning conveyed here. The wording—the word "given" in the verse—conjures a ceremony where the recipient is being honored for his achievements, or installed in a position of authority. Having been recently bequeathed, the rider is now out on a hunting expedition to bag an even bigger trophy. Together, the crown and the bow mean this.

But what of the color white? In the Bible white indubitably means righteousness. This is one reason some have identified the rider as Jesus. But if the rider is a hunter and not Jesus, how does white relate in this case? In truth, the white rider is one of Revelation's mysteries. The commentators struggle to explain it. Although white may have been a sacred color to the Parthians, soldiers aren't clad in white. And this, if for no other reason, is because it's next to impossible to keep a garment white while out on maneuvers, what with no change in clothes and no laundry service. Certainly not the peasants who've historically filled the ranks of archers.

Historically, white is also a symbol for terror. (The whale in *Moby Dick* is white, and so is the color of God's throne [20:11].) But does this make sense in the context of the four horsemen? It does jive with the rider's attributes. The third horse is black; the event is famine. Does black signify famine any more than white signifies terror? But, on the other hand, if the horse's white is a symbol of the righteousness of the rider, then it must be a self-righteousness, and not a godly one. Or, righteousness in the eyes of others. Collating the righteousness of white with the rider's bow and crown: the rider, a newly appointed commander, fancies himself on a righteous quest to hunt wild beasts—big game—in behalf of the people ostensibly, for his own vanity in actuality. Perhaps. Or the rider on the prowl strikes terror into the heart of those who might oppose him. It's left to the reader to decide what's correct.

Several have said that the first horseman is the antichrist. The white-righteousness of the horse, in this case, is a deception. He has a bow but no arrows, meaning he has a bark but no bite. Perhaps this is so, perhaps not. An assumption therein is that the seals are opened at the beginning of the seven year Tribulation, and since the antichrist comes on the scene at this time, the rider is the antichrist. Revelation does not say that he doesn't have any arrows, only that he has a bow. One cannot conclude that he has no arrows. But if this rider is indeed the antichrist, the picture of him going out as a hunter fits well—in fact, it fits better than a vision of the anti-

*Part III: The Visions*

christ going out to war. Those who believe he's the antichrist reach this conclusion after having developed a tight timeline for the events in end-time prophecy, with the majority of the judgments in Revelation occurring during the Tribulation. Those not adhering to this view, that the rider is the antichrist, usually don't adhere to the timelines either.

The four horsemen may be cascading events, each one triggering calamities that cause the next. If this is the case, then the first rider, symbolizing a conqueror on the prowl, causes the next rider, war. But one thing most experts are united on is this: the first horseman does *not* represent Jesus, in spite of the white. A few reasons for this. First, this denigrates the lordship of Jesus Christ. Second, Jesus would be pictured with a sword, not a bow. Third, Jesus comes at the culmination of events, not the inception.

## 4. The Second Seal: War (6:3–6:4)

> 6:3 When He broke the second seal, I heard the second living creature saying, "Come."
> ⁴And another, a red horse, went out; and to him who sat on it, it was granted to take peace from the earth, and that men would slay one another; and a great sword was given to him.

War, the second rider, is the logical conclusion of the ambitions of the first. This one is given a sword, the preferred weapon of warfare in John's era. Like the crown for the first, the sword for the second is given to the rider, instead of him taking it for himself. The giving of the sword insinuates the assignment of a mission. The rider is granted to take peace from the earth, which implies that there's a general state of peace prior to the loosing of the second seal.

Here the case can be made that the seals have already been opened. As chronicled in the *Decline and Fall of the Roman Empire*, the Empire of the late first century A.D. was still basking in the peace and prosperity of Pax Romana. The Empire's borders, having been established by prior conquest, were positioned along rivers and other defensible boundaries, then secured with walls, fortifications, and billeted troops. This succeeded in keeping the barbarians out. The Romans controlled all the territories adjacent to the Mediterranean Sea, resulting in a lucrative trade from one end of the Empire to the other, as the Sea, centrally located, made for an effective trade conduit. Roman law and administration, which has

## Part III: The Visions

formed the foundation of nations until this present day, kept society stable. In addition, Roman excellence in engineering wasn't surpassed until modern times. For example, only in the nineteenth century did Europe and America develop public water supply and sewage systems comparable to ancient Rome's.

But a hundred years after John's apocalypse, society began its decline. Compromise and corruption were seeping into Roman institutions. As apathy set in, the populace became softer, and the rigors of military service were shunned. The third century saw government-sponsored persecution, hampering the Christians from engaging in society. But while the civilization was decaying from the inside, the Church was growing. Heresy and schism, threats as severe as persecution—if not worse—had been systematically suppressed. As a result, one uniform church was emerging: the Catholic Church.

Then Constantine in the early fourth century lifted forever the ban against Christianity. The expression of faith, however, had been slowly changing. The gifts of the Spirit had disappeared. Pentecostalism, having the same excesses and fanaticism then as now, withered and vanished. Christians, slandered and persecuted, had as a result developed an other-worldly mentality, where the emphasis was shifted from this world to the world to come. Heaven and hell, eternal rewards and punishments, the judgment to come—Christians became preoccupied with these, supplanting Judaism's focus on this present life. This obsession is not entirely unscriptural, as a couple NT references attest:

> Matt. 5:11 "Blessed are you when people insult you and persecute you, and falsely say all kinds of evil against you because of Me.
> [12]"Rejoice and be glad, for your reward in heaven is great;
>
> 1 Pet. 1:4 ...to obtain an inheritance which is imperishable and undefiled and will not fade away, reserved in heaven for you,
> . . . . . . . . . .
> [6]In this you greatly rejoice, even though now for a little while, if necessary, you have been distressed by various trials,
> [7]so that the proof of your faith, being more precious than gold which is perishable, even though tested by fire, may be found to result in praise and glory and honor at the revelation of Jesus Christ;

## Part III: The Visions

The NT offers consolation in the form of a deferred hope of heavenly rewards to those suffering persecution, to encourage them to endure. But also, Revelation is an encouragement and comfort of a different type: those who persecute will assuredly one day receive their retribution. But to those not suffering persecution, the NT exhorts that these live a godly life, that they be vigilant, and that they persevere in good works, applying their faith to their daily routine. In the fourth century the transformation of Rome from a pagan to a Christian empire transpired over a few decades. The Christians, however, having acquired the upper hand, could not readjust their emphasis on the next life to a balanced emphasis between this life and the one to come. As the institutions of the Empire disintegrated, Christians inherited powers that had hitherto been denied them. They had the moral fiber requisite to undergird society, but refused to do so. In other words, Rome had always intertwined their pagan worship with everything from holidays to military duty. Christians would have nothing to do with it—and rightly so. But once the things reprehensible were removed, Christians wouldn't reconsider their involvement in the government, the military, or anything else Roman. When Rome was no longer the host to the gladiator spectacles, and the state sponsor of paganism, Rome became worth saving—but the Christians would have no part in it. At this juncture, had they infused their strength and will into the military, they could have prevented the impending debacle.

By the end of the third century, the army was beginning to recruit barbarians, as a career in the military suited their uncivilized ferocity. Meanwhile, overpopulated Germanic lands to the east of Roman Europe began to exert pressure on the borders of the Empire, as these hordes were in need of food. According to the historian J.B. Bury, these tribes looked up to the Romans, and had no intention of destroying the Empire. They merely wanted a slice of its prosperity. As the Empire by this time had been in existence for several hundred years, no one could fathom a pending collapse, so great was its prestige, the greatest of all empires. For a while Constantine had stemmed the slide, which originated from a series of incompetent emperors, but as the fourth century waned, the barbarian soldiers infiltrated higher and higher ranks, until one finally assumed control of the western Roman forces. Then Rome committed a blunder: when one of the tribes penetrated its borders, rather than repulsing them, it placated them by allowing them to form a *federation*—an enclave of barbarians settled within the Empire. A couple years later, as their unrest could not be pacified, these barbarians went on a rampage, blazing a trail of destruction through

*Part III: The Visions*

the Empire. Others followed. The Vandals, Goths, and Visigoths fragmented the Empire. New nations eventually emerged.

One could argue that the breaking of the first seal unleashed the barbarian tribes: the hunter on horseback represents the migration of the tribes; their prey, the riches of the Empire. Peace and prosperity ended, chaos ensued. The second horseman, clothed in red, the color of war and aggression, followed on the heals of the first. Since the collapse of Rome, Europe has been afflicted by an unending host of poachers in the form of one nation rising against another—and mostly for frivolous reasons. War has been the norm in Europe from the disintegration of Rome onwards.

On the other hand, the first and second seals may not have been broken yet. True, there have been instances one can point to as fulfillment of these prophecies. But ambition and warfare are commonplace throughout history, to the point where it's difficult to distinguish the fulfillment of prophecy from the noise. Furthermore, the episodes described previously as potential fulfillment of the prophecies do not take a global perspective, but are limited to the western half of the Roman Empire. The Empire, for reasons of efficiency, had been split into two administrative realms, with Rome in the west and Constantinople in the east. Though the barbarians penetrated the west, the east was never breached. In fact, the eastern Roman Empire lingered until the fifteenth century. But though a couple of millennia ago the world was centered around Rome, China and India, for example, were thriving as well. The horseman was "granted to take peace from the earth"—not just a slice of it.

Neither does Revelation say how long the horsemen are unleashed for. This is as crucial as when they're unleashed. Are they loosed for two or for three years? Or are they instructed to run roughshod over the human race until the Second Coming? If these first two seals have been broken already, who's to say that the horsemen aren't still out and about on a perpetual, multi-century rampage? When compared to mankind's violent history, would anyone notice a remarkable difference?

## 5. The Third Seal: Famine (6:5–6:6)

The third horseman is the consequence of the first two. The vision progresses seamlessly:

*Part III: The Visions*

6:5 When He broke the third seal, I heard the third living creature saying, "Come." I looked, and behold, a black horse; and he who sat on it had a pair of scales in his hand.
⁶And I heard something like a voice in the center of the four living creatures saying, "A quart of wheat for a denarius, and three quarts of barley for a denarius; and do not damage the oil and the wine."

What does "three quarts of barley for a denarius" equate to in today's prices? Because of the conversion's complexity, assumptions and crude estimates must be used, the derivation of which is specified in Appendix A. Suffice to say, the setting of the price of barley in 6:5 indicates a 5-to-1 increase in the cost of goods and services.

But why would the wheat cost three times as much as the barley? It's difficult to say what, if any, distinction there was between wheat and barley in the ancient world. It appears from 6:6 that, in the ancient world, barley was more common, or easier to grow—in drought conditions especially—than wheat. But, faced with the conditions defined by the third rider, folks would be buying barley, not wheat, just to survive. This is the first odd thing about the prices. The second is that the cherub orders the rider not to "damage the oil and wine". The word "damage" implies famine, insect damage, or some other crop-spoiling natural disaster. Whatever it was, it affected the wheat most severely, followed by the barley, but didn't affect the olives and grapes, from which oil and wine come. So the wheat crop is ruined, the barley crop is severely affected, but the olive and grape yields are unchanged. The grains are the staples; the oil and wine are not. Olive oil was plentiful throughout the ancient world, and was shipped in large volumes around the Mediterranean. But unlike olive oil, wine has few practical uses. It was mixed with drinking water as a sterilizing agent, or simply to add flavor. Because oil can be used as lamp fuel, or as a soothing balm, and not just as a food stock, some commentators jump to the obvious symbolism of oil and wine in the NT. Wine is a biblical symbol of joy, and the light-headedness is analogous to the affects of the Holy Spirit. It suppresses the natural inclination to refrain from frivolousness, so is used to liven up parties, as the serving and consumption of wine was central in the wedding in Cana in John 2.

To understand the meaning of the third horseman, it should be emphasized again that John's vision is in terms of the world he lived in. It would've been no use for him to view objects not yet invented. Barley and olive oil—even wine for that matter—are not the staples nowadays that they were in John's time. In this light, it was as if the judgment limited the bulk of the food supply, but didn't affect the variety of it. This is one explanation of the barley and wheat vs. the oil and wine. The other explanation, the more popular one, is that the cherub wants to protect the symbols of the Holy Spirit. Neither theory makes sense completely, however. In any case, sparing the oil and wine means that the judgment's severity is not total—there's worse to come. The conditions brought about by the third rider mean that there's food to live on, but not without a lot of scraping and scrounging. Some will starve to death, most will lose weight, all will be strained—but it's survivable.

Has the third seal been broken already? If so, when was the famine? Like the first and second horseman, planet earth has known so many famines that it's difficult to pinpoint the singular epoch that has fulfilled this already. Famine occurs almost continuously. Not until the twentieth century, with quantum improvements in farming, has starvation due to widespread famine become controllable, at least in developed countries. But as Revelation's curses continue to unfurl, it will become increasingly clear that the majority of the judgments could not have transpired yet.

## 6. The Fourth Seal: The Grim Reaper (6:7–6:8)

> 6:7 When the Lamb broke the fourth seal, I heard the voice of the fourth living creature saying, "Come."
> ⁸I looked, and behold, an ashen horse; and he who sat on it had the name Death; and Hades was following with him. Authority was given to them over a fourth of the earth, to kill with sword and with famine and with pestilence and by the wild beasts of the earth.

The word "death" was translated "pestilence" in 2:23, and again in 6:8b. Both *pestilence* and *death* can be alternately translated as *the Plague*. But in 6:8a the translators chose "Death" rather than *pestilence* because of the context. The context is *Death and Hades*, the duo showing up again in 20:13, and, based on the usage there, Hades denotes the afterlife that's the alternative to heaven. "Death and Hades" in Revelation is a figure of speech. A modern equivalent is *the Grim Reaper*.

Continuing on to the latter half of 6:8, there's precedence for not interpreting literally the phrase, "wild beasts of the earth". Here's the precedence:

*Part III: The Visions*

1 Cor. 15:32 If from human motives I fought with **wild beasts** at Ephesus, what does it profit me?

Paul never fought any actual wild animals at Ephesus. What he's referring to is recorded in Acts 19. Paul was performing miracles in that city, drawing the people away from the Ephesian pagan deity Artemis. To oppose Paul, Demetrius the silversmith stirred up those whose business depended on the worship of Artemis. This handful of people are the "wild beasts" Paul refers to in v. 32—not animals in the literal sense. The phrase *wild beasts* or something similar is used in both the OT and NT. For example:

> Ps. 22:12 Many bulls have surrounded me; Strong bulls of Bashan have encircled me.
> [13]They open wide their mouth at me, As a ravening and a roaring lion.

This is a Psalm David wrote in his anguish, when his enemies were pursuing him. It's also a prophecy of Jesus on the cross, as he was quoting from Ps. 22, "My God, my God, why have You forsaken me?" But David was never surrounded and pursued by animals (neither was Jesus). His problem was with Saul.

Again, the phrase *wild beasts* is used in the Gospels:

> Mark 1:12 Immediately the Spirit impelled Him to go out into the wilderness.
> [13]And He was in the wilderness forty days being tempted by Satan; and He was **with the wild beasts**, and the angels were ministering to Him.

The Children's Bible has an illustration of this verse. Jesus is sitting calmly in the desert, and gathered around him are a lion and a few other wild animals, as though it was a petting zoo. Unfortunately, few, if any, commentators point out that the "wild beasts" in Mark 1:13 is a figure of speech—Jesus was never waylaid by beasts in the wilderness. Pictures such as these from illustrated Bibles (not to mention movies-for-television) form lasting impressions more so than a thousand words. These unfortunately have led many to the wrong conclusion of who Jesus was.

In the Bible phrases along the lines of being surrounded by wild beasts, or fighting wild beasts, are equivalent to the phrases, *has his back against the wall,* and, *fighting for his life*. It means an intense

*Part III: The Visions*

struggle, or means a life-or-death peril, or means a confrontation with opponents who are out to destroy you. This should be remembered when, later in Revelation, the beast of Revelation makes his debut. He's called *the beast* because his purpose is to kill and destroy. The cherubim, although they have animal heads, are not called *beasts* but *living beings*, because *beast* has an evil connotation.

So 6:8's reference to the "wild beasts of the earth" refers to people, not animals. Since beasts in the biblical sense are out to destroy people, the first horseman is himself a beast of sort. Who are these wild beasts? They may have been loosed by the horsemen. This would make sense: the authority given to the fourth rider (perhaps two riders, Death and Hades) in 6:8 is to finish what the first three horsemen began. This completes the group as a cohesive set. And if they are a set, it stands to reason that all four riders are loosed within a short duration of one another. The Plague in the sixth and fourteenth centuries killed one-third of the civilized world's population on each occurrence, whereas the fourth rider kills one-quarter of the earth's population. Either of these two plagues could fulfill the prophecy of the fourth rider. But the fourth rider kills not only by plague but also by war and famine. So the Justinian Plague of the sixth century and the Black Death of the fourteenth—terrible as they were—don't quite fulfill the judgment of the fourth seal. But it's easy to see how someone could point to these or other calamities as proof that the riders have been unleashed.

## 7. The Fifth Seal: A Pause for the Martyrs (6:9–6:11)

Back in the third chapter, in the scene around the throne, John never mentioned an altar. Using the definite article in 6:9, he takes it for granted that the reader knows of it. But what is it?

> 6:9 When the Lamb broke the fifth seal, I saw underneath the altar the souls of those who had been slain because of the word of God, and because of the testimony which they had maintained;

By definition, an altar is a table used as part of a sacrificial ritual. In this dispensation the church altar originated from the early Christian communion table, and also perhaps from the connotations that the Catholic doctrine of transubstantiation carries with it,

*Part III: The Visions*

since this has dominated Christendom for centuries. Denominations that are far removed from the mother-church, no longer adhering to this doctrine, have inherited the word, but have modified its original meaning, first referring to a table of service, later referring to the front of the church. But somewhere along the way, a biblically correct understanding of an altar's use has been misplaced. Misconceptions persist. People picture an altar as a table where a priest slays an animal (or, in a savage pagan rite, a person). Though this may be true for pagan rituals, it's not biblically sound.

In the OT animals weren't slain on the altar, but instead were slain in close proximity to it. Then, depending on the type of offering, part or all of its body was burned on the altar. This practice was first recorded in reference to Noah. Notice how he used the altar to burn the offering:

> Gen. 8:20 Then Noah built an altar to the LORD, and took of every clean animal and of every clean bird and offered burnt offerings on the altar.

When God told Abraham to sacrifice Isaac, Abraham consequently built an altar (Gen. 22:9). The primary purpose was to offer Isaac as a burnt offering, burning Isaac's corpse upon it; only incidentally was it used to slay him upon it. That's why he laid him on a stack of wood that was over the altar. In the Law altars were used mostly to burn animal parts, the animals having been sacrificed either close to it (a burnt offering) or far from it (a sin offering), but rarely on it. A sign of devotion to the Lord, burnt offerings were offered as a thanksgiving, or in remembrance of a covenant. This God received, as several Scriptures attest to the pleasing aroma yielded by these offerings (Gen 8:21; Exod. 29:18; Eph. 5:2; Phil. 4:18, to name but a few).

The OT type that Jesus fulfilled utilizes the altar in a way that's contrary to popular perception. Unlike the slaying of the lion on the altar in C.S. Lewis's *The Lion, the Witch, and the Wardrobe*, Jesus' OT sacrificial type was not slain in this manner. Heb. 9:24 specifically, and the ninth chapter generally, along with Heb. 8:4,5, state that the temple and its trappings are copies of the heavenly prototype. Now, the earthly altar is in the Tabernacle courtyard, outside of the Holy Place, half of which is the Holy of Holies. Jesus is the anti-type of the sin offering, where the animal is slain far from the altar. He was killed outside the city; as Heb. 13:11-13 points out, Jesus was crucified "outside the camp", far from the altar. After he rose from the dead, he entered the heavenly Holy of Holies, where God's throne is. Taking with him his blood, like the High Priest did

*Part III: The Visions*

once a year in the earthly Holy of Holies, he sprinkled it on the heavenly Mercy Seat, the inner-altar.

In the Bible the Brazen Altar, the altar in the Tabernacle courtyard, later moved to the temple, is the only altar of the Mosaic Law—not the Mercy Seat. Most Scriptures, OT or NT, that mention sacrifices, or that are metaphors of the same, refer to this altar. It was in use throughout the year; in fact, the Law commands that a fire burn continuously on it (Lev. 6:12). To this altar the Israelites went, the priests slaughtering their offerings nearby, then pouring the blood around the base, the fire on the altar consuming the carcass. As the smoke rose to the sky, the heavens, the Lord symbolically received the sacrifice. The blood soaked into the ground around the altar's base.

Hence, the heavenly altar in 6:9 corresponds to the working altar in the tabernacle courtyard. Their lives having been given entirely to the Lord, the martyrs have, symbolically speaking, ascended to heaven in the smoke of the offering burning on the altar. Their blood, however, is left at the base of the altar. In 6:9 they appear under the altar, close to where the blood saturated the soil on the earthly one. Just as the blood of Abel cried out from the ground (Gen. 4:10), so too, figuratively speaking, the blood of the martyrs cries out. This is what they say:

> 6:10 and they cried out with a loud voice, saying, "How long, O Lord, holy and true, will You refrain from judging and avenging our blood on those who dwell on the earth?"

How long is the longsuffering of God? Longer than the longsuffering of the martyrs. These who laid down their lives without a struggle cry out for justice and vengeance, God's wrath to be loosed. The target of their vengeance is not those who killed them, but "those who dwell on the earth". Is the seal broken in the lifetime of the parties responsible for their martyrdom? Or is this proxy judgment, judging future generations who persist in the sins of their forbearers? Both cannot be true, but if the former is, then the fifth seal, and by consequence the first four, were broken in Roman times. That question aside, the martyrs are entitled to justice—a theme of Revelation—and their request, spoken in righteousness, God will acquiesce to. It's a matter of *when*, and not *if*. It's their fellow martyr Jesus who dictates the time, as he's the one opening the seals.

\*

*Part III: The Visions*

A side note before proceeding to the next verse. It's the norm, the expected—it's God's will—that Christians suffer persecution. Jesus promised this in the Sermon on the Mount:

> Matt. 5:10 "Blessed are those who have been persecuted for the sake of righteousness, for theirs is the kingdom of heaven.
> [11]"Blessed are you when people insult you and persecute you, and falsely say all kinds of evil against you because of Me.
> [12]"Rejoice and be glad, for your reward in heaven is great; for in the same way they persecuted the prophets who were before you.

A jog through 1 Pet. repeats the same; notice the multiple occurrences of the word *suffer*:

> 1 Pet 1:21 For you have been called for this purpose, since Christ also **suffered** for you, leaving you an example for you to follow in His steps,
> [22]WHO COMMITTED NO SIN, NOR WAS ANY DECEIT FOUND IN HIS MOUTH;
> [23]and while being reviled, He did not revile in return; while **suffering**, He uttered no threats, but kept entrusting Himself to Him who judges righteously;

> 1 Pet 2:14 But even if you should **suffer** for the sake of righteousness, you are blessed AND DO NOT FEAR THEIR INTIMIDATION, AND DO NOT BE TROUBLED,

> 1 Pet. 4:1 Therefore, since Christ has **suffered** in the flesh, arm yourselves also with the same purpose, because he who has **suffered** in the flesh has ceased from sin,

> 1 Pet. 4:12 Beloved, do not be surprised at the fiery ordeal among you, which comes upon you for your testing, as though some strange thing were happening to you;
> [13]but to the degree that you share the **sufferings** of Christ, keep on rejoicing, so that also at the revelation of His glory you may rejoice with exultation.
> [14]If you are reviled for the name of Christ, you are blessed, because the Spirit of glory and of God rests on you.
> [15]Make sure that none of you **suffers** as a murderer, or thief, or evildoer, or a troublesome meddler;

*Part III: The Visions*

¹⁶but if anyone **suffers** as a Christian, he is not to be ashamed, but is to glorify God in this name.

As used in 1 Pet., the word "suffer" is specifically *to suffer persecution*. While arguing that it's God's will that Christians suffer sickness and disease, some have quoted one or two of the above verses, assuming that the suffering Peter talks about is an umbrella that includes illnesses of all sorts. This is not true. Peter is talking about suffering in relation to persecution, and not in relation to anything else. For example, 1 Pet. 4:14 uses the word "reviled", demonstrating that the context of the suffering is mistreatment by ungodly men. And 1 Pet. 4:15 instructs Christians to walk in a morally upright manner lest they "suffer" as a result of immoral behavior, the suffering inflicted by society and not disease. The debate over healing aside, Peter affirms the words of Jesus, namely that, on occasion, it's God's will for Christians to suffer persecution.

The Holy Spirit informs a believer of impending persecution. Jesus knew from a young age that he would die on a cross. John delivered a prophecy to the church at Smyrna of what they would suffer. It was prophesied to Paul, years ahead of time, that he would suffer persecution:

> Acts 9:15 But the Lord said to him, "Go, for he is a chosen instrument of Mine, to bear My name before the Gentiles and kings and the sons of Israel;
> ¹⁶for I will show him how much he must suffer for My name's sake."

> Acts 21:10 As we were staying there for some days, a prophet named Agabus came down from Judea.
> ¹¹And coming to us, he took Paul's belt and bound his own feet and hands, and said, "This is what the Holy Spirit says: 'In this way the Jews at Jerusalem will bind the man who owns this belt and deliver him into the hands of the Gentiles.'"
> ¹²When we had heard this, we as well as the local residents began begging him not to go up to Jerusalem.
> ¹³Then Paul answered, "What are you doing, weeping and breaking my heart? For I am ready not only to be bound, but even to die at Jerusalem for the name of the Lord Jesus."
> ¹⁴And since he would not be persuaded, we fell silent, remarking, "The will of the Lord be done!"

*Part III: The Visions*

Martyrdom is the logical epitome of persecution. Writing his last epistle, Paul knew that his life of persecution was over—only to end in his execution. Later in Revelation, a prophecy is given that others will face martyrdom (13:10).

\*

The ones in 6:11, those in heaven, are given white robes, an acknowledgement of their righteousness in death, and the justness of their cause:

> 6:11 And there was given to each of them a white robe; and they were told that they should rest for a little while longer, until the number of their fellow servants and their brethren who were to be killed even as they had been, would be completed also.

They are to wait until a predetermined number are killed. This is predestined judgment. God decides that judgment is coming, even though the recipients have yet to fill up the measure of his longsuffering, and have yet to commit the deeds warranting judgment. The two opposing ends of the stick—God's sovereignty and man's free will—are always in play; this time both ends are being worked. On the one hand, it's as though the clock is ticking, and there's nothing man can do to escape. This is the sovereignty end. On the other hand, man is in control of his destiny—the other end. God's trigger point won't be reached until more Christians die at the hands of the ones being judged. But God knows the hearts of all men, the wicked included. It's not that they cannot repent, but that they will not. Their evil hearts are fixated on a path of destruction. But though God knows this, justice will not be meted until action—not propensity—merits it. God doesn't judge based on the inclination of man's heart but on his deeds. But this same inclination invariably culminates in works meriting judgment. So in 6:11 he waits for more to be killed.

## 8. The Sixth Seal: All Is Shaken (6:12–6:17)

Those believing that the hitherto events in Revelation occurred prior to the twenty-first century make convincing arguments, though not conclusive ones. This changes with the sixth seal. History has no record of the likes of these fantastic prophecies.

*Part III: The Visions*

6:12 I looked when He broke the sixth seal, and there was a great earthquake; and the sun became black as sackcloth made of hair, and the whole moon became like blood;

Joel's prophecy, the sun turning black and the moon like blood (Joel 2:31), is finally fulfilled. Or is it? Peter quoted from Joel 2 in his Pentecost sermon. Addressing the crowd that gathered after hearing the commotion, Peter asserts that this is the fulfillment of Joel's prophecy.

Acts 2:15 "For these men are not drunk, as you suppose, for it is only the third hour of the day;
[16]but this is what was spoken of through the prophet Joel:

He goes on to quote a section of the chapter, including Joel 2:31:

Acts 2:19 'AND I WILL GRANT WONDERS IN THE SKY ABOVE AND SIGNS ON THE EARTH BELOW, BLOOD, AND FIRE, AND VAPOR OF SMOKE.
[20]'THE SUN WILL BE TURNED INTO DARKNESS AND THE MOON INTO BLOOD, BEFORE THE GREAT AND GLORIOUS DAY OF THE LORD SHALL COME.
[21]'AND IT SHALL BE THAT EVERYONE WHO CALLS ON THE NAME OF THE LORD WILL BE SAVED.'

According to Peter, Joel's prophecy—up to and including the sun and moon part—was fulfilled on Pentecost. There's no record of this happening, however. One might argue that the sun turning into darkness is an eclipse, maybe even a severe storm cloud. But these things happen regularly. What good is a prophecy if it predicts a common occurrence? And what about the "blood, and fire, and vapor of smoke"? Two possibilities. Either Peter was prophesying himself, while quoting Joel, and these things were to be fulfilled after Pentecost, or their meaning is figurative and not literal. One cannot imagine how the sun could turn into darkness and the moon into blood. And, in so imagining, an unspoken stipulation is inserted, namely that all of God's judgments are natural phenomena, howbeit gigantically magnified. Though usually it's the case that God's wrath is poured out in this way, like some of the ten plagues that fell on Egypt, it has not always been so. Sodom and Gomorrah are a prime example: no natural phenomenon can explain their sudden destruction. Those who attempt to explain what could cause the sun to turn to darkness in 6:12 often limit to natural means

*Part III: The Visions*

God's fulfillment of the prophecy. It takes a wilder imagination to predict how the moon might "become like blood", however.

In acute circumstances God uses astrological signs to convince man of his intervention. Jesus' birth was accompanied by a star that only a few could see. In its proper place, used by God, astrology is not the occult perversion that man has made it into. Those who pursue astrology in its occult form are without excuse when they see God using these same stars for supernatural signs. In other words, there're those like Herod, who, at the birth of Christ, was told of the heavenly sign by the Magi, yet chose not to heed it. The longsuffering of God's patience compels him to go the extra mile in reaching out to recalcitrant man. But man's dereliction after having irrefutably witnessed supernatural signs exhausts God's patience. God's intervention through astrological portents seals a foreordained, predestined judgment, and Joel's prophecy concerning the sun and the moon fits the groove.

> 6:13 and the stars of the sky fell to the earth, as a fig tree casts its unripe figs when shaken by a great wind.

Figs have a round shape, and, hanging on a fig tree, appear from a distance as scattered orbs, somewhat like stars in the sky. The stars fall to the earth; like the verses preceding 6:13, it's anyone's guess just how this might come to pass. It's rash to suggest that this has already happened. And this means that at a minimum there're one or two seals yet to be opened. If, like some have asserted, the previous seals were opened and their judgments dispensed many years ago, then there must've been a gap of several hundred years of earth-time between seal openings. If this is the case, then what John was watching, though brief in heaven-time, spanned several hundred years of earth-time. In spite of the array of prognosticators who've tried to ascertain the earth-time of these events, they have nevertheless failed to address many a question.

John compares the stars falling to earth like figs falling from a tree. Framed in terms of his understanding, the description presupposes that the stars hover in the sky in relatively close proximity to the earth. Hence they are affected by gravity, hence they can fall like figs. As far back as the Egyptians, the ancients knew that the stars were far, far away, as they were used as fixed reference points when designing the wonders of Egypt. The Greeks knew that the earth is round, and even calculated to a surprising accuracy its circumference. A few centuries before Columbus's expedition to the New World, the educated class also knew the world was round, but, unlike the modern world, with the proliferation of the printed word,

*Part III: The Visions*

this knowledge was not widespread. Likewise, someone like John would have been ignorant of the knowledge that the earth is round, and would have believed that the world is flat, has four corners, that the sun makes a journey across the sky each day, and that the stars are suspended in the sky. He cannot describe things but from his own frame of reference, that is, his own understanding. Therefore the stars fall from the sky as though the invisible force that keeps them hanging is removed, and gravity takes its course. (Appendix B examines the practical difficulties with a literal interpretation of 6:13.)

> 6:14 The sky was split apart like a scroll when it is rolled up, and every mountain and island were moved out of their places.

In 6:14 John is describing a scroll as it appears from one of its ends, like one would look through a telescope. A scroll forms a cylindrical shape when rolled up—but only approximately, as the swirls from the layers of the roll don't form a tight circle. Otherwise, John could've described the sky as a circle or a tube. For this reason his description sounds like a massive funnel cloud of some sort, the result of which affects mountains and islands. No storm can displace mountains and islands like that; that requires an earthquake at a minimum. But again, this attempts to explain Revelation by natural causes. Should the mountains and islands move more than a few meters, the resulting earthquakes and tsunamis would cause enormous damage to the surrounding area. They moved only a noticeable distance, one surmises, otherwise, the damage inflicted would kill too many people for that not to have been noted in Revelation. From these verses it appears that some cataclysmic catastrophe affects both sky and land simultaneously.

\*

To understand 6:16, one must know that in the Bible speaking to a mountain is a figure of speech (Mark 11:23 for example). Saying to a mountain to fall on oneself (Hos. 10:8) is a similar figure of speech, whose meaning is self-evident. In any event, as the wrath of God is dispensed, the principle, "Blessed are they who did not see, and yet believed", has been obsoleted. The unseen God becomes visible. There will be no more mercy...

> 6:15 Then the kings of the earth and the great men and the commanders and the rich and the strong and every slave and

*Part III: The Visions*

free man hid themselves in the caves and among the rocks of the mountains;
¹⁶and they said to the mountains and to the rocks, "Fall on us and hide us from the presence of Him who sits on the throne, and from the wrath of the Lamb;
¹⁷for the great day of their wrath has come, and who is able to stand?"

...Nor do men seek it. The expectation that there will be huge multitudes of heathens who flock to the Lord during this judgment is unfounded, as the above verses attest. Though all mankind shrinks from God's wrath, the masses are not crying out in repentance—only in protection of self. It's not that God won't receive them if they turn from their sins, it's that they won't turn. Just as Pharaoh's heart was hardened, so is mankind's at this juncture. God predestines judgment to come when man's heart is hardened like in the days of Noah. And as the rich man looked across the chasm to Lazarus, being succored in the bosom of Abraham, and as his cry was only for relief and not one of repentance, so these in 6:15 cry out in the same way. Remove them from their peril, and quickly they would forget the rude interruption, and continue along their path of iniquity.

## 9. The Bond-Servants Are Sealed (7:1–7:8)

7:1 After this I saw four angels standing at the four corners of the earth, holding back the four winds of the earth, so that no wind would blow on the earth or on the sea or on any tree.

Both Greek mythology and the OT (Dan. 7:2) believed that the earth, being flat, has four corners and four winds. They believed that the four winds are the engines that drive the weather and the seasons. Stopping them up is like damming a river: energy builds continuously while it's contained. When the dam bursts, a torrent is let loose.

When does this occur? Some say that these angels reappear in 9:14, and that in that chapter they're released. Are these one and the same? Probably not. But if these are a different set of angels, what does holding back the four winds result in? It's hard to tell. Perhaps the natural disasters in the eighth chapter. Since holding back the winds radically disrupts the course of nature, the results must affect nature.

*Part III: The Visions*

> 7:2 And I saw another angel ascending from the rising of the sun, having the seal of the living God; and he cried out with a loud voice to the four angels to whom it was granted to harm the earth and the sea,

The "rising of the sun" is the east, of course. A universal symbol, the sun symbolizes the powers that determine the current status quo, or simply the status quo, the state of affairs (Eccles. 4:3,7, etc.). In respect to nations, a *rising sun* is an emerging power that will reshape the political equilibrium. Thus, the significance of the angel with the seal, a written mandate, coming from the rising of the sun could be a new power emerging.

> 7:3 saying, "Do not harm the earth or the sea or the trees until we have sealed the bond-servants of our God on their foreheads."

The influence of Ezekiel is apparent:

> Ezek. 9:4 The LORD said to him, "Go through the midst of the city, even through the midst of Jerusalem, and put a mark on the foreheads of the men who sigh and groan over all the abominations which are being committed in its midst."

Putting a mark or remembrance on the forehead, or describing the aspects of one's forehead, is a common figure of speech from the Bible (Exod. 13:9,16; Exod. 28:38; Deut. 6:8; Deut. 11:18; Isa. 48:4; Ezek. 3:8-9, 9:4). Those who take this expression literally have a tenuous grasp of the OT. In 7:3 John does not mean that the angel will actually place a seal, or any sort of mark for that reason, on the bond-servants' foreheads. In Scripture, the differing body parts denote various personal aspects—instead of the actual part itself. This is a Semitic figure of speech. Since the OT and several NT authors were Semitic, metaphors using parts of the body are scattered throughout their books. For example, "If your hand offends you, cut it off", is not literal. One's hand is not the problem—one's mind and heart is. Since it's through one's hands that actions are performed, hands then represent actions. Eyes represent meditation on one's heart's desire. In English this is used in the exclamation, *I've got my eye on a new car*. This understanding clarifies Jesus' statement,

*Part III: The Visions*

> Matt. 6:22 The eye is the lamp of the body; so then if your eye is clear, your whole body will be full of light.

In other words, Jesus said that the desires that a person meditates on fill his or her body (actions, lifestyle, plans, etc.). If one rids himself or herself of meditating on impure desires, his or her lifestyle will become purified as a result.

In the context of Revelation, a forehead seal is the mark of God's or the beast's ownership, put there for the entire world to see. In the Bible the forehead is the radiance of a person's identity, and also a personal reminder of the same.

> 7:4 And I heard the number of those who were sealed, one hundred and forty-four thousand sealed from every tribe of the sons of Israel:
> ⁵from the tribe of Judah, twelve thousand were sealed, from the tribe of Reuben twelve thousand, from the tribe of Gad twelve thousand,
> ⁶from the tribe of Asher twelve thousand, from the tribe of Naphtali twelve thousand, from the tribe of Manasseh twelve thousand,
> ⁷from the tribe of Simeon twelve thousand, from the tribe of Levi twelve thousand, from the tribe of Issachar twelve thousand,
> ⁸from the tribe of Zebulun twelve thousand, from the tribe of Joseph twelve thousand, from the tribe of Benjamin, twelve thousand were sealed.

Those selected are evenly distributed among the twelve tribes. These are named according to the twelve sons of Jacob, from which the tribes originated. The practical difficulties of getting 12 thousand from each of the twelve tribes are addressed in Appendix C.

## 10. The Multitude of the Righteous from the Great Tribulation (7:9–7:17)

The drama shifts as John writes, "I looked, and behold". As he began by saying, "After these things", there was either a pause or a significant change in the unfolding of the vision, like the act in a play.

*Part III: The Visions*

> 7:9 After these things I looked, and behold, a great multitude which no one could count, from every nation and all tribes and peoples and tongues, standing before the throne and before the Lamb, clothed in white robes, and palm branches were in their hands;
> [10]and they cry out with a loud voice, saying, "Salvation to our God who sits on the throne, and to the Lamb."

(Max & Mary reword 7:10, "Salvation be ascribed to God".)

> 7:11 And all the angels were standing around the throne and around the elders and the four living creatures; and they fell on their faces before the throne and worshiped God,
> [12]saying, "Amen, blessing and glory and wisdom and thanksgiving and honor and power and might, be to our God forever and ever Amen."
> [13]Then one of the elders answered, saying to me, "These who are clothed in the white robes, who are they, and where have they come from?"

In 7:13 the word "answered" should be understood to mean *declared* or *stated*. Posed as a reply to a question, the elder's remark is thus emphasized. In a similar way, in the Garden, after Adam sinned, God called to him asking, "Where are you?" As a literary technique the Bible poses rhetorical questions; the answer is known, but the statement framed as a question leaves an impression on the hearer.

> 7:14 I said to him, "My lord, you know." And he said to me, "These are the ones who come out of the great tribulation, and they have washed their robes and made them white in the blood of the Lamb.

The elder addresses John as "My lord"; *sir* or *my good man* conveys the meaning a bit more clearly. Later in the verse, the phrase "made them white" is one word in Greek; a more exact translation is *bleached*. The blood of Jesus is a bleaching agent. It turns white, or purifies, anything it touches. There's an ugliness that comes with sin, and those who practice it have a sort of filthiness about their countenance, in the way they walk, talk—in mannerisms. After coming to know the Lord, this is eradicated to the extent that one yields himself to Christ, affecting changes in personality and habits, touching mundane details. In some cases, the

## Part III: The Visions

change is so pronounced that it causes others to give their hearts to the Lord. The blood of Jesus not only wipes away sin, but bleaches the heart and mind, making it a brilliant white. Even the saints in John's vision, those who endured the tribulation—their toughness and perseverance and sacrifice, laudable as it is, is not sufficient to warrant the righteousness of God. They need Jesus' blood the same.

The words in 7:14 should be capitalized, reading *the Great Tribulation*, to more accurately capture the intention in the Greek. John writes about it as though the reader knows the epoch he's referring to. Nevertheless, this is the first—and only—explicit reference to the Great Tribulation in Revelation. It's commonly taught that this tribulation is the same as the seven-year tribulation in Daniel and later in Revelation. Because they're both severe trials, and because John speaks of it as though the reader understands it, and because Daniel and Jesus speak of a period of trial in the final days, it's assumed they are one and the same. As end-time theories correlate prophetic Scriptures throughout the Bible to create a unified model, fragments such as these are coerced into the greater framework of events and timelines. And ironically, Revelation isn't the best book in the Bible for constructing a prophetic timeline. When attempting to predict the future, eschatologists tend to avoid the book because its symbolic imagery is too ambiguous. Looked at another way, the prophecies from the other books are not so ambiguous and therefore easier to construct a future model from. Thus, the Great Tribulation is synonymous with the seven years. Nevertheless, it's possible that the two are not the same.

> 7:15 "For this reason, they are before the throne of God; and they serve Him day and night in His temple; and He who sits on the throne will spread His tabernacle over them.
> [16]"They will hunger no longer, nor thirst anymore; nor will the sun beat down on them, nor any heat;

The literal reading of the end of 7:15 is that God will *put his tent over them*, referring to the tents that nomads used, and hence the sanctuary that the tents provided. Inherited from the nomad Abraham, the tent-metaphor had become ingrained in Israel's psyche (Prov. 14:11 and Isa. 54:2 are examples), the metaphor continuing long after the nomadic tribes became a settled nation. John uses it in 7:15, and the verse continues saying that the multitude will no longer endure the deprivations of hunger and thirst, nor have the "sun beat down on them, nor any heat". The thirst in 7:16 is caused by a long trip; therefore, the afflictions must mean the general hardships of life, as nothing else fits the bill. Poverty produces hun-

## Part III: The Visions

ger but not thirst. Persecution results in restricted freedom, financial hardship, imprisonment and even death, but none of those things cause thirst. Thirst occurs for short durations. The sun's rays afflict from time to time, when toiling in the day's heat or the like. And listed alongside thirst and heat, one assumes that the hunger in 7:16 is the same: not a steady path to starvation, but sporadic pangs. Verses 7:15,16 must refer to the shelter and hospitality that a traveler receives when, after a long trip, he arrives back at his own tent or that of a neighbor; thirst, hunger, and a lack of shelter are used in a metaphor to a nomad who endures these on a journey, but, having arrived, his thirst and hunger ends and he finds shade—7:16 alludes to this arrival.

Obviously, the Great Tribulation is a period of hardship, but not necessarily the result of persecution, not entirely at least. Throughout Christian history there've been so many epochs of tribulation that any could fit the description; just one of these might've been the fulfillment. Or perhaps John is saying that for any Christian to live in a fallen world is a trial—this lifetime is the Great Tribulation. The multitude John saw, "from every nation and all tribes and peoples and tongues" (7:9), could be the host of the Faithful spanning all generations, who served the Lord all the days of their short, toilsome lives, who'll attend the marriage supper of the Lamb, and who'll enter into the eternal reward for their faithfulness.

In spite of the promises in the Bible of the Father's provision (Matt. 6:30-34; Phil. 4:19; Ps. 37:25; 1 Cor. 9:7), and the blessings of the Mosaic covenant (Deut. 28), believers too often don't realize these in practice. Like Lazarus, who sat outside the gate of the rich man, each day begging for a morsel of food, throughout the centuries Christians have seldom walked in the light of the promises that God will provide their needs. Revelation vows that this too will end:

> 7:17 for the Lamb in the center of the throne will be their shepherd, and will guide them to springs of the water of life; and God will wipe every tear from their eyes."

The heavenly reward, spiritual in nature and eternal in duration, overshadows the temporary, physical suffering. This is a NT theme, and is a comfort to Christians suffering for whatever reason in this present life. Beyond the recompense of judgment that Revelation promises the wicked, it assures those who belong to the Lord that their sorrows are but temporary.

*Part III: The Visions*

## 11. The Seventh Seal (8:1–8:13)

> 8:1 When the Lamb broke the seventh seal, there was silence in heaven for about half an hour.

The half-hour of silence is a mystery, but one that builds suspense in the mind of the reader, as the seventh seal—seven, the number of completion—is about to be broken. The wrath to be revealed in this last seal exceeds any of the previous.

> 8:2 And I saw the seven angels who stand before God, and seven trumpets were given to them.

The last of the horseman was dispatched with the fourth seal, but now, peeling the layers of the onion of God's wrath, this last seal releases seven angels, the agents of active judgment. The intensity is increasing—the first seals were merely a prelude. The angels of 8:2 are given trumpets, presumably to sound commands, or herald an arrival or departure. But before the seven angels sound their trumpets, another angel appears in the vision, not to loose calamities, but to burn incense.

> 8:3 Another angel came and stood at the altar, holding a golden censer; and much incense was given to him, so that he might add it to the prayers of all the saints on the golden altar which was before the throne.

The incense and the altar mimic the use of the same in the Tabernacle in the Wilderness. The heavenly altar is the same one the martyrs were under in 6:9. The utensils are golden, like the ones used for service in the Tabernacle. Unlike the horsemen and the angels with trumpets, the incense simply accompanies God's judgment, setting the mood under which it transpires, just as the incense saturated the Tent of Meeting. It will be burned while the judgments from the seven angels are in motion. The angel gathers the incense's ingredients from two sources, combining the two into one. The first comes from God, the second from man. God's justice, comprised of his infinite wisdom and knowledge, tempered by his longsuffering, is the first part. The saints' supplication uttered while under persecution is the second part. As God was waiting for Jesus to take the scroll, so he waits for his servants to pray. Like a king having a coterie, God relinquishes his self-sufficiency, allowing himself to be turned, persuaded, and influenced by his favorites.

*Part III: The Visions*

Just as incense can be stored for a long time before use, the prayers form a resin to be ignited later, at a designated time. These intercessions have not fallen on deaf ears, as it might have seemed when offered, but rather have been accumulated for later recollection. Just as the incense in the earthly tabernacle was holy, so Christians' prayers are in heaven.

> 8:4 And the smoke of the incense, with the prayers of the saints, went up before God out of the angel's hand.

A coal was taken from the altar to keep the incense smoldering for the duration of the seven trumpets:

> 8:5 Then the angel took the censer and filled it with the fire of the altar, and threw it to the earth; and there followed peals of thunder and sounds and flashes of lightning and an earthquake.

On the Brazen Altar, some sacrifices had to be incinerated entirely, so embers were always available (a requirement actually, Lev. 6:13). Each morning a priest placed a new charge of incense on the Altar of Incense (Exod. 30), and, if a coal were needed, the Brazen Altar would readily supply it. In heaven the fire from the same altar that consumed the saints as burnt offerings is used to light the incense. In 8:5 the censor is thrown to earth so that the aroma from the incense will permeate the earth, establishing the ambiance for the seven angels to unleash their fury: God's righteous judgment combined with the shed blood of persecuted Christians is this setting.

> 8:6 And the seven angels who had the seven trumpets prepared themselves to sound them.
> ⁷The first sounded, and there came hail and fire, mixed with blood, and they were thrown to the earth; and a third of the earth was burned up, and a third of the trees were burned up, and all the green grass was burned up.
> ⁸The second angel sounded, and something like a great mountain burning with fire was thrown into the sea; and a third of the sea became blood,
> ⁹and a third of the creatures which were in the sea and had life, died; and a third of the ships were destroyed.

*Part III: The Visions*

¹⁰The third angel sounded, and a great star fell from heaven, burning like a torch, and it fell on a third of the rivers and on the springs of waters.
¹¹The name of the star is called Wormwood; and a third of the waters became wormwood, and many men died from the waters, because they were made bitter.
¹²The fourth angel sounded, and a third of the sun and a third of the moon and a third of the stars were struck, so that a third of them would be darkened and the day would not shine for a third of it, and the night in the same way.

The upheavals from the first four angels have this in common: they all cause something to fall from the sky or cause signs in the sky. And one-third of this or that is destroyed. This signals to mankind that God is involved, that these are not just random natural phenomena. Again, some have tried to assign probable causes for these events, saying that a meteorite collides with the earth in 8:10, or that 8:8 describes a gigantic volcanic eruption. No one, however, can come up with an explanation for the blood (8:7) that pelts the earth. Or why in 6:13 the stars fell to the earth, but then they fall again here in 8:12. This leads to the greater question: why try to explain these in the first place? If God turned the Nile River to blood, then he can rain down blood from the sky. Scripture simply states it; why should man be concerned about tying down loose ends that only God can manage in the first place?

While it's true that God is slow to wrath, once his patience has been exhausted, and judgment is aroused, it's always thorough and it always results in irreversible devastation. God's judgment that falls on a Christian is alternatively called *discipline*. The Lord prefers to discipline a believer, rather than judge him. The temporary affliction of discipline results in repentance (Heb 12:4-13), which in the long-term rectifies bad behavior. The Father's plan is to thus correct his children, so that they will mature into Christ's image. Judgment is punishment, and is invoked only after God has abandoned any hope of correction.

> 8:13 Then I looked, and I heard an eagle flying in midheaven, saying with a loud voice, "Woe, woe, woe to those who dwell on the earth, because of the remaining blasts of the trumpet of the three angels who are about to sound!"

God is unleashing his wrath, but he's hardly finished.

*Part III: The Visions*

## 12. The Fifth Angel and the One Who Destroys (9:1–9:12)

> 9:1 Then the fifth angel sounded, and I saw a star from heaven which had fallen to the earth; and the key of the bottomless pit was given to him.

The words "had fallen" mean that, at the time the events in this vision are occurring, this star will have already been ejected from heaven, the Greek tense emphasizing that the angel had already fallen before John's vision. Obviously, the star here is not an actual star, as the next verse says, "he opened". Stars are symbolic of agents, or leaders of prowess. This star is an angelic being, though not necessarily an angel per se. He had apparently been kicked out of heaven because of his wickedness, as the word *fallen* used in 18:2 and Luke 10:18 imply the same. This leads credence to the theory in 12:4 that Satan, when he was kicked out of heaven, took a third of the angels with him. Some further assert that the fallen angels are the demons mentioned in the NT. The star of 9:1 could be a demon, or Satan himself, though the latter is not likely.

In Greek the "bottomless pit" literally reads *the pit of the abyss*. This same word *abyss* Paul uses in Rom. 10:7, and also in 20:3; they are the same. In other books of the Bible, it refers to the underworld or hell; in Revelation this place is simply a pit that holds foul creatures, and is kept shut to both keep the creatures in and keep the stench out. At the time the fifth angel sounds off, the fallen spirit of 9:1 is in standby, waiting for a key to be given him. One surmises that what this being unleashes is so foul that God uses a demonic creature, instead of one of his angels, to release it, to spare one of his angels from having to get too close to the pit. The question is, why would this evil spirit collude with the Lord in dispensing his wrath? It's because he can't help but to indulge in the momentary elation of opening the floodgate here. Like wicked men, Satan and his cohorts live for the moment; as a result God in his wisdom can manipulate them. With glee the demon is waiting for the key to be handed to him, driven by his love of being able to harm so many in one shot.

> 9:2 He opened the bottomless pit, and smoke went up out of the pit, like the smoke of a great furnace; and the sun and the air were darkened by the smoke of the pit.

## Part III: The Visions

The smoke that comes out of the pit is like a "great furnace". Furnaces, like the one John compares this to, were used to smelt ores. A steel mill's blast furnace is the closest modern equivalent, but nowadays these are hard to come by in the United States, and even so they no longer do justice to John's simile, as anti-pollution improvements have removed much of the noxious fume-producing byproducts. Back in the 1940s in the city of Pittsburgh, when the city was still producing a large percentage of the world's steel, the pollution was so severe that the street lights had to be turned on at noon, while the people walked around with gauzes over their mouths to shield themselves from the unbearable odor. The city developed a tradition called *spring cleaning*: each spring they emptied their cupboards to wipe away the grime that had accumulated. All this John saw—only worse.

> 9:3 Then out of the smoke came locusts upon the earth, and power was given them, as the scorpions of the earth have power.
> ⁴They were told not to hurt the grass of the earth, nor any green thing, nor any tree, but only the men who do not have the seal of God on their foreheads.

Locusts are a type of grasshopper that travel in great swarms. In the Middle East back in biblical times, a swarm would arrive suddenly, consume entire crops, then depart as quickly as it came. The locusts that come out of the abyss are to attack the human race, and so must leave the vegetation alone. They're also commanded to leave Christians alone. Like in 7:3 all bond-servants of God will have the seal of God on their foreheads.

To be a bond-servant of God, a person must accept Christ as savior. There are no exceptions, nor will there ever be. A bond-servant is one who's given his or her entire life to Jesus, and consequently has the seal of God (figuratively speaking) on his or her forehead. Whether this applies to lukewarm Christians or not isn't something Revelation addresses. Nor do other Scriptures, such as,

> 1 Cor. 6:9 Or do you not know that the unrighteous will not inherit the kingdom of God? Do not be deceived; neither fornicators, nor idolaters, nor adulterers, nor effeminate, nor homosexuals,
> ¹⁰nor thieves, nor the covetous, nor drunkards, nor revilers, nor swindlers, will inherit the kingdom of God.

*Part III: The Visions*

Based on the above verses, does God give allowance for marginal Christians? The answer is that these two verses do not recognize nor consider carnal Christians. Other verses do, but not these. This is the Semitic mindset: one is either a Christian, and therefore acts like one, or one is not. There's no such thing as in between, or on the fence.

So it is with the seal of God in Revelation. Christians have it. Unbelievers don't. A third category isn't considered. The 144 thousand Israelites back in the seventh chapter who were sealed on their foreheads gave their lives totally to Christ, and that's when God sealed them. But how is it that they're not the only ones sealed? It's because the epochs in Revelation where the wrath of God is poured out on mankind are intended for sinners, not saints, just as Paul said,

> 1 Thess. 5:9 For God has not destined us for wrath, but for obtaining salvation through our Lord Jesus Christ,

Therefore the locusts are instructed to leave those with the seal of God on their forehead alone. Therefore the seal of God must be on all believers (the case of carnal Christians not considered). Since all Christians are sealed at this point, and since there presumably are more Christians than the 144 thousand (who're also sealed), one can conclude that the seal of God on one's forehead is synonymous with being a Christian.

> 9:5 And they were not permitted to kill anyone, but to torment for five months; and their torment was like the torment of a scorpion when it stings a man.
> ⁶And in those days men will seek death and will not find it; they will long to die, and death flees from them.

Some have taught that 9:6 means that people will try to commit suicide but will be unable to do so, but what John means is best understood by the paraphrase, *they will wish they were dead*. A person could easily kill himself, should he decide to do so, but the will to live is too strong. It's doubtful that God would supernaturally intervene each time one afflicted tries to kill himself because the locusts are tormenting him—9:6 is a hyperbole.

But as the writers of the Bible tend to understate, rather than overstate, truth, the torment from these locusts is unimaginable, as John further elaborates:

*Part III: The Visions*

9:7 The appearance of the locusts was like horses prepared for battle; and on their heads appeared to be crowns like gold, and their faces were like the faces of men.
⁸They had hair like the hair of women, and their teeth were like the teeth of lions.
⁹They had breastplates like breastplates of iron; and the sound of their wings was like the sound of chariots, of many horses rushing to battle.
¹⁰They have tails like scorpions, and stings; and in their tails is their power to hurt men for five months.

The description of these locusts creates an image difficult to imagine. What does a horse look like when it's prepared for battle? It has lots of bridles and other straps running across it, and if it has armor, the armor is usually painted with an insignia, or the horse is draped with a distinctive-patterned tunic over which the armor is placed. What John describes as a crown, to the modern eye would be a wreath. Having a face like men means they have two eyes, a nose, and a mouth, like most animals. In fact, they have a few mammal-like features. They have hair like women—which is long. They have a good set of fangs like a lion. But they have insect-like characteristics also. Describing the exoskeleton of an insect, the breastplate of iron is a smooth, hard plate. They have stingers in their tails. And they make a loud sound when they fly. Adjusted for weight, insects are much louder than birds. But John's description of the sound they make, that of horses and chariots, is not a high-pitched sound, but more of a rumble. This sound is caused by the flapping of their wing; the frequency of that flapping can be estimated based on the pitch of galloping horses. To make this sound the wings would likely flap between 10 and 30 times a second. It would take a large, dense swarm to equal the volume level of several chariots.

> 9:11 They have as king over them, the angel of the abyss; his name in Hebrew is Abaddon, and in the Greek he has the name Apollyon.

Apparently, the creature of 9:1,2 is the "angel of the abyss" of 9:11. John identifies him as an angel called "Abaddon". Metzger calls Abaddon *the destroyer*. The Greek omits the article from before his name; that, coupled with the Semitic significance of assigning a name, means that his name is a description: *one who destroys* or *one who's nature it is to destroy*. The name confirms the suspicion that this is an evil spirit. The angels who serve God might be sent on a mission to destroy something or someone, but it's not their nature to do so. Jesus said the thief (Satan) comes but to steal, kill, and destroy. Hence, interpreting 9:1,2 and 9:11 in conjunction: after having been cast out of heaven, this demon resides in hell, where he waits with his legion of underlings to wreak destruction on the human race.

> 9:12 The first woe is past; behold, two woes are still coming after these things.

Yet another layer is uncovered, as the onion of God's wrath continues to be peeled.

## 13. The Sixth Angel (9:13–9:21)

> 9:13 Then the sixth angel sounded, and I heard a voice from the four horns of the golden altar which is before God,

This is the same altar where sacrifices pleasing to God are offered, the same altar that the saints are under. The voice from the horns of the altar speaks.

> 9:14 one saying to the sixth angel who had the trumpet, "Release the four angels who are bound at the great river Euphrates."

Are these the same four angels in 7:1, the ones who're positioned at the four corners of the earth and told to stay there until the bondservants are sealed? There's agreement with 7:1 because both were bound, then released. But there's disagreement also. The four were positioned at the four corners, but here they're in the center of the earth. The Euphrates is mentioned in Genesis as flowing out of Eden. John would've considered Eden to be the center of the earth, since that's where creation began. Furthermore, how is it that these angels are bound, and the angels in the seventh chapter were not? And why were the angels from the seventh chapter holding back the wind, but in this chapter are released to kill? These angels are bound because they like to kill, and must be restrained like wild animals, to prevent them from starting their rampage too soon.

*Part III: The Visions*

> 9:15 And the four angels, who had been prepared for the
> hour and day and month and year, were released, so that they
> would kill a third of mankind.

They are placed in the center of the map, to be released in four directions, one towards each of the four corners of the earth. Verse 9:15 marks a specific point in earth-time when they'll be loosed—evidence of the concrete correlation between heaven-time and earth-time.

The next few verses are odd. In spite of the abrupt transition that leaves a loose association between the angels and horsemen, the angels evidently control a huge army, the size of which exceeds the first century's estimated population.

> 9:16 The number of the armies of the horsemen was two
> hundred million; I heard the number of them.
> [17]And this is how I saw in the vision the horses and those who
> sat on them: the riders had breastplates the color of fire and
> of hyacinth and of brimstone; and the heads of the horses are
> like the heads of lions; and out of their mouths proceed fire
> and smoke and brimstone.

Starting with the destruction of Sodom and Gomorrah, "fire and brimstone" is used throughout the Bible as a means of God's punishment. Brimstone is the sulfuric residual deposit that collects around volcanic vents. Sulfur has a foul odor, and in the open easily converts to sulfuric acid, making it caustic and corrosive.

> 9:18 A third of mankind was killed by these three plagues, by
> the fire and the smoke and the brimstone which proceeded
> out of their mouths.
> [19]For the power of the horses is in their mouths and in their
> tails; for their tails are like serpents and have heads, and with
> them they do harm.

It's anyone's guess as to what these horsemen and riders are, but whatever they are, they haven't visited the earth yet. The folks who claim that the events in Revelation have already occurred in reality only claim that some of these things have happened.

> 9:20 The rest of mankind, who were not killed by these
> plagues, did not repent of the works of their hands, so as not
> to worship demons, and the idols of gold and of silver and of

## Part III: The Visions

brass and of stone and of wood, which can neither see nor hear nor walk;

Seeing that these verses have yet to be fulfilled, and that the worship of physical idols has been virtually eradicated from the civilized world, it's difficult to imagine that even the wicked would revert to blatant paganism. Furthermore, the materials used to construct these idols are limited to the ones available in John's time—not even iron is mentioned. In the unlikely event that one were to make an idol in this day and age, it would be cheaper to mass-produce it from steel, aluminum, or plastic than it would be to use the other materials listed in 9:20. As John does not seem to be speaking figuratively here, one guess is that this is proxy judgment: since modern-day humanists walk in the footsteps of the ancient pagans, John speaks to the prototype humanists, the pagans of his day, and this covers all who follow their godless beliefs, though not their exact practices.

9:21 and they did not repent of their murders nor of their sorceries nor of their immorality nor of their thefts.

Murders, sorceries, immorality (fornication), and thefts can be construed with leeway, as they're used metaphorically in other verses in the Bible. But even if they're not metaphors, man in his fallen state is capable of these sins. Though they ebb and flow from age to age, their resurgence is as certain as the change in seasons. The plagues are unleashed on all of mankind, save the righteous. Revelation's view of man's nature is one of wickedness, perpetual sin, and constant rebellion against God. This stands in contrast to the humanist's view of man, that he's essentially good in spite of his shortcomings. The humanist believes that, though man is sinful, in time and with toil in the pursuit of goodness he will shed his sinful nature—perhaps not all of it, but the most egregious portions. The Judeo-Christian world-view, built in part from verses such as these from the ninth chapter, has influenced political philosophies whose wisdom has culminated in the United States Constitution, which assumes a political society comprised of men capable of and prone to sin. The Constitution established checks and balances to prevent a handful of wicked men from subverting the entire government. On the opposite hand, humanistic philosophy spawned communism, which makes no provision for the sinfulness of man. As a result, every communist government has been despotic.

Seven broken seals, four horsemen, and six angelic trumpet blasts later, the hearts of the survivors are still recalcitrant. Even if they were cast into hell for a thousand years, then released, the hearts of those afflicted by God's wrath would be unchanged the moment the agony was lifted. Though in 9:21 God gives them yet another chance to repent, their judgment is predestined, their fate is sealed. They go back to their wicked ways.

In the NT one repents and turns to the Lord by believing in Jesus and receiving him by faith. There's no mention of this in 9:20,21; instead their refusal to repent is inferred by their works. This kind of repentance, one where a person replaces bad works with good works, is reminiscent of episodes in the OT (Isa. 1:16,17 for example). The Western mind has a problem with this, the same problem it has with, "faith, if it has no works, is dead" (James 2:17). The Semitic writers James and John have no issue—they know that faith and works are inextricably connected. Thus, the refusal of the wicked in 9:20,21 to turn from their deeds is synonymous with their rejection of Jesus. One who believes in the Lord will obey him; by logical induction 9:20,21 proves that faith in God and continuing in wickedness are mutually exclusive.

## 14. The Strong Angel with the Little Book (10:1–10:11)

The end of the ninth and continuing into the tenth chapter is a transition in Revelation. With few interruptions a series of plagues have transpired. The scene shifts to "another strong angel":

> 10:1 I saw another strong angel coming down out of heaven,
> clothed with a cloud; and the rainbow was upon his head,
> and his face was like the sun, and his feet like pillars of fire;

Some say the strong angel is Jesus; most say he's not. The brilliance of this angel reminds one of the description of Jesus in 1:13-15, but any being stationed in the presence of God Almighty acquires brilliance, just as Moses, after he had seen the Lord, had to veil his face while speaking to the Israelites (2 Cor. 3:7). The strong angel could be Jesus, but that's doubtful. There's nothing in the description that alludes to his death, resurrection, or resulting authority. Neither does it fit in the flow of events, nor does one expect Jesus to be introduced as an angel.

Insofar as much of Revelation is a mystery, one speculates who the angel of 10:1 is. Gabriel and Michael are prime candidates. The term "strong angel" implies a class above the average angel. Mi-

*Part III: The Visions*

chael appears later in Revelation, but there, like in other places in the Bible, he's engaged in combat with Satan and his minions. For this reason, Michael is eliminated. This leaves Gabriel. Gabriel dwells in the presence of God (Luke 1:19), and would therefore radiate God's splendor of holiness. Perhaps it is he.

> 10:2 and he had in his hand a little book which was opened. He placed his right foot on the sea and his left on the land; ³and he cried out with a loud voice, as when a lion roars; and when he had cried out, the seven peals of thunder uttered their voices.
> ⁴When the seven peals of thunder had spoken, I was about to write; and I heard a voice from heaven saying, "Seal up the things which the seven peals of thunder have spoken and do not write them."
> ⁵Then the angel whom I saw standing on the sea and on the land lifted up his right hand to heaven,

It's anyone's guess why this angel is standing with one foot on the sea and one on the land, but this angel is puzzling to begin with. But, in any case, the know-it-alls who have a ready explanation for every detail in Revelation (and have no tolerance for any opinion that contradicts their own) can take a short break, as, according to 10:2, the seven peals of thunder are hidden. Even if the meaning of the peals were revealed, it would be just one less mystery in a book full of mysteries. Nevertheless, it adds to the suspense.

In 10:4 John says he was "about to write". This leads one to conclude that John was seeing a series of visions, with enough time between the visions for him to write what he had just seen before the next vision ensued. It also implies that John wrote Revelation without the aid of a scribe. This would explain why, according to Summers, there's so many grammatical errors in the book, since Greek was not John's native language, and had John been dictating to a scribe, the scribe would've corrected the grammatical errors as a matter of course. It would also mean that the visions occurred over the duration of several hours, most probably more than a single day, as it would take that amount of time just for John to compose all twenty-two chapters of Revelation—the time for the visions not included. One who reads Revelation from start to finish finds himself or herself having difficulty sorting out the details, remembering which beast is which, etc. Had John seen all the visions at once, then had to write in one burst what he'd seen, chances are he

*Part III: The Visions*

would've forgotten or confused a lot of it (unless he was granted a supernatural ability to remember).

> 10:6 and swore by Him who lives forever and ever, WHO CREATED HEAVEN AND THE THINGS IN IT, AND THE EARTH AND THE THINGS IN IT, AND THE SEA AND THE THINGS IN IT, that there will be delay no longer,
> ⁷but in the days of the voice of the seventh angel, when he is about to sound, then the mystery of God is finished, as He preached to His servants the prophets.

Who are "His servants the prophets" in 10:7, and what is the "mystery"? The prophets are primarily the OT prophets Daniel, Ezekiel, and Zechariah, whose prophecies of the future are the mystery. The "delay" in 10:6 is from the time of the prophets' writings to the sounding of the seventh angel. What John's saying is that the fulfillment of the prophecies of these OT prophets will be completed with the seventh angel. The next few chapters of Revelation show the fulfillment of these prophecies.

> 10:8 Then the voice which I heard from heaven, I heard again speaking with me, and saying, "Go, take the book which is open in the hand of the angel who stands on the sea and on the land."
> ⁹So I went to the angel, telling him to give me the little book. And he said to me, "Take it and eat it; it will make your stomach bitter, but in your mouth it will be sweet as honey."
> ¹⁰I took the little book out of the angel's hand and ate it, and in my mouth it was sweet as honey; and when I had eaten it, my stomach was made bitter.

Verses 10:9,10 are copied almost verbatim from Ezekiel:

> Ezek. 3:1 Then He said to me, "Son of man, eat what you find; eat this scroll, and go, speak to the house of Israel."
> ²So I opened my mouth, and He fed me this scroll.
> ³He said to me, "Son of man, feed your stomach and fill your body with this scroll which I am giving you." Then I ate it, and it was sweet as honey in my mouth.

*Part III: The Visions*

Not only intuitive in and of itself, the significance of John eating the scroll is verified by this passage in Ezekiel. By eating the scroll, John takes to himself the full impact of the message. It becomes an integral part of his psyche. The taste is sweet in his mouth, meaning John likes it when he first hears it. But it becomes bitter in his stomach, meaning that the consequences, as they manifest themselves, cause John anguish and remorse.

The scene in the tenth chapter is not complete.

> 10:11 And they said to me, "You must prophesy again concerning many peoples and nations and tongues and kings."

As 10:7 states that the OT prophetic writings will be appended with the content of the subsequent chapters of Revelation, so the above verse reveals another direction of the visions to come, and therefore aids in fitting the next several chapters into a larger framework. According to 10:11 the visions to come will concern peoples, nations, tongues—the phrase used multiple times in Revelation—and kings. From the end of the message to the churches up to chapter ten, the visions have been a serial revelation of the wrath of God, which wrath unfolds systematically as steps in a predetermined program.

## 15. Measuring the Temple (11:1–11:2a)

On several occasions in the OT, God speaks to man instructing him to build. God not only tells him to erect a structure, but also specifies the dimensions for it. It's not only the construction of buildings, facilities, utensils, etc. that the Creator gives precise instructions for, but he also specifies the exact way to perform rituals, or carry out other duties. It's only after an object is built according to his specifications, or something is executed according to his exact methods, that the Lord's pleased. Man's compliance is a test of his obedience. After the object has been built according to God's dimensions, then the Almighty deigns himself to utilize it for his own purposes, which are always for man's benefit. This is an OT means by which God communes with man.

Noah's ark (Gen. 6:14-16) is the first case where God tells man to build to specification. The instructions for building the ark anticipate and solve problems for Noah. How many animals will be sheltered in the ark? Noah didn't know, but Jehovah knew the ark's

*Part III: The Visions*

necessary size. In this case God's specifications were for practical purposes. But they were also a test of Noah's obedience.

Skip on over to the wilderness, where God instructs Moses how to build the Tabernacle:

> Exod. 25:8 "Let them construct a sanctuary for Me, that I may dwell among them.
> [9]"According to all that I am going to show you, as the pattern of the tabernacle and the pattern of all its furniture, just so you shall construct it.
> [10]"They shall construct an ark of acacia wood two and a half cubits long, and one and a half cubits wide, and one and a half cubits high.

Starting with the above passage from Exodus and continuing into the other books of the Law, God dictates the specifications of the Tabernacle and its trappings. The details for making the Tabernacle are exact, as are also the instructions for the priestly duties, the instructions for preparing sacrifices, and instructions for other articles of worship. And God promises that he'll "dwell among them" once the sanctuary is complete—in spite of Israel's sin. Because it's built according to God's directives, the sanctuary is holy. This allows God to dwell in it, and he's pleased to do so. The adherence to precise dimensions enables imperfect man to create perfection, which is required of man by God, but in reality cannot be supplied by man. The adherence to precise dimensions and tedious protocols is analogous to faith in the NT. Faith is the means of having the Lord tabernacle in one's heart, and if pursued according to the instructions of God's Word, it brings the holy and perfect God to man's habitation, making him accessible.

The Law of Moses is the bedrock for the rest of the OT. Skipping over to the prophets, the symbolism of dimensions and measurements is thus inherited and imported from Moses. In one of Ezekiel's visions, Ezekiel is shown a man who measures the temple, the temple's courtyard, and all the surroundings:

> Ezek. 40:3 So He brought me there; and behold, there was a man whose appearance was like the appearance of bronze, with a line of flax and a measuring rod in his hand; and he was standing in the gateway.
> [4]The man said to me, "Son of man, see with your eyes, hear with your ears, and give attention to all that I am going to

show you; for you have been brought here in order to show it to you. Declare to the house of Israel all that you see."
⁵And behold, there was a wall on the outside of the temple all around, and in the man's hand was a measuring rod of six cubits, each of which was a cubit and a handbreadth. So he measured the thickness of the wall, one rod; and the height, one rod.

This goes on for a couple of chapters. Understanding it is crucial to understanding the start of Revelation 11, because what John wrote in the eleventh chapter (twenty-first too) mimics what Ezekiel wrote. What does measuring the temple mean? It's proof that the temple has been correctly prepared and is acceptable for God to come and reside in, like in the tabernacle of old. Therefore, applied to Revelation, it means that the Lord will again live in the midst of Israel, and that he will again be their God, their advocate and protector. Prior to the vision in the fortieth chapter, the end of Ezek. 39 is a promise that Israel will be restored. Preparing the temple is prerequisite, however. The measurements taken in Ezek. 40-42 begin with the temple and work their way out to the gate. The end of this passage concludes with these verses:

> Ezek. 43:4 And the glory of the LORD came into the house by the way of the gate facing toward the east.
> ⁵And the Spirit lifted me up and brought me into the inner court; and behold, the glory of the LORD filled the house.

Just as when Moses built the Tabernacle, then consecrated it, and afterwards the glory of the Lord descended on it and remained in it, after Israel is restored from captivity, Ezekiel is shown the glory of the Lord filling the house. This completes the restoration of Israel—not simply the repossession of the promised lands, but the restoration of God's glory. But for both Moses and Ezekiel, had they not built to exacting specifications, God's glory would not have descended on the assembly.

Another instance where the temple, the courtyard, the walls, or Jerusalem are measured is in Zechariah.

> Zech 1:16 'Therefore thus says the LORD, "I will return to Jerusalem with compassion; My house will be built in it," declares the LORD of hosts, "and a measuring line will be stretched over Jerusalem."'

*Part III: The Visions*

¹⁷"Again, proclaim, saying, 'Thus says the LORD of hosts,
"My cities will again overflow with prosperity, and the LORD
will again comfort Zion and again choose Jerusalem."'"

Zech 2:1 Then I lifted up my eyes and looked, and behold,
there was a man with a measuring line in his hand.
²So I said, "Where are you going?" And he said to me, "To
measure Jerusalem, to see how wide it is and how long it is."

Just like in Ezekiel, Zechariah's vision is of Jerusalem being measured. The implication of the act of measuring is that it verifies compliance with God's requirements, and thus God will be pleased to dwell again in the city.

So skipping over to Revelation 11, the scene repeats itself:

11:1 Then there was given me a measuring rod like a staff;
and someone said, "Get up and measure the temple of God
and the altar, and those who worship in it.
²"Leave out the court which is outside the temple and do not
measure it, for it has been given to the nations; and they will
tread under foot the holy city for forty-two months.

The symbolism is carried over from the previous passages. The temple meets God's standards; God will inhabit it. At the end of 11:1 it says to measure "those who worship in it"—they are also approved by God. The temple court is not measured; 11:2 says it has been given to the nations. Though the temple premises are desecrated, the holy parts of the temple are not.

\*

These two verses embark upon a couple mysteries. First, the existence of the temple. John wrote Revelation roughly between 90–100 A.D., after the destruction of the second temple; for this prophecy to be fulfilled, the temple needs to be rebuilt. A few of John's visions allude to a temple. Since it did not exist at the time of the writing of the book, and it hasn't been rebuilt since, this means the visions could not have come to pass yet. Some insist that Revelation was written earlier, perhaps 68 or 69 A.D., but they insist so partly because the temple was still in existence—this way it can be argued that the prophecies requiring a standing temple have been fulfilled.

And there're other unfulfilled prophecies that require a temple. Bible scholars assert that the Abomination of Desolation in Daniel's prophecies (Dan. 9:27, 11:31, 12:11) refers to a pagan idol that's erected in the temple and worshipped in place of God. Jesus said

*Part III: The Visions*

that the Abomination was yet to be fulfilled (Matt. 24:15-26; Mark 13:14). The completion of OT mysteries, the promise of 10:6,7, occurs after the sounding of the last angel. One of these mysteries is the Abomination. The Revelation visions are an obvious continuation of Daniel's prophecies. If the prophecies are to be taken literally, then there must be a third temple in Jerusalem. And not only a temple, but the reinstatement of the sacrifices.

The barriers to rebuilding the temple are formidable. One of the holiest shrines in Islam, the Dome of the Rock, sits on the site where the temple would go. Muslims have jurisdiction over the site. Furthermore, only a handful of Jewish religious extremists have even the slightest interest in rebuilding the temple—the vast majority of the nation could care less. Nor do they have any interest in performing Levitical sacrifices. Hard as it is to imagine, these obstacles are nevertheless subject to change. Years ago, could anyone have imagined that the Jews, after an almost two millennia hiatus, would not only have retained their religious and ethnic identity, but would also return to the land from which they were expelled? And speak the original language? Rebuilding the temple—as preposterous as the idea sounds—is subject to change. But a larger mystery is the post-resurrection role of a Judaic temple.

After Jesus died on the cross, the veil of the temple tore from top to bottom (Mark 15:38). No longer shielded by the veil inside the Holy of Holies, God's holy presence departed. In its place the Holy Spirit indwells Christians; collectively *they* are the temple (1 Cor. 6:19; 2 Cor. 6:16). Christians were never commanded to visit the temple. Jerusalem is not the center of their spiritual lives, a departure from the OT. Christ lives in his disciples by the person of the Holy Spirit. This was not available under the Jewish covenant, nor was salvation readily available to all nations. Because the average believer in OT days didn't have the Holy Spirit in him, he had to rely on both the priest as his link to God and the temple as the house of his God. The new covenant is better than the old because it fixes the deficiencies of the old.

With a hypothetical third temple, would the Father's visitation with man revert to OT means? If the Jews were to reinstate the system of sacrificial atonement—far-fetched as that would be—how could this supplant the remission of sin through the blood of Jesus? The blood of bulls and goats was a temporary measure until Jesus died as the ultimate sacrifice once and for all. There's no need for further sacrifices, neither would God receive such. Furthermore, Jesus himself is our High Priest. Believers are made priests unto God, so even if the Jews were to revive the priesthood, it would mean nothing in God's eyes. What's more, should a third temple be

*Part III: The Visions*

built, God would not come and dwell in it. Though it's possible that the Jews could physically build a third temple, it would just be a building—nothing special.

So what of the prophecies of Daniel and Revelation that make reference to a temple? These prophecies identify the temple as the center of spiritual life. There're only two possibilities: either they've already been fulfilled or the temple's figurative, not literal. Though the synchronization in Revelation of heaven-time and earth-time is not thoroughly known, logic demands the sequential ordering of the breaking of the seals and of the angels' trumpet blasts. In other words, it's possible for a six month delay (in earth-time) between the breaking of the first and second seals, followed by a hundred year delay from the second to the third, but it's not possible for the third seal to be broken before the second. From the time John wrote Revelation to the present, it's safe to assume that the plagues from the sixth seal (6:12) onwards have not occurred. By this reasoning alone, Revelation 11 hasn't happened yet, therefore the prophecies of Daniel and Revelation 11 could not have already happened.

By process of elimination, this leaves one possibility: the temple referred to by Daniel and Revelation 11 is figurative, and not physical. Principles in biblical interpretation have to be bent to accommodate this conclusion, but if it's true, then it might explain 11:1,2. The temple merely symbolizes God's protective hand over Israel. The temple is measured, proving that God still watches over Israel, but the courtyard is not measured, as the nations "tread under foot", a phrase in Scripture (Mic. 7:19; Luke 21:24) meaning *occupy or dominate*, Jerusalem. The Gentiles treading under foot the temple court signifies how close the Gentiles come to overrunning Israel entirely—but God has measured the temple; they will not gain entrance; the Lord is pleased to dwell in it.

## 16. The Two Witnesses (11:2b–11:19)

Reading the eleventh chapter, the continuity of Revelation with the Book of Daniel is obvious. Revelation is the fulfillment of Daniel's prophecy of the seventy weeks. Scholars agree that the word *week* actually refers to one year, not an actual week. Halfway through the last of Daniel's seventy weeks is the seven-year tribulation, which is split in half, forming two 3½ year (42 month, or 1278 days) segments, the first appearing in 11:2,3:

*Part III: The Visions*

> 11:2 "Leave out the court which is outside the temple and do not measure it, for it has been given to the nations; and they will tread under foot the holy city for forty-two months.
> ³"And I will grant authority to my two witnesses, and they will prophesy for twelve hundred and sixty days, clothed in sackcloth."
> ⁴These are the two olive trees and the two lampstands that stand before the Lord of the earth.

According to 11:6, the witnesses (lifted straight out of Zechariah) prophecy, which means they speak God-given words, but not necessarily predicting future events. Forth-telling, not fore-telling.

> 11:5 And if anyone wants to harm them, fire flows out of their mouth and devours their enemies; so if anyone wants to harm them, he must be killed in this way.
> ⁶These have the power to shut up the sky, so that rain will not fall during the days of their prophesying; and they have power over the waters to turn them into blood, and to strike the earth with every plague, as often as they desire.

Moses had the power to turn water into blood. Elijah shut up the sky so it wouldn't rain, and the Lord took him to heaven rather than let his body die (see 11:12 also). These witnesses walk in their footsteps. They have the power to directly kill those who would harm them—something no other prophet, OT or NT, had. They walk in the tradition of the OT, and not the NT. When it comes to their adversaries, they're not sheep led to the slaughter (Rom. 8:36)...except for one incident:

> 11:7 When they have finished their testimony, the beast that comes up out of the abyss will make war with them, and overcome them and kill them.

The beast first appears. Like in 6:8, the beast is a creature whose singular mission is to destroy. Since human beings are born into the earth, and the beast comes out of the abyss, the beast cannot be human unless he's resurrected from the damned. He's therefore a demonic creature of some kind, probably like the destroyer in 9:11. But probably not the same beast as in the twelfth chapter either.

## Part III: The Visions

11:8 And their dead bodies will lie in the street of the great city which mystically is called Sodom and Egypt, where also their Lord was crucified.

The "great city"—the subtleties of the Greek could justify a slight rewording to *Great City*—the place the Lord was crucified, if interpreted literally, is Jerusalem. The word "mystically" is actually *spiritually*. This city, spiritually-speaking, is Sodom and Egypt: a haven of sin, worldliness, and false gods. The words *Great City* (if not taken literally) and the reference to where the Lord was crucified would mean apostasy and hatred of God. But this must be a real city, as the subsequent context of 11:13 gives details of a real place.

11:9 Those from the peoples and tribes and tongues and nations will look at their dead bodies for three and a half days, and will not permit their dead bodies to be laid in a tomb.
[10]And those who dwell on the earth will rejoice over them and celebrate; and they will send gifts to one another, because these two prophets tormented those who dwell on the earth.
[11]But after the three and a half days, the breath of life from God came into them, and they stood on their feet; and great fear fell upon those who were watching them.
[12]And they heard a loud voice from heaven saying to them, "Come up here." Then they went up into heaven in the cloud, and their enemies watched them.
[13]And in that hour there was a great earthquake, and a tenth of the city fell; seven thousand people were killed in the earthquake, and the rest were terrified and gave glory to the God of heaven.

But even these two witnesses' miracles and their miraculous resurrection do not dissuade those still alive. God unleashes plagues, followed by a pause, but repentance is not forthcoming. To continue the judgment, the seventh seal is comprised of seven angels, as God uses the last seal to begin another round of calamities, each successively worse—more onion layers.

11:14 The second woe is past; behold, the third woe is coming quickly.

But first the scene shifts back to heaven:

> 11:15 Then the seventh angel sounded; and there were loud voices in heaven, saying, "The kingdom of the world has become the kingdom of our Lord and of His Christ; and He will reign forever and ever."
> [16]And the twenty-four elders, who sit on their thrones before God, fell on their faces and worshiped God,
> [17]saying, "We give You thanks, O Lord God, the Almighty, who are and who were, because You have taken Your great power and have begun to reign.
> [18]"And the nations were enraged, and Your wrath came, and the time came for the dead to be judged, and the time to reward Your bond-servants the prophets and the saints and those who fear Your name, the small and the great, and to destroy those who destroy the earth."

Thus, the above passage summarizes the Book of Revelation. The era in which man is free to live in rebellion to God comes to a close. It's time for the rewards and punishments.

> 11:19 And the temple of God which is in heaven was opened; and the ark of His covenant appeared in His temple, and there were flashes of lightning and sounds and peals of thunder and an earthquake and a great hailstorm

God continues to reveal himself in his holiness. The mercy and grace of the NT are set aside in place of the frightful holiness that Moses wrote of.

## 17. The Woman and Child (12:1–12:6)

Like a novel that jumps from one thread to another, and by jumping goes back in time, so starting in the twelfth chapter the previous narrative, the dispensing of God's wrath, is halted, and another is picked up. With the next vision it'll be obvious that, in the process, the clock has been rewound.

> 12:1 A great sign appeared in heaven: a woman clothed with the sun, and the moon under her feet, and on her head a crown of twelve stars;

*Part III: The Visions*

²and she was with child; and she cried out, being in labor and in pain to give birth.

The child she gives birth to is Jesus; therefore the woman is Israel. The biblical symbolism of the sun and the moon is rooted in Gen 1:16 and Gen. 37:9.

> Gen. 1:16 God made the two great lights, the greater light to govern the day, and the lesser light to govern the night; He made the stars also.

The day symbolizes righteousness, and the night unrighteousness. The two bright lights, the sun and the moon, symbolize the players that control the day and night respectively. The sun directs the events of mankind during the day; the moon directs at night. The sun symbolizes God's involvement in the affairs of man; the moon is Satan's involvement. The woman is clothed with the sun, symbolizing God's covenant with her. It wraps her entire being, meaning that Israel is immersed, or baptized, by this relationship. The moon is pictured under her feet. What's placed under one's feet is the thing that one has dominion over. God placed Israel above her neighboring nations, whose orb is the moon, the darkness (Deut. 28:1).

Since stars symbolize agents, angels, notable personalities, dominating individuals, or peoples, the twelve stars are obviously the twelve sons of Jacob, which became the twelve tribes of Israel. The woman, so attired, is an apparition in "heaven" (12:1), actually *the heaven* in Greek. According to the context, this is both the sky above and the spirit-realm—but it's not the heaven where God lives, as what transpires in the next several verses precludes this possibility. That this isn't the heaven of God's throne is suggested by John's leading phrase, "A great sign appeared", which rings of an astrological sign, like the ones in prior chapters. In this vision, the sky is the stage on which the cast performs. The woman is about to give birth, but another actor enters the scene.

> 12:2 and she was with child; and she cried out, being in labor and in pain to give birth.
> ³Then another sign appeared in heaven: and behold, a great red dragon having seven heads and ten horns, and on his heads were seven diadems.

## Part III: The Visions

At this point Revelation shifts subtly—when referring to the devil, John hereafter prefers the word *dragon* over *Satan*. The dragon is Satan when he's on a warpath, when he's out to conquer and subdue. The color red, the same as the second horseman in 6:4, highlights the dragon's belligerency. Earlier in Revelation when John wrote to the churches, he used the word Satan—henceforth (but not exclusively) he uses the word *dragon*, as the devil prepares his final assault on mankind.

The dragon's seven heads and his ten horns are reiterated in the beast's description in 13:1, and what they symbolize is likely the same for both. But like 13:1, both the dragon and the beast have diadems and not crowns (*stephanos*) like the woman Israel in this passage, or the twenty-four elders. Neither the dragon nor the beast merited a *stephanos*, so in accordance with their nature they usurped diadems.

Many have taught that Satan, when he was cast out of heaven, took with him one-third of the angels, and that these fallen angels became demons. They base it on the following:

> 12:4a And his tail swept away a third of the stars of heaven and threw them to the earth.

They say that the stars are angels. However, in this context it's unclear whether the stars are angels. One cannot point back to 1:16 and say that the stars in Jesus' hand are angels—they are not—and use that as evidence that the stars in 12:4a are also angels. Just as the stars in the woman's head (12:1) are the twelve tribes of Israel, the stars in 12:4a could be a number of things. Furthermore, the word "heaven" here is vague, alluding to the spiritual realm, encompassing more than the traditional sense of heaven. This "heaven" cannot be God's heaven, as Satan, having been cast out long before, can gain no more admittance. It must be the world of spirits. It's where Satan is poised ready to pounce on the child that the woman gives birth to.

> 12:4b And the dragon stood before the woman who was about to give birth, so that when she gave birth he might devour her child.

God established a nation as a vehicle to bring the Messiah into the world. But it took Jehovah years of working with the nation Israel to arrive at the "fullness of time" (Gal. 4:4). This was achieved with successive covenants and prophecies, and by means of the faithfulness of the remnant. Several times it looked like Israel would be either destroyed by her enemies or go awry by her own sin. All of these are the birth pains the woman in this chapter experiences. The dragon crouched by the woman is the devil's attempts to annihilate the woman's child, and thereby thwart the plan of God.

Satan has always hated Israel and has tried to destroy the Jews, even to the present time. He hates the nation because they were chosen by God to be his people, because they brought forth the Messiah, and because of the prophecies concerning her. Antisemitism is driven by the wicked spirits that Paul listed in Eph. 6. Demonic influence fuels the persecution of the Jews. The nations where well-known waves of Jewish persecution occurred, such as the eastern European pogroms or the Spanish Inquisition, are provinces, often backwards, where evil is rampant and freedom is scarce. In these countries Satan has free reign. Controlled by those who hold anti-Christian philosophies, the United Nations has issued an overwhelming number of resolutions against Israel. The hatred of Israel by the Arabs and the European nations evades logical explanation. It's the demonic force in the spiritual realm that animates this opposition. This is not to say that Israel is blameless in all her ways. But looking at this from a historical perspective, throughout the centuries there have been nations who've persecuted the Jews and nations who've allowed the Jews to live in peace. When a Jewish populace is granted freedom, their work ethic will naturally bring prosperity to themselves, and not only themselves but also to the nation at large. In modern times there are a few of Jewish heritage who've become so liberal that they're a detriment to society, but this is as much, if not more, caused by their abandonment of Judeo-Christian philosophy, combined with their upper middle-class upbringing. But a cornerstone of American economic production is comprised of hard-working Jews who have established their own businesses or excel in their chosen vocations.

> 12:5 And she gave birth to a son, a male child, who is to rule all the nations with a rod of iron; and her child was caught up to God and to His throne.

Wuest's translation of the NT says that the "male child" has "the peculiar qualities of masculinity-power and vigor". He's born to rule, and will one day, but this messianic prophecy, echoed from the OT, has yet to be fulfilled. In the above verse the Greek word for "rule" is the same as *shepherd*, and "rod" is the same as *staff* (also *scepter*), so one might say he will *shepherd with a staff of iron*. In

*Part III: The Visions*

other words, his rule will be total; nothing will escape the scrutiny of his government. In the Bible iron symbolizes hegemony. The dragon's attempt to destroy this child by having him crucified backfires. Because of Jesus' obedience, God appoints him Lord of all, and by this act he's "caught up to God and to His throne".

This twelfth chapter demonstrates how the synchronization between heaven-time and earth-time isn't always linear and proportional. In other words, John sees a vision that apparently is of short heaven-time duration, but the events span centuries and millennia of earth-time, the distant past, the recent past. But also the future:

> 12:6 Then the woman fled into the wilderness where she had a place prepared by God, so that there she would be nourished for one thousand two hundred and sixty days.

The 1260 days of Daniel's vision has yet to be fulfilled, but in this vision the woman fled from the dragon, a picture in the spirit world of the Jewish diaspora in the first century A.D. and of the ensuing persecution by the nations. But this verse promises that Israel will be protected by God when the last week of Daniel's vision takes place.

## 18. The Battle in the Spirit World (12:7–12:17)

There're a few places in Scripture that show the battles that go on in the spiritual world against Satan. One of these is in the tenth chapter of Luke:

> Luke 10:17 The seventy returned with joy, saying, "Lord, even the demons are subject to us in Your name."
> ¹⁸And He said to them, "I was watching Satan fall from heaven like lightning.
> ¹⁹"Behold, I have given you authority to tread on serpents and scorpions, and over all the power of the enemy, and nothing will injure you.

Unfortunately, the true meaning of what Jesus said has been misplaced, as this is one of the most misinterpreted passages in the NT. To begin with is the failure to adequately translate the Greek imperfect tense of Jesus' words "was watching" in v. 18. The NASB is one of the few translations that even attempts to translate the continuous action of the tense—most others translate these words

*Part III: The Visions*

as *saw* instead of *was watching*. A better rendering is *kept on seeing*. In addition, when in v. 18 Jesus names Satan, he's actually referring to demons, not Satan himself. Since all demonic spirits are subject to Satan, in the NT one sometimes stumbles across the word *Satan* used instead of the word *demon*, where *demon* would be more accurate. For example, Matt. 12:26, "If Satan casts out Satan, he is divided against himself". Obviously Matt. 12:26 refers to a demon casting out another demon. Also, Luke 13:16, "And this woman, a daughter of Abraham as she is, whom Satan has bound for eighteen long years…" A demon spirit, and not Satan himself, caused the disease which bound the woman. Another key to v. 18 is that, like in Revelations 12, the word "heaven" should be translated *spirit world*. And finally, in v. 18 the word "fall" means that a person or being had been forcibly ejected from their sphere of power or influence. Putting all these pieces together, vv. 18 and 19 are better translated:

> [18]And He said to them, "I saw one demon after another being forcibly ejected from its spiritual stronghold, and each time it looked like lightning striking."
> [19]"You see, I have given you authority to tread on serpents and scorpions, and over all the power of the enemy, and nothing will injure you.

Jesus was not reminiscing over Satan's first sin, which was prior to the creation of man, but instead was having a vision in the spiritual realm (the gift of discerning of spirits [1 Cor. 12:10]) at the same time his disciples were casting out devils. As his disciples were healing the sick and casting out demons, Jesus was seeing one demon after another get the smack-down. Viewed in the light of this alternate translation, the narrative makes more sense. Jesus had given instructions to the seventy, then sent them out, as he remained behind. When they came back and reported the success they had casting out demons, his reply is relevant to the conversation—instead of the spaced-out remark that most think that he made.

The passage in Luke sheds light on Revelation. The vision that John sees continues:

> 12:7 And there was war in heaven, Michael and his angels waging war with the dragon. The dragon and his angels waged war,

## Part III: The Visions

Just as there's warfare in the natural world, there's also warfare in the spiritual world ("heaven" in 12:7). The archangel Michael is commissioned with protecting the nation of Israel (Dan. 12:1). According to 12:7 he has a legion at his command with which he fights the dragon.

> 12:8 and they were not strong enough, and there was no longer a place found for them in heaven.
> ⁹And the great dragon was thrown down, the serpent of old who is called the devil and Satan, who deceives the whole world; he was thrown down to the earth, and his angels were thrown down with him.

The dragon is "thrown down", meaning that he loses the battle. Many claim that this occurred when Satan sinned the first time and was cast out of heaven, and that John's vision here is a replay. That's not true. This is a different event. In 12:8 the phrase, "there was no longer a place found for them in heaven", implies that Satan lost a spiritual stronghold, which implies that he had one to begin with. Satan has various spiritual dominions; an example was the passage from Luke 10. Satan has a "place in heaven" when he controls a person through the obvious, demonic possession and disease, but also through vain reasonings. When Jesus' disciples cast out demons and healed the sick, Jesus, as he spoke in Luke 10, saw Satan fall from that place in heaven. So, what's the stronghold Satan has in Revelation 12 that Michael expels him from? The answer is found in 12:9: it's a stronghold of deception. In this verse John calls him "the serpent of old", referring to Satan's cunning nature, and the one "who deceives the whole world". Though they may not appear to harm people like demon possession or sickness does, strongholds of deception are not trivial. Revelation 12 is a case in point. This battle pits not just Satan against one of the highest ranked angels in the kingdom of God, but it also involves legions of angels and demons.

Through deception Satan inflicts tremendous damage on the human race, howbeit indirectly. The deception prevents the Word of God from taking hold in the lives of men and women, rendering them defenseless against the less powerful demons who do the legwork of killing, stealing, and destroying. This is analogous to the U.S. Air Force's strategy employed in the first Gulf War. The advanced attack aircraft, like the F-117 and B-2, were used in the opening campaign to gain air superiority and suppress the antiaircraft capabilities of the enemy. Once air superiority was established, the venerable B-52s were free to prey on ground targets with

*Part III: The Visions*

impunity. These low-tech, vulnerable bombers dropped more bombs by weight than any other U.S. aircraft in the war. This is the same way Satan and his cohort work.

This twelfth chapter summarizes the nature of the devil. He manifests himself as the serpent and as the dragon. He prefers the first to the second. As the serpent he deceives the human race by false religions and by strange philosophies. When one thinks of a philosophy, he or she is inclined to imagine formal philosophies, what's taught in philosophy courses—existentialism, Aristotle, Nietzsche, etc. But often philosophies are ad hoc, mixed with religion, and personalized. One might have the idea that heaven is a boring place where good but nevertheless dull people retire—but on the other hand, hell, in spite of being a bit dangerous, is one long, wild party. Or one might believe that a long, tedious road of good works cancels one's sins, i.e. is a means of salvation. Goethe's *Faust* is an example. Faust's good works nullified his pact with the devil. Lodged in the minds of the willing or naïve, these philosophies disqualify a person from the kingdom of God.

On the other hand, manifested as the dragon, Satan overwhelms the human race by force: threats of violence, persecution, poverty, sickness. As the dragon, he's a forthright, devouring beast.

In addition to a strategy of deception, Satan attempts to gain a stronghold in heaven by accusing the brethren:

> 12:10 Then I heard a loud voice in heaven, saying, "Now the salvation, and the power, and the kingdom of our God and the authority of His Christ have come, for the accuser of our brethren has been thrown down, he who accuses them before our God day and night.
> [11a] "And they overcame him because of the blood of the Lamb and because of the word of their testimony,

The devil (*diabolos*, the slanderer) demands an audience with God for the purpose of reciting the sins of the righteous, in order to sever their access to the Father. In this way Satan also torments the brethren with thoughts and images, reminding them of the sins they committed, especially those that were done before a person knew Christ or walked with him. Many through ignorance, guilt, or a lack of faith succumb to his accusations, and their relationship with the Father is damaged because they don't understand their righteousness in Christ. Satan gains a spiritual stronghold over a person if he or she capitulates under the weight of his accusing voice. Because it hits a nerve deep in a person's heart, this kind of assault should not be disdained. As it says in 12:11a, it's only through the blood of the Lamb that one overcomes these accusations.

*

One of the most important verses in Revelation...

> 12:11b and they did not love their life even when faced with death.

...is not quoted much in churches these days, being thrust aside in lieu of more 'relevant' messages—bullet-points in neatly structured PowerPoint presentations that promise to fix one's problems, delivered in a such a tidy manner that it makes it appear as easy to do as changing a burned-out light bulb, the Word of God presented like so much psychology. Absent the lifestyle of sacrifice spelled out in 12:11b, the listeners forget the sermon before Monday morning has rolled around, only to repeat the process the next Sunday, in the vain hope that maybe this time the magic will work. They love their lives too much to devote themselves to prayer; sermons, skits, and inspiring music can never compensate.

When the devil is ejected from his spiritual stronghold, he's cast down to earth. This means that he changes his modus operandi from deception and slanderous accusations to blunt persecution and affliction; the serpent becomes the dragon. These latter tactics are not as effective as the former—that's why Satan fought so hard against Michael to retain the former, and to not have to resort to the latter. Even still, the following verse has for years caused Christians to tremble:

> 12:12 "For this reason, rejoice, O heavens and you who dwell in them. Woe to the earth and the sea, because the devil has come down to you, having great wrath, knowing that he has only a short time."

Although the prior verse says that the devil's wrath is directed against the entire human race, the next verse says that it's particularly severe against Israel, dispelling any doubt that forces of wickedness are aligned against this nation.

> 12:13 And when the dragon saw that he was thrown down to the earth, he persecuted the woman who gave birth to the male child.

*Part III: The Visions*

The word "persecuted" in the above context is more appropriately translated *pursued*, specifically, *pursued with the intent to harm*. Once he hits the ground, the dragon starts chasing the woman. To elude the dragon, in 12:14 the woman grows a pair of wings, those of the great eagle.

Gleaned from the Greek text, a "great eagle" in 12:14 implies a specific species of bird. The word *eagle* in Greek also means *vulture* (like in Matt. 24:28). In biblical literature eagles and vultures are categorized in the same family, whereas nowadays eagles and hawks are lumped together. The list of unclean animals in Lev. 11 enumerates the creatures by similarity (in the writer's mind), similar creatures being listed adjacent to one another. Lev. 11:13 groups eagles and vultures together, but one has to skip down to Lev. 11:16 to find the reference to hawks. In the Hebrew mind both eagles and vultures are unclean, but it's hard to imagine that eagles were considered as disgusting as vultures. In the NT, if the context has any ambiguity, the translators will prefer *eagle* to *vulture*. Of course, the scale is tilted away from *vulture* and towards *eagle* because of a few OT cross-references to eagle wings (Exod. 19:4; Isa. 40:31). Nevertheless, it's possible that 12:14 refers to a vulture, and not an eagle. John is talking about a huge set of wings, large enough to carry a woman. Of all the types of birds in the world, vultures and albatrosses have the largest wingspans. Albatrosses are not indigenous to the Middle East, so this leaves vultures. Condors are the largest vultures, but they're only in the Western Hemisphere. In John's locale the largest species of vultures are the Griffon Vulture (wingspan 230-269 cm) and the Lappet-faced Vulture (wingspan 250-300 cm). Picking the larger of the two, John's "great eagle" wings could be those of the Lappet-faced Vulture.

The timeframe for the events corresponding to this vision spans from before Christ's birth up to Daniel's last week. It's difficult to tell if parts of this panorama have been completed or not. The dragon pursuing the woman could take place over many centuries, but at least part of it coincides with Daniel's seven year period, as 12:14 uses the phrase "time and times and half a time"—3½ years. Furthermore, Satan's great wrath noted in 12:12 may have already started, seeing that Satan may have already been cast down.

> 12:14 But the two wings of the great eagle were given to the woman, so that she could fly into the wilderness to her place, where she was nourished for a time and times and half a time, from the presence of the serpent.

¹⁵And the serpent poured water like a river out of his mouth after the woman, so that he might cause her to be swept away with the flood.
¹⁶But the earth helped the woman, and the earth opened its mouth and drank up the river which the dragon poured out of his mouth.
¹⁷So the dragon was enraged with the woman, and went off to make war with the rest of her children, who keep the commandments of God and hold to the testimony of Jesus.

The children of the woman Israel are obviously Christians, perhaps Jewish, perhaps the 144 thousand. But they are not Jews in the traditional sense, i.e. ones who don't accept Christ. The fate of the Jews is a question of interest in the Bible, both OT and NT. Revelation, the last book of the Bible, is expected to bring closure to such biblical questions, but answers are not so forthcoming from this book.

## 19. The Two Beasts (13:1–13:15)

At the end of chapter 12, the enraged dragon, having failed to get the woman, then turns to go after the Faithful. The scene that started in 12:1 continues.

> 13:1a And the dragon stood on the sand of the seashore.

A few of the less reliable manuscripts altered 13:1a to say, *I stood* instead of "the dragon stood". Earlier editions of the NASB translate it "he stood", faithful to the Greek. Later editions are correct, as the dragon is the antecedent of *he*, but the clarification is an inexact rendering. Using *he* emphasizes the continuity. The dragon turns to pursue the brethren. His next action is to go to the seashore and summon the beast, his lieutenant in persecuting Christians:

> 13:1b Then I saw a beast coming up out of the sea, having ten horns and seven heads, and on his horns were ten diadems, and on his heads were blasphemous names.
> ²And the beast which I saw was like a leopard, and his feet were like those of a bear, and his mouth like the mouth of a

*Part III: The Visions*

lion. And the dragon gave him his power and his throne and great authority.
³I saw one of his heads as if it had been slain, and his fatal wound was healed. And the whole earth was amazed and followed after the beast;
⁴they worshiped the dragon because he gave his authority to the beast; and they worshiped the beast, saying, "Who is like the beast, and who is able to wage war with him?"
⁵There was given to him a mouth speaking arrogant words and blasphemies, and authority to act for forty-two months was given to him.

These words are familiar. Reading Daniel's vision, the connection between his and John's becomes obvious:

> Dan. 7:2 Daniel said, "I was looking in my vision by night, and behold, the four winds of heaven were stirring up the great sea.
> ³"And four great beasts were coming up from the sea, different from one another.
> ⁴"The first was like a lion and had the wings of an eagle. I kept looking until its wings were plucked, and it was lifted up from the ground and made to stand on two feet like a man; a human mind also was given to it.
> ⁵"And behold, another beast, a second one, resembling a bear. And it was raised up on one side, and three ribs were in its mouth between its teeth; and thus they said to it, 'Arise, devour much meat!'"
> ⁶"After this I kept looking, and behold, another one, like a leopard, which had on its back four wings of a bird; the beast also had four heads, and dominion was given to it.
> ⁷"After this I kept looking in the night visions, and behold, a fourth beast, dreadful and terrifying and extremely strong; and it had large iron teeth. It devoured and crushed and trampled down the remainder with its feet; and it was different from all the beasts that were before it, and it had ten horns.
> ⁸"While I was contemplating the horns, behold, another horn, a little one, came up among them, and three of the first horns were pulled out by the roots before it; and behold, this horn possessed eyes like the eyes of a man and a mouth uttering great boasts.

*Part III: The Visions*

John's vision is so similar to Daniel's that the former cannot be interpreted in isolation from the latter. First, the beasts in both visions come up out of the sea. The sea in the Bible is supposed to represent the masses of humanity—at least that's what's taught. The problem is that those who teach this are short on supporting Scripture references. But in the Bible the sea means several different things. It forms the practical boundary of Israel's world. Alongside it live several heathen nations. It is vast, is tumultuous, and in its unexplored depths dwell mysteries, creatures like Jonah's whale. And other monsters, great and terrible, lie submerged. Thus, out of the sea Daniel's four beasts come. Most who interpret his dream do not identify the four beasts as four men, neither is it likely that the beast of Revelation 13 is a man, considering the parallels between Daniel and Revelation.

Just like the ending of the vision of Revelation 12, the meaning of the beast in Revelation is a matter of speculation. It has heads and horns, and these must signify nations or something. What exactly is unknown, but to claim that the beast's horns correspond to Roman emperors, for example, errs by coercing historical events to fit the vision. This is just as much speculation as extrapolating current events into a futuristic scenario where the visions are fulfilled. The underlying problem is the certitude wherewith theories are promulgated.

And the beast is given authority, but 13:7 does not name from whom the authority is given.

> 13:6 And he opened his mouth in blasphemies against God, to blaspheme His name and His tabernacle, that is, those who dwell in heaven.
> ⁷It was also given to him to make war with the saints and to overcome them, and authority over every tribe and people and tongue and nation was given to him.
> ⁸All who dwell on the earth will worship him, everyone whose name has not been written from the foundation of the world in the book of life of the Lamb who has been slain.
> ⁹If anyone has an ear, let him hear.
> ¹⁰ᵃ If anyone is destined for captivity, to captivity he goes; if anyone kills with the sword, with the sword he must be killed.

In the *UBS Greek New Testament*, 13:10a appears as poetic stanza. The next sentence 13:10b is the epilogue to this poem. (13:10a again dispels any doubt whether it can be God's will for a

*Part III: The Visions*

Christian to suffer persecution.) In poetic form this verse permeates the heart of those who must suffer, as suffering is an inevitability one has no control over. Meditating on it gives a Christian the strength to endure, as 13:10b attests:

> 13:10b Here is the perseverance and the faith of the saints.

But returning to the question posed by 13:7, the answer is in 13:4—the dragon gave the beast authority to overcome the saints, and over all the peoples of the earth. But what kind of authority does Satan have here? He cannot give what he doesn't have, nor will he fail to relinquish to the beast any authority he might posses. Satan exercises authority over the human race through the power of suggestion that results in sin, resulting in a darkening of the heart. A person ultimately chooses whether he or she will follow Satan's prompting, but having succumbed, his or her nature is corrupted as a result. Subsequent promptings grow coercive. The vast majority in the kingdom of darkness are not subject to Satan's every command. Most of the ungodly are only susceptible to certain suggestions. But this link constitutes a kingdom with Satan as king. His grip is both individual and collective. It can be broken, should one turn to the Lord, but as prior chapters of Revelation have shown, those on earth resist God. One's own callous heart keeps one firmly in the darkness, and as long as that's the case, Satan will have a kingdom to rule over.

This authority, handed over to the beast, impels the ungodly to persecute the godly. The more hardened the heart, the more inclined to demonic suggestion, the whispers of which inevitably are against the saints. As 13:15 attests, mankind is split between those who will worship the beast, and those who worship the true God.

> 13:11 Then I saw another beast coming up out of the earth; and he had two horns like a lamb and he spoke as a dragon. [12]He exercises all the authority of the first beast in his presence. And he makes the earth and those who dwell in it to worship the first beast, whose fatal wound was healed. [13]He performs great signs, so that he even makes fire come down out of heaven to the earth in the presence of men. [14]And he deceives those who dwell on the earth because of the signs which it was given him to perform in the presence of the beast, telling those who dwell on the earth to make an image to the beast who had the wound of the sword and has come to life.

*Part III: The Visions*

¹⁵And it was given to him to give breath to the image of the beast, so that the image of the beast would even speak and cause as many as do not worship the image of the beast to be killed.

This is the third beast. The first comes out of the abyss (11:7), but acts independent of the other two. The second comes out of the sea (13:1), the third out of the earth (13:11). This last beast has human attributes, since he comes out of the earth, is able to perform signs, and acts with the authority of the previous beast.

It's no surprise that the beast seeks universal worship. It has always been Satan's goal to extinguish all other religions, and to replace them with one mandatory worldwide religion that exalts himself. An example is Nimrod and the Tower of Babel. Notes about Gen. 10:8,9 by Bullinger say that Nimrod's name means *rebel*, and that he was a mighty one in defiance to (actual translation of "before") the Lord. Genesis says that Nimrod was a mighty hunter; according to the historian Josephus, he was a hunter of men. Nimrod created an empire on the plains of Mesopotamia with Babel, listed first, as the chief city:

> Gen. 10:10 "The beginning of his kingdom was Babel and Erech and Accad and Calneh, in the land of Shinar."

Nimrod conquered cites, annexing them into the empire. Since empires upheld by threats of violence are unstable, Nimrod devised two contrivances to bind the fledgling provinces: language (Gen. 11:1) and religion. Bullinger notes that the literal translation of Gen. 11:4, the phrase, "whose top may reach into heaven", is *and its top with the heavens*. Many, including him, interpret this as a false religion. It was never God's will for man to aggregate within the confines of a single geographical area (Gen. 9:1), but for him to spread out, and thus spawn a diversity of language and culture (and perhaps race as well). On the contrary, it became man's will to bind mankind together, enforcing uniformity in language and religion. Universality of language extends beyond the obvious; it's also the agreement in thought and intention, implied by the following verse:

> Gen. 11:1 Now the whole earth used the same language and the same words.

This unity in purpose with an absence of dissention meant that they could accomplish anything they set their mind to.

*Part III: The Visions*

Gen. 11:6 The LORD said, "Behold, they are one people, and they all have the same language. And this is what they began to do, and now nothing which they purpose to do will be impossible for them.

This unity was grounded in a common religion. On the whole, ancient civilizations in Mesopotamia and Egypt bound functions of society and of day-to-day affairs to their religion.

With this God was not pleased, and went down to "confuse their language" (Gen. 11:7)—disagreement entered; unity of purpose left. Construction on the tower stopped; the empire crumbled; the inhabitants spread throughout the earth, which was God's original intention. Had God not intervened and had they continued on their path unimpeded, they would've accomplished what they set their mind to—the unification of the world under one empire, having one religion. The righteous line on the earth would've been extinguished, and along with it God's plan of salvation. Nimrod's plan is the same plan that the devil uses in Revelation 13, with an economic twist added.

## 20. The Mark of the Beast System (13:16–13:18)

13:16 And he causes all, the small and the great, and the rich and the poor, and the free men and the slaves, to be given a mark on their right hand or on their forehead,
$^{17}$and he provides that no one will be able to buy or to sell, except the one who has the mark, either the name of the beast or the number of his name.
$^{18}$Here is wisdom. Let him who has understanding calculate the number of the beast, for the number is that of a man; and his number is six hundred and sixty-six.

Mention the number 666 to someone, and he'll reply *antichrist*, and go on to say that when the antichrist comes, no one will be able to buy anything without the number written on his forehead. Close, but not correct. It's the beast, not the antichrist. The second beast, actually. And the number is on the hand or forehead, not just forehead. And it's both buying and selling, not just buying. And so on, and so on—there's a pile of books on the subject.

Recapitulating 7:3, putting a mark on one's hand or forehead is a phrase having its origin in the OT. The forehead is the tablet on

*Part III: The Visions*

which is inscribed one's purpose in life; the hand holds a self-reminder of something of importance. Having these numbers written on oneself is not to be taken literally. It would be silly for folks to walk around with the number 666 on their foreheads. Plus, there has been so much literature about the significance of 666 that, should the number ever come into vogue, it must be construed as an act of defiance against God and the Bible. It's been two millennia since Revelation was written. The Bible is the best-selling book in the history of mankind. No one can be taken by surprise with a 666-system—coerced perhaps, but not duped.

Now, for years many have insisted that the technology was already available to implement the mark-of-the-beast-system—the elimination of paper currency in lieu of an all-electronic financial system, whereby select individuals can be locked out of the system, preventing them from buying or selling. As far back as the 1980s books have been written that warned that such a system could be put into place in short notice. This is absurd. There's no way that a world-wide electronic system that replaces all cash transactions could have been implemented in the 1980s (see Appendix D). Even in the twenty-first century the West is not ready to eliminate paper currency. And except for the rich, those in developing countries have limited access to electricity, let alone electronic banking facilities.

This begs a greater question: how could so many be so wrong? Back then, most Christians were convinced that the mark-of-the-beast-system could be implemented on short notice. Born-again computer experts swore that the technology was already in place. Where did they go wrong? To begin with, by nature a strong movement of the Spirit is pregnant with the conviction that Jesus will return soon. In that atmosphere Christians search for evidence of his imminent return, and forego skepticism. Furthermore, the experts who testified that the technology was in place were not experts by today's standards. The computer industry was still young and unsophisticated, and, while these so-called experts had degrees in computer science and had worked with information technology, most of them had never worked on a large, networked application, simply because they didn't exist at the time. Having no experience with a real system, they couldn't fathom the problems involved in not only creating such a system, but making it practicable for day-to-day use.

Take the analogy of crossing the Atlantic Ocean in an airplane. The first trans-Atlantic flight was made by Charles Lindbergh in 1929. But years went by before travel by air over the Atlantic replaced travel by ship. Just because Lindbergh made one flight over

*Part III: The Visions*

the ocean didn't mean that the aviation industry was thenceforth capable of shuttling masses of paying customers on routine trans-Atlantic flights. Lindbergh's airplane was so heavy that it barely cleared the tree line on takeoff. The plane had no windshield. Who would trust his or her life to such a machine? The same was with computer technology in the late '70s and into the '80s. Simply because funds could be transferred electronically across the country from one account to another didn't mean that it was feasible to do every transaction electronically. When people hear about a new technology, in the excitement they overlook the engineering improvements necessary to make the technology feasible for everyday use. All problems must be solved: cost, security, reliability, maintainability, ease of use, etc. Just the potential of failure is an obstruction to prevent the deployment of a new technology. Aircraft fly-by-wire flight control systems are an example. It wasn't until 1995 that Boeing put one in a commercial airliner, even though the technology had been around for years.

So, several years ago, the computer experts who wrote or were consulted in the writing of end-time prophecy books were in over their heads. But still another factor contributing to the belief in the soon-coming mark-of-the-beast-system is this: Christians are prone to hysteria, tend to believe information without verifying the source's credibility, tend to indulge in urban legend, and tend to defend irrational propositions with the same zeal that they defend the Bible. (To this extent the world has a reason to fear the hysteria of the Religious Right.)

Those who've speculated on the form of the mark-of-the-beast-system imagine a system that is totally electronic, the elimination of cash. But is this assumption necessary? Could a system that's only partially electronic be used to the same end, i.e. to block a list of people from buying and selling? Suppose an alternative mark-of-the-beast-system is implemented; the same goal but by different means. Could the current financial network, with relatively minor changes, be modified to enforce mandated blacklists to lock out select individuals? Assuming a rogue government in collusion with a majority of the citizenry, what measures could be taken by them to block certain buying and selling? First, banks and other financial firms would be instructed to cancel the accounts for ostracized clients and to seize their assets. Second, employers would be required to pay through direct deposit only. Third, retailers and grocery stores, at least the larger ones, would be forbidden to accept cash payments—additionally enforced by mandating that banks not accept cash deposits from commercial enterprises. Fourth, all cash transactions above a certain amount, say $1,000, would, by re-

*Part III: The Visions*

quirement of law, be reported to the authorities, along with the buying and selling of large items such as real estate or automobiles. With these relatively simple controls in place, it would be difficult for one targeted by such a system to earn a living and to pay for household commodities. Not impossible, but difficult. The system could be enhanced over time, with the government increasingly clamping down on extant paper transactions. Private industry would react by contriving a more convenient means of exchanging money, like, for example, a more efficient and extensible checking system. Over time cash would dry up—the government would encourage this by decreasing the volume of currency in circulation, and by seizing the stockpiles of cash locked up in bank vaults.

Movies often reflect the public's paranoia, and there have been many a film made about the government perpetrating nefarious schemes against innocent citizens. How many movies cast the government in the role of the bad guy? After such media inundation, how would a democratic populace permit this? Perhaps the result of two factors. First, the gradual intrusion of government into the private sector by entitlement spending, the appendage to socialism. A once-prosperous society in moral decline loses its vigor and becomes docile. The citizens, seeking shelter from the vicissitudes of the economy, exchange their self-sufficiency for government guarantees, having become conditioned to look to the government, their Jehovah Jireh, to provide for them.

Second, a reaction against an increase in criminal activity would call for the imposition of a strong, central government. The West has lived in tranquility for so long that it's forgotten what a menace a rogue element can be. The chaos accompanying a resurgence of crime would be intolerable. Technology would offer solutions. Putting computer checks on purchases could be used as a means of reigning in illegal activity: instead of catching the criminal in the act, catch him trying to spend his money. A computerized system could be devised which runs audits on income and purchases, looking for anomalies, such as someone who spends much more than he makes. The computer would scan transactions, keeping the information confidential, and only suggest investigating those who score above a statistical threshold, without naming any egregious purchases. To a small extent the IRS does this already.

In fact, this system could be used to snare would-be terrorists. In the contemporary atmosphere of political correctness, profiling those who're likely to be terrorists, such as young, male, foreign-born Moslems, is taboo. But with computer technology brought to bear, the political problem could be skirted. Say, if the government mandated that, prior to boarding an aircraft, all must be inter-

*Part III: The Visions*

viewed and searched, it could then provide a means by which the average person could obtain a waiver. Prior to arriving at the airport, a background audit would be run, checking for credit rating, employment status, age, and other statistical attributes unrelated to the obvious correlating factors of religion, country of birth, etc. An easily achievable score would then exempt the 60 year-old lady from Omaha from a rigorous examination, subjecting only a small percentage of the population to strip searches. This would be an effective method of screening terrorists.

But a system that could do such audits would require coalesced data from disparate databases. In other words, the computer would need to pull tax records from the IRS, birth records from the state the subject under question was born in, credit information from another source, criminal records, etc. This information would have to be accessible on a network similar to the Internet, but one that has restricted access and enhanced security. Call this network *Govnet*. It would tie all government computers together, and exchange information with peer systems running in foreign countries. It could be used to catch drug lords, terrorists, or other criminal elements. And the IRS would run more effective audits with it, while streamlining the tax collection system. It could also be used to control immigration, cutting down on aliens, illegal employment, and a host of other immigration-related problems. In short, it would solve a host of problems. And it would be the perfect tool for a mark-of-the-beast-system.

But while many over the years have missed the mark, claiming that the technology was in place to eliminate cash transactions, a steady progression has been contributing the missing pieces to the puzzle. The technology to implement such a system will mature in time, even though it has taken longer than expected. Though the world does not progress as quickly as many a Revelation-fanatic imagines it does, it does march forward, and one day people will realize that, with a flip of a switch, a rogue government could control all financial transactions. That realization will have come like a thief in the night.

## 21. The New Song, the Final Warning, and the Wine Press (14:1–14:20)

In spite of misconceptions, Revelation's theme is not Satan and his emissaries tormenting mankind, but rather the unveiling of God's righteous judgment upon those who've persistently disobeyed

*Part III: The Visions*

him. Satan's attempt at a world order is featured in the thirteenth chapter, and parts of the twelfth, but that's all the limelight he'll enjoy. Revelation is about what God is doing—not Satan. Satan is a spectacular failure, as the eschatologist Hilton Sutton is fond of repeating. As the fourteenth chapter commences, the dragon and the beast cease being the center of attention. God's plan continues. With the reappearance of the familiar Hebrew idiom, John starts another vision:

> 14:1 Then I looked, and behold, the Lamb was standing on Mount Zion, and with Him one hundred and forty-four thousand, having His name and the name of His Father written on their foreheads.

It's reasonable to assume that these are the same 144 thousand from chapter 7. Recalling from 7:4 that the 144 thousand were "sealed", and noting in 14:1 that the same have names "written on their foreheads", one deduces that the two are equivalent, i.e. having a name written on the forehead means that one is sealed. The two mean the same thing: a distinguishing sign of authenticity and ownership. In any event, the vision is not a scene from earth, but one from the spirit-world—or so it would appear. Jesus would not appear in the flesh with a large crowd on the real Mt. Zion before his triumphant coming. This amplifies the debate concerning these 144 thousand, whether they're literal blood-descendants from the twelve tribes or not.

As a side note, the age-old stereotype of angels or deceased humans lounging on clouds playing harps may have originated from the reference to harps in 14:2b.

> 14:2 And I heard a voice from heaven, like the sound of many waters and like the sound of loud thunder, and the voice which I heard was like the sound of harpists playing on their harps.
> ³And they sang a new song before the throne and before the our living creatures and the elders; and no one could learn the song except the one hundred and forty-four thousand who had been purchased from the earth.

In 14:3 a "new song" rises out of the depths of the hearts of those surrounding the Lamb. Although music accompanies this chapter's song (not all songs in the Bible are set to music), the spectacle is that "no one could learn the song except the 144 thousand who had

*Part III: The Visions*

been purchased from the earth". The theme in their hearts was seeded by their having been purchased by the blood of the same Lamb, the one they gather to at Zion in 14:1. Others cannot learn the song, either because they have not been purchased by the Lamb, or because what Jesus did for them does not stir their hearts deeply. Their ability to learn the song is synonymous with their seal, the name of the Father and the Son on their foreheads.

> 14:4 These are the ones who have not been defiled with women, for they have kept themselves chaste. These are the ones who follow the Lamb wherever He goes. These have been purchased from among men as first fruits to God and to the Lamb.
> ⁵And no lie was found in their mouth; they are blameless.

The phrase, "for they have kept themselves chaste", (or something similar) is in most modern translations. The KJV, rendering the Greek literally, reads, "for they are virgins". One wonders if the newer translations purposefully steer away from the literal wording just to avoid advocating a connection between celibacy and dedication to God. The Roman Catholic requirement that priests remain celibate has support in the NT, as this and other verses attest that the one who's unmarried can better dedicate himself or herself to the Lord. Forcing this upon the clergy, rather than allowing God to reveal to those who're called in this manner, is where the practice deviates from Scripture.

So which translation is correct? To answer this, one must rewind the clock to earlier days and consider society from that perspective. Keep in mind that an abundance of singles (defined as those who for any reason live autonomously) is a recent phenomenon. Before household appliances, running water, and refrigeration, the tasks of preparing meals and washing clothes were difficult, time consuming, labor intensive, and relatively expensive. People aggregated in households out of necessity, not necessarily by choice. Single women seldom lived alone. If a woman fell on hard times and lost her immediate family, it was the moral duty of a relative to take her into his (or occasionally her) household. In the Bible a widow is a woman who through misfortune has become stranded and has to fend for herself. They, along with orphans, were on the last rung of the economic, and hence social, ladder. This is why the Bible has so many moral invectives concerning the treatment of widows.

But strictly speaking, in biblical times a *virgin* is a girl who has reached the age of eligibility for marriage, but is still in the custody of her father or a surrogate. Paul in 1 Cor. 7:34 makes a distinction between two categories of women, "The woman who is unmarried, and the virgin". The "unmarried woman" is one who had previously been married but had returned to her father's or a relative's household, probably because her husband had passed away. The difference between these two, the unmarried and the virgin, is that the latter has never been married, and that she is probably younger as well. A virgin is one who's under the authority of her father and has never left her household. She's physically pure, of course, but she's also without the responsibility and care for a husband, for children, or for a household. She can therefore dedicate herself to the things of the Lord. As Paul continues in 1 Cor., a virgin is "...concerned about the things of the Lord, that she may be holy both in body and spirit...."

This is the meaning conveyed in 14:4; both the NASB and KJV are correct, but incomplete. The 144 thousand, having always been a part of the Lord's household, are dedicated to serving him. And they're sexually pure. The word "defiled" in 14:4 conjures up the image of an OT priest, the state of ritualistic purity requisite to serve as an attendant in the Tent of Meeting, housing the Lord's presence. In the same way, sexual sin disqualifies a man from accessing God's holy presence. Too often Christians have preached the practical side of abstinence: emotional well-being and the prevention of venereal disease. While these inducements might be sufficient to obey God's commandment, this is not the principal reason for doing so. Sexual sin defiles a man, interfering with his relationship with the Lord. Only looking at the natural, heathens cannot be persuaded to observe the NT demarcation of permitted sexual behavior, as the commandments invoke the holiness of God, of which they have no comprehension. While the world concurs with the OT taboo against adultery, the tightened NT restrictions concerning sex (namely the prohibitions against fornication) are not embraced. Christians ought to accept that the world cannot be persuaded to adhere to their understanding of sexual purity.

To an extent, sexual sin affects men and women differently. As 14:4 shows, a man's sexual impurity corrupts him, preventing him from serving God. Immorality would stymie an OT priest from fulfilling his duties as a minister in the presence of the Almighty. The repercussions are spiritual. When Israel neglected their attendance to the Tabernacle or the Temple, they lost the Lord's supernatural blessing, resulting in poverty and in their enemies gaining dominion over them. Analogous to this, if a man commits sexual sin, the resulting defilement hinders his ability to walk in the Spirit, to receive supernatural assistance from the Father. In the Mosaic covenant, God required that a men present himself before the Lord

*Part III: The Visions*

three times a year (Exod. 23:17). In this covenant God requires that, from time to time, a man withdraw from his day-to-day activities to present himself before the Lord in prayer, entering his holy presence in worship. Failure to do so displeases God, and his displeasure reverberates throughout the man's natural life. A man might fail to appear before the Lord for one of several reasons: he might do so out of ignorance, out of negligence, or he might be disqualified because of defilement—in this case, sexual sin.

On the other hand, when a woman transgresses sexually, family and society suffer the consequences. According to the Law (Deut. 22:13-29), a promiscuous woman was punished much more severely than a man. Feminists decry such verses as sexist, despising the wisdom of the Law, but God places the bulk of the responsibility of society's preservation of sexual mores on the woman, and not the man. The twentieth century decline in sexual morality, having propagated to all strata of society, has been accompanied by a rise in divorce, a rise in illegitimacy, and the breakdown of the traditional family, which in turn correlates to increased crime, drug abuse, and illiteracy, to name but a few ills. The demise of sexual morality began with the sex revolution of the 1960s. In reality, this so-called revolution was the abandonment of sexual morals by women. For the most part, the revolution didn't cause men to become immoral—they already were. The immorality of women gave opportunity for men to indulge.

\*

According to the next verses, God is neither finished with his judgments, nor is he remiss in giving sinners one more chance. The below phrase "eternal gospel" is different than *the Gospel*, the NT message of hope and salvation. The word "gospel" would be better translated *proclamation* in this context.

> 14:6 And I saw another angel flying in midheaven, having an eternal gospel to preach to those who live on the earth, and to every nation and tribe and tongue and people;
> [7]and he said with a loud voice, "Fear God, and give Him glory, because the hour of His judgment has come; worship Him who made the heaven and the earth and sea and springs of waters."

This is the first of three angels who proclaim the judgments that God is about to do. Quite out of the blue, the second angel proclaims judgment on Babylon the harlot, introducing another player in Revelation.

*Part III: The Visions*

> 14:8 And another angel, a second one, followed, saying, "Fallen, fallen is Babylon the great, she who has made all the nations drink of the wine of the passion of her immorality."

Again, the word "immorality" in 14:8 obscures the meaning of the Greek word *porneia*. Babylon is a harlot; fornication is her business. *Porneia* as used in the NT means deviant or immoral sexual behavior, often extreme. Preachers ranting against fornication have too often harped on sex between an unmarried man and woman, skewing the comprehension of this NT word. Fornication includes adultery. The difference between fornication and adultery is that fornication emphasizes the deviancy of a sexual act, whereas adultery emphasizes the breaking of the marriage pact.

But the harlot is an apparition in a vision. She's not an actual person, but is the personification of an illicit spiritual phenomenon. The phrase, "drink of the wine of the passion of her immorality", means, *participate in the ferocity by which she commits fornication*. The harlot's forte is her ability to attract partners. Prostitutes that are effective at their trade have one thing in common: they're experts in alluring men into bed. This calling-card will be mentioned later in the eighteenth chapter.

> 14:9 Then another angel, a third one, followed them, saying with a loud voice, "If anyone worships the beast and his image, and receives a mark on his forehead or on his hand, [10]he also will drink of the wine of the wrath of God, which is mixed in full strength in the cup of His anger; and he will be tormented with fire and brimstone in the presence of the holy angels and in the presence of the Lamb.

Warning those against receiving the mark of the beast, the third angel employs the old metaphor of drinking of the cup (Matt. 20:22,23). In this case it's the cup of mixed wine (Ps. 75:8; Prov. 9:2,5) that a host prepares for guests. As noted in the Bible, wine was frequently mixed with water. Because of the hot climate in the Middle East, large quantities of fluid are needed; much water must be consumed. Adding wine to water purified the water, and added flavor to it, and also diluted the potency of pure wine, as pure wine only aggravates one's thirst. In addition, myrrh and other spices were added for flavor. This was the ancient's substitute for cocktails, which are diluted, distilled beverages. Ancient hosts prepared these drinks for guests in the same way that cocktails might be

*Part III: The Visions*

served before a dinner party. The 14:10 metaphor has God preparing a special concoction for the guests—only one that's not diluted.

> 14:11 "And the smoke of their torment goes up forever and ever; they have no rest day and night, those who worship the beast and his image, and whoever receives the mark of his name."

John in the next verse repeats the introductory phrase from 13:10, "here is the perseverance of the saints". Embedded in the diatribe of judgments comes this word of encouragement. Odd that it should be here.

> 14:12 Here is the perseverance of the saints who keep the commandments of God and their faith in Jesus.
> [13]And I heard a voice from heaven, saying, "Write, 'Blessed are the dead who die in the Lord from now on!'" "Yes," says the Spirit, "so that they may rest from their labors, for their deeds follow with them."

The encouragement is but a short tangent off the curve of God's judgment, which continues to the end of the chapter. This vision of the fourteenth chapter is an overview of the dispensations of wrath from the fifteenth chapter onwards, and therefore summarizes the subsequent plagues.

> 14:14 Then I looked, and behold, a white cloud, and sitting on the cloud was one like a son of man, having a golden crown on His head and a sharp sickle in His hand.

John's remark "like a son of man" is not a reference to Jesus the Son of man. In this context "son of man" means *a perfectly proportioned man*. This ideal man has a sickle, but he's not the only one reaping. An angel joins in. Why the two and not one is a mystery.

In the next few verses God's wrath is conveyed in the two metaphors, both different kinds of harvest, wheat harvest and grape harvest. From this, the title of Steinbeck's *The Grapes of Wrath* has its origins.

> 14:15 And another angel came out of the temple, crying out with a loud voice to Him who sat on the cloud, "Put in your sickle and reap, for the hour to reap has come, because the harvest of the earth is ripe."

*Part III: The Visions*

¹⁶Then He who sat on the cloud swung His sickle over the earth, and the earth was reaped.
¹⁷And another angel came out of the temple which is in heaven, and he also had a sharp sickle.
¹⁸Then another angel, the one who has power over fire, came out from the altar; and he called with a loud voice to him who had the sharp sickle, saying, "Put in your sharp sickle and gather the clusters from the vine of the earth, because her grapes are ripe."

In ancient times harvesters cast grapes on a bed and crushed them with their feet, 14:20 alluding to this.

> 14:19 So the angel swung his sickle to the earth and gathered the clusters from the vine of the earth, and threw them into the great wine press of the wrath of God.
> ²⁰And the wine press was trodden outside the city, and blood came out from the wine press, up to the horses' bridles, for a distance of two hundred miles.

A river is formed by the blood of the slain wicked, the majority of earth's population. The height of the river is given—a horse's bridle (horses were smaller then), approximately 1.4 m (4.5 ft)—but the width is not. If there are 8-10 pints of blood in the average person, averaging children in will adjust this down to perhaps 6-7 pints (1.4–3.3 l) per person. The last variable, the width of the river, is a wide-open guess based on a sense of proportion. One might picture a river having a width 10–100 times its depth. The length, 1600 stadia (29.3 km, 960,000 ft., 181 miles) is specified, so the volume of the river is anywhere from 409,000-4,09,000 cubic meters. With 1 cubic meter equal to 1000 liters, the blood from 426 people (using 2.35 l of blood per person) fills a cubic meter. Using the range of river width estimates, to fill a river like that takes 175 million to 1.75 billion people. Assuming that two-thirds of the world's population had died in previous plagues, the earth's population before God's wrath is unleashed would've been from 525 million to 5.25 billion. The upper figure is not so far off from the earth's present population. If only the Bible specified the river's width, the Revelation prognosticators could estimate an approximate date of this judgment through population growth projections.

*Part III: The Visions*

## 22. Finishing the Wrath of God (15:1–16:21)

The beast and his followers persecute the righteous any chance they get, as 14:12,13 indicated. But it's only a short duration until the Lord sets things straight. In anticipation, a song of victory is in the heart of the overcomers, the "song of Moses" and the "song of the Lamb". Moses reminds of past triumph; the Lamb for impending triumph.

> 15:1 Then I saw another sign in heaven, great and marvelous, seven angels who had seven plagues, which are the last, because in them the wrath of God is finished.
> ²And I saw something like a sea of glass mixed with fire, and those who had been victorious over the beast and his image and the number of his name, standing on the sea of glass, holding harps of God.
> ³And they sang the song of Moses, the bond-servant of God, and the song of the Lamb, saying, "Great and marvelous are Your works, O Lord God, the Almighty; Righteous and true are Your ways, King of the nations!
> ⁴"Who will not fear, O Lord, and glorify Your name? For You alone are holy; For ALL THE NATIONS WILL COME AND WORSHIP BEFORE YOU, FOR YOUR RIGHTEOUS ACTS HAVE BEEN REVEALED."
> ⁵After these things I looked, and the temple of the tabernacle of testimony in heaven was opened,
> ⁶and the seven angels who had the seven plagues came out of the temple, clothed in linen, clean and bright, and girded around their chests with golden sashes.
> ⁷Then one of the four living creatures gave to the seven angels seven golden bowls full of the wrath of God, who lives forever and ever.
> ⁸And the temple was filled with smoke from the glory of God and from His power; and no one was able to enter the temple until the seven plagues of the seven angels were finished.

The angels are clothed in linen (15:6) just as the priests were when ministering in the earthly temple. The smoke that fills the heavenly temple (15:8) also filled the earthly temple (Exod. 40:34; 1 Kings 8:10; 2 Chron. 5:13). The plagues issued are reminders of what God worked in Egypt.

*Part III: The Visions*

16:1 Then I heard a loud voice from the temple, saying to the seven angels, "Go and pour out on the earth the seven bowls of the wrath of God."
²So the first angel went and poured out his bowl on the earth; and it became a loathsome and malignant sore on the people who had the mark of the beast and who worshiped his image.
³The second angel poured out his bowl into the sea, and it became blood like that of a dead man; and every living thing in the sea died.
⁴Then the third angel poured out his bowl into the rivers and the springs of waters; and they became blood.

The long sentence of 16:5,6, appended by the short sentence, "They deserve it", summarize the theme of Revelations chapters 4-20, although the principal theme of Revelation in its entirety is repeated out of the blue in 16:15—"Behold, I am coming like a thief". Being vigilant and ready is the message to Christians, past, present, and future.

> 16:5 And I heard the angel of the waters saying, "Righteous are You, who are and who were, O Holy One, because You judged these things;
> ⁶for they poured out the blood of saints and prophets, and You have given them blood to drink. They deserve it."

In this vision inanimate objects speak. For too long having witnessed the blood of the righteous sprinkled around it, the heavenly altar can remain silent no more.

> 16:7 And I heard the altar saying, "Yes, O Lord God, the Almighty, true and righteous are Your judgments."

But though God scorches sinners with fire, their stubborn hearts still will not budge. The Almighty in his foreknowledge knows this, yet it's implied that he would accept should they repent. He knows that they won't, and has pre-ordained more plagues to follow.

> 16:8 The fourth angel poured out his bowl upon the sun, and it was given to it to scorch men with fire.
> ⁹Men were scorched with fierce heat; and they blasphemed the name of God who has the power over these plagues, and they did not repent so as to give Him glory.

## Part III: The Visions

> [10]Then the fifth angel poured out his bowl on the throne of the beast, and his kingdom became darkened; and they gnawed their tongues because of pain,
> [11]and they blasphemed the God of heaven because of their pains and their sores; and they did not repent of their deeds.

This next section of the vision fast-forwards to the triumphant return of Jesus (19:11-19). A throng will gather to waylay him upon his reentry into the world, another indication of the hardness of mankind's heart and the vindication of God's wrath. The audacity and foolishness of this endeavor is mind-boggling. Prerequisite to assembling in anticipation of his return is the belief that he will return. If he can return from heaven, then certainly he is the Lord of Hosts, capable of defeating any earthly army. This sled of delusion must be greased with demonic deception (16:13), in this case demons like frogs.

> 16:12 The sixth angel poured out his bowl on the great river, the Euphrates; and its water was dried up, so that the way would be prepared for the kings from the east.
> [13]And I saw coming out of the mouth of the dragon and out of the mouth of the beast and out of the mouth of the false prophet, three unclean spirits like frogs;
> [14]for they are spirits of demons, performing signs, which go out to the kings of the whole world, to gather them together for the war of the great day of God, the Almighty.
> [15]("Behold, I am coming like a thief. Blessed is the one who stays awake and keeps his clothes, so that he will not walk about naked and men will not see his shame.")
> [16]And they gathered them together to the place which in Hebrew is called Har-Magedon.

The army that comes out of the east is a favorite source of speculation for the end-time enthusiasts. They point to 9:16 and say that there's a 200 million strong army that'll gather at Armageddon. Supposedly, the angel in 16:12 dries up the Euphrates to allow passage over this river. Fording such a river was difficult for ancient armies, but there're bridges nowadays, not to mention that modern armies lay pontoons for river crossings. But 200 million is a large army, and a single bridge would take over a month for that number to cross. Crossing a dry river bed would be quicker.

China is the favorite choice when speculating where this army will originate, selected because it's the only country with a suffi-

*Part III: The Visions*

ciently large population to field such an army. But why China, why not India? For the last few decades, China has had policies to control population growth by limiting families to a single child. In a few years the population of India should surpass that of China. This is another example of an end-time theory that appeared plausible when it was conceived, but with the passage of time has become outdated.

> 16:17 Then the seventh angel poured out his bowl upon the air, and a loud voice came out of the temple from the throne, saying, "It is done."
> [18]And there were flashes of lightning and sounds and peals of thunder; and there was a great earthquake, such as there had not been since man came to be upon the earth, so great an earthquake was it, and so mighty.

In 16:18 God caused an earthquake, but does this mean that God causes earthquakes in general? Assuming that the Lord does inflict devastation through earthquakes (or if they occur because of the sinfulness of those inflicted), then why do earthquakes predominantly occur along tectonic plate boundaries, happening in the same places year after year? Are the nations who live there inherently wicked? If they were to swap locations with Christians, would the occurrences of earthquakes change as well? Is the 1964 Alaskan earthquake, a magnitude 9.2, one of the highest ever recorded, proof that Anchorage is a sinful city? Or have they cleaned up their act, since no earthquake of such magnitude has happened since? Why has New York City received neither earthquake nor hurricane? For a given geographic location, is there any correlation between spiritual revival and earthquake frequency? Would God still bring an earthquake knowing that a few of the godly would be killed in it? If so, what's the maximum number of Christians that God would allow to perish therein?

> 16:19 The great city was split into three parts, and the cities of the nations fell. Babylon the great was remembered before God, to give her the cup of the wine of His fierce wrath.
> [20]And every island fled away, and the mountains were not found.
> [21]And huge hailstones, about one hundred pounds each, came down from heaven upon men; and men blasphemed God because of the plague of the hail, because its plague was extremely severe.

*Part III: The Visions*

## 23. Babylon the Mother of Harlots (17:1–17:5)

> 17:1 Then one of the seven angels who had the seven bowls came and spoke with me, saying, "Come here, I will show you the judgment of the great harlot who sits on many waters, ²with whom the kings of the earth committed acts of immorality, and those who dwell on the earth were made drunk with the wine of her immorality."

The harlot is painted with symbols that have specific meanings. She "sits on many waters"; according to Summers, "The waters upon which she sits are symbolical of the people over whom she reigns." Many scholars agree. She manages to seduce the "kings of the earth", in addition to "those who dwell on the earth."

If it's not obvious that the woman is a spiritual apparition, John says he was carried way in the Spirit:

> 17:3 And he carried me away in the Spirit into a wilderness; and I saw a woman sitting on a scarlet beast, full of blasphemous names, having seven heads and ten horns.

The spiritual vision and the wilderness as the harlot's lair recall Jesus' statement concerning demons in Matt. 12:43. Jesus says there that, "when the unclean spirit goes out of a man, it passes through waterless places seeking rest, and does not find it." The "waterless places" is a desert or wilderness, and symbolizes a lack of human receptivity to demonic infiltration. The unclean spirit leaves one person and seeks an abode in another, but fails to find an alternate host because deserts are uninhabitable. The same with the harlot—her surroundings are an uninhabitable wasteland. It's of her own doing, as the harlot mars the lives of those whom she touches.

She undoubtedly has power over the red beast that she sits upon. Red, the color of the dragon and the color of the rider war, is the beast, a creature that savages the human race. Having blasphemous names, the beast is arrayed against God. Commentators have debated the symbolism of the seven heads and ten horns. Many agree that they stand for nations, leaders, or some political entity.

> 17:4 The woman was clothed in purple and scarlet, and adorned with gold and precious stones and pearls, having in

her hand a gold cup full of abominations and of the unclean things of her immorality,

The purple clothing and expensive jewelry denote wealth or royalty; the scarlet again is for one who goes forth to kill. She entices her lovers to drink of her cup, to partake of her fornication, to have sex with her. The fornication symbolizes their participation in a false religion or in the worship of false gods. The "unclean things" bar the participants from any relationship with the true God.

One of a few occurrences in Revelation to having something written on one's forehead, the harlot has such. Here is displayed the intentions of her heart and the course of her pursuits.

> 17:5 and on her forehead a name was written, a mystery, "BABYLON THE GREAT, THE MOTHER OF HARLOTS AND OF THE ABOMINATIONS OF THE EARTH."

John says the name is a "mystery" (Greek *mustarion*), the word appearing in critical passages throughout the NT. *Mustarion* means not only the obvious—a mystery—but also refers to a matter that's not easily grasped, one that requires meditation to comprehend the profound significance of. A *mystery* also refers to something that's marveled over: in the next two verses John "wonders greatly" about the woman, and the angel explains the mystery.

Paul uses this same sense in Eph. 1:19, "the mystery of His will". In spite of centuries dominated by theology that contradicts common sense, God's will is not a mystery in the sense that it cannot be understood or that God commits or condones perverse acts that would be denounced had the same been committed by human hands. God's will is not mysterious. It's plainly written in the Bible. Even simple folk understand it (and are thereby saved). God's will is more often than not cast in black and white; the challenge for the disciple is in doing it—not understanding it. Addressing Christians, Paul in Col. 1:26,27 refers to Christ as a mystery. What he means is that the knowledge of Christ, his death and resurrection, his position in the Trinity, is deep and profound. Of course, the Christians whom Paul addressed knew Christ already, but Paul encouraged them to ponder the deep things of this simple truth: Christ died for our sins. So the harlot's "mystery" of 17:5 refers to something that must be pondered to grasp its magnitude and profoundness. It's a mystery why false religion has had and continues to have a stranglehold on the human race. Religious folk are dead certain that their religion is the correct one—not just correct in general but in every minutia of doctrine as well. A hundred have such certitude,

*Part III: The Visions*

and not one agrees with another, but none has ever paused to consider that he might be wrong, and one of the ninety-nine right. This is just one of the mysteries of religion.

\*

She is the city Babylon, and as symbolic biblical cities aggregate citizens for a common purpose, all the citizens partake of the cup of the harlot's fornication. But why is the city named Babylon? There are few, if any, metaphorical or symbolic references to Babylon in the Scriptures. Some have attempted to link Revelation's Babylon to the Babel of Genesis, but there're few correlations aside from geographic location. Babylon was simply the land of exile for Judah. But as such it's the antithesis of the Promised Land—it's the land of punishment, the place where God did not intend his people to be.

Examining what the Bible says about Babylon, Daniel's vision of the statue places it at the head with subsequent empires comprising the chest, thighs, legs, and feet:

> Dan. 2:31"You, O king, were looking and behold, there was a single great statue; that statue, which was large and of extraordinary splendor, was standing in front of you, and its appearance was awesome.
> $^{32}$"The head of that statue was made of fine gold, its breast and its arms of silver, its belly and its thighs of bronze,
> $^{33}$its legs of iron, its feet partly of iron and partly of clay.
> . . . . . . . . . .
> $^{38b}$ You are the head of gold.
> $^{39}$"After you there will arise another kingdom inferior to you, then another third kingdom of bronze, which will rule over all the earth.
> $^{40}$"Then there will be a fourth kingdom as strong as iron; inasmuch as iron crushes and shatters all things, so, like iron that breaks in pieces, it will crush and break all these in pieces.

The progression of metals from head to toes is not random, but has symbolic meaning. Of all the statue's metals, gold is the most beautiful. It does not tarnish and lose its luster. It's the easiest to forge, requires the least amount of skill and knowledge to work, and is extremely malleable. But of the metals listed, gold is the least common and has the least practical use. On the other hand, silver has some practical uses, more so than gold, but not as many as bronze, which before the Iron Age was used for weaponry and for armor (the ancients' interest in metals was foremost for imple-

*Part III: The Visions*

ments of warfare). Progressing down the statue, the metal's ores become more common, but require more resources and technology to smelt and to forge into weapons. Bronze is an alloy comprised mostly of copper, but is stronger than copper because of the tin. Replacing copper with bronze was a technological breakthrough in the ancient world.

The last of the statue's metals is iron. When the Bible speaks of iron, it's talking about both iron and steel. Steel is iron with a residual amount (perhaps a couple percent) of carbon—but this alone is insufficient to make steel, as the impurities, particularly sulfur and phosphorous, must be purged, otherwise the steel will have no strength. Owing to these difficulties, steel could not be mass-produced until modern times. The ancients knew of steel, but had difficulty making it. In their eyes it was still iron, howbeit in a strengthened form. Converting iron to steel was a time-consuming, delicate, and arduous process. Revelation prophesies that Jesus will rule "with a rod of iron" (2:27; 12:5; 19:15). Obviously the "rod of iron" is strong. It's actually a rod of steel; an iron rod, iron absent refinement, would be too brittle and would break too easily, and therefore cannot be the rod John wrote about. Iron, however, is in many ways the opposite of gold. The ore is very common—the earth's core is iron; that's why there're magnetic poles. Smelting iron from its ore is difficult (whereas extracting gold is easy), requiring a high level of technology, large furnaces, and plenty of charcoal. (In fact, some have speculated that Europe was deforested to supply the quantities of charcoal necessary to convert iron into steel.)

These metals symbolize empires; scholars attribute the golden head to Babylon, the silver chest to the Medes and Persians, the bronze thighs to the Greeks and Macedonians, and the legs to the Romans. As the empires are traversed head to foot, the sophistication of each increases, and therefore its longevity. The older, Mesopotamian empires rose up swiftly and disappeared overnight because they hadn't the infrastructure of civilization to sustain them. On the opposite end of the spectrum was Rome, which lasted several hundred years, whose laws and religion were folded into the barbarian countries that it spawned. Rome likewise had infused in it the culture of the Greeks, who taught mankind what the mind is for, how to think abstractly. Though Alexander the Great's Macedonian Empire didn't last long, it, together with the Greeks, dominated the Mediterranean for a couple centuries. Its influence has lasted until modern times, like Rome. Roman law, the Roman army, Roman engineering—these in combination with their success in annexing and assimilating their neighbors—prevented them

*Part III: The Visions*

from disintegrating in the same way that the Babylonians did. In these respects the empires resemble their metals in the vision of the statue.

But Babylon is gold, and Rome iron. Gold is beautiful, and iron at best is plain. How does Babylon resemble the glitter of gold? Perhaps the luster and beauty of the metals symbolize each government's sponsorship of religion as the main purpose of human existence. The Babylonians stand in for their contemporaries the Egyptians, who built the pyramids out of their superstitions concerning death and the afterlife. On the other hand, the Greek, and subsequently Roman, gods served to explain the irrational turn of events in human affairs, but Greek intellectual thought was untethered from religion, explaining scientific phenomena without reference to the gods. The Romans followed in course. Although they had cultic devotion to their gods, by the time of the Romans the government was severed from the sponsorship of any single pagan religion, in contrast to the Babylonians.

These attempts to explain the reference in Revelation to Babylon are as much speculation as fact, seeing that there's not much Scripture to support any theory. But the objects in these visions must mean something, and if they have meaning, then God intends for them to be deciphered. At least that's the age-old wisdom.

## 24. The Mystery of the Woman (17:6–17:18)

Though a spiritual apparition, the harlot is described with such detail to make her one of the easier of Revelation's figures to place. As prior verses attest, her trade is prostitution, and her clientele has made her rich. According to the next verse, she delights in persecuting the saints:

> 17:6 And I saw the woman drunk with the blood of the saints, and with the blood of the witnesses of Jesus. When I saw her, I wondered greatly.

The beast with its heads and horns corresponds to rulers and kingdoms on the earth. Beasts in Scripture are out to conquer and devour. This one comes out of the abyss, home to foul creatures.

> 17:7 And the angel said to me, "Why do you wonder? I will tell you the mystery of the woman and of the beast that carries her, which has the seven heads and the ten horns.

> [8] "The beast that you saw was, and is not, and is about to come up out of the abyss and go to destruction. And those who dwell on the earth, whose name has not been written in the book of life from the foundation of the world, will wonder when they see the beast, that he was and is not and will come.

The "was and is not and will come" from 17:8b is alluded to in 17:10. The time synchronization is clear: some of it had been fulfilled by the first century, while more of it was to be fulfilled. The symbolism of the vision is intended to be understood by "the mind which has wisdom". If this can't be figured out, what in Revelation can be?

> 17:9 "Here is the mind which has wisdom. The seven heads are seven mountains on which the woman sits,
> [10] and they are seven kings; five have fallen, one is, the other has not yet come; and when he comes, he must remain a little while.
> [11] "The beast which was and is not, is himself also an eighth and is one of the seven, and he goes to destruction.
> [12] "The ten horns which you saw are ten kings who have not yet received a kingdom, but they receive authority as kings with the beast for one hour.
> [13] "These have one purpose, and they give their power and authority to the beast.

Since the beast on which the harlot sits existed in John's day, the harlot must've too. With glee, Bible scholars name the Roman emperors who are the kings in these verses. But the harlot is the central figure, not the beast that supports her. The harlot symbolizes the practice of pagan, idolatrous worship, and by extension symbolizes any religion in opposition to the truth, which opposition is again confirmed by the next verse:

> 17:14 "These will wage war against the Lamb, and the Lamb will overcome them, because He is Lord of lords and King of kings, and those who are with Him are the called and chosen and faithful."

On a side note, water equated to peoples has its biblical grounds in the next verse:

*Part III: The Visions*

17:15 And he said to me, "The waters which you saw where the harlot sits, are peoples and multitudes and nations and tongues.
¹⁶"And the ten horns which you saw, and the beast, these will hate the harlot and will make her desolate and naked, and will eat her flesh and will burn her up with fire.
¹⁷"For God has put it in their hearts to execute His purpose by having a common purpose, and by giving their kingdom to the beast, until the words of God will be fulfilled.

The woman is either loved or hated, and though the masses swoon in their support of the harlot called paganism, the empire, presumably represented by the beast, and the leaders of this empire, represented by the horns, are jealous and fearful of the sway she has over the populace. Thus, they see her as a competitive threat to their own fortune and well-being, and so, not complacent with their position in subordination to her, rebel against her. Such is the case in history: an oppressive religion's stranglehold poses a political threat to the ruling class, resulting in enmity between the two. The harlot is hated even by sinners.

Pitting the forces of good against the forces of evil is so ingrained in the mind that one tends to frame all conflicts in this manner. This is not the case. Not all evil men move in unison. In 17:16 there is a power struggle of wicked men contending against other wicked men. Revelation insinuates that Satan does not have direct control over the thoughts and actions of mankind. Once a man is corrupted with sin, the lusts so implanted impel the man to evil deeds, but nevertheless deeds independent of the devil's direct control. Satan therefore cannot animate mankind in coordinated action, 17:16 being an example. In 17:17 God uses this to work his own ends, demonstrating his sovereignty even over those who are in opposition, whose free wills are unconstrained. It's by his wisdom that God manipulates those who oppose him.

17:18 "The woman whom you saw is the great city, which reigns over the kings of the earth."

## 25. The End of Babylon (18:1–19:3)

As Revelation is the end of many things, the whore must meet hers. The word "fallen" in 18:2 means just that.

*Part III: The Visions*

18:1 After these things I saw another angel coming down from heaven, having great authority, and the earth was illumined with his glory.
²And he cried out with a mighty voice, saying, "Fallen, fallen is Babylon the great! She has become a dwelling place of demons and a prison of every unclean spirit, and a prison of every unclean and hateful bird.

Agreeing with what the Gospels teach, in 18:2 "demons" is used interchangeably with "unclean spirits". There're demons that roam this earth looking for minds to inject unclean thoughts into—unclean, leveraged from the Law's concept of clean and unclean but applied to spiritual beings. Sexual perversion, violence, abuse, foul language—these are readily recognized as having a demonic origin. Religion is not. Demons were at work in the frenzy over Artemis in Acts 19. So they are today, only they dwell in certain churches (they did in Jesus' day [Mark 1:23]) and seminaries and universities, which are haunts of unclean spirits, analogous to the foul birds in 18:2 that prey on dead carcasses, which Moses wrote were odious (Lev. 11:13). These unclean spirits wail whenever they hear of the virgin birth or the deity of Jesus. The Babylonian woman attracts these spirits—and so do those who are opposed to the truth.

The rulers' promotion of false religion in 18:3 is compared to an orgy:

18:3 "For all the nations have drunk of the wine of the passion of her immorality, and the kings of the earth have committed acts of immorality with her, and the merchants of the earth have become rich by the wealth of her sensuality."

The descriptions of the beast that this woman sits on and the specific prophecies point to a fulfillment in John's time. Since events in prior chapters have yet to come to pass, the sequence of fulfillment of John's visions is not progressive with respect to earth-time. On the other hand, the harlot is a prototype for all ungodly religious systems, so one expects to find her straddling centuries of history.

Some have said that the harlot is the Roman Catholic Church. The error in this assertion is committed by taking a character in a spiritual vision and connecting it to a single earthly institution, a denomination in this case. The Catholic Church is nearly two thousand years old, and its disposition has turned throughout the centuries. Although the Reformation Protestants were quick to identify

## Part III: The Visions

the harlot as the Roman Church, in this century only one devoid of understanding would make the same claim. But some do, and they reach back several hundred years for damning evidence. Are Germans an aggressive and bellicose people who gravitate towards authoritarian governments? In the first part the twentieth century they were—but they've changed since then. Catholicism has changed over the course of time. So has Protestantism. When given the upper hand, Protestants, and not just Catholics, didn't tolerate any who disagreed with them. Few contradict the consensus of the age in which they live, though most pride themselves in being free thinkers. In the sixteenth century, religious tolerance was not esteemed as a virtue, Catholic and Protestant alike.

> 18:4 I heard another voice from heaven, saying, "Come out of her, my people, so that you will not participate in her sins and receive of her plagues;

One marvels at why an angel admonishes Christians to refrain from participating in the sins of the harlot, but the extent to which Christians indulge in sin comes as no surprise to those who've attended church for any length of time. Since the whore is associated with pagan gods, there must've been Christians participating in such idolatry. Christians can fall into idolatry just like any other sin, hence the need for John to end his first epistle with this warning:

> 1 John 5:21 Little children, guard yourselves from idols.

Contrast the above to what Paul writes:

> Eph 5:5 For this you know with certainty, that no immoral or impure person or covetous man, who is an idolater, has an inheritance in the kingdom of Christ and God.

Doctrines concerning sin will always be controversial for these reasons.

> 18:5 for her sins have piled up as high as heaven, and God has remembered her iniquities.
> 6"Pay her back even as she has paid, and give back to her double according to her deeds; in the cup which she has mixed, mix twice as much for her.
> 7"To the degree that she glorified herself and lived sensuously, to the same degree give her torment and mourning; for she

*Part III: The Visions*

says in her heart, 'I SIT AS A QUEEN AND I AM NOT A WIDOW, and will never see mourning.'
⁸"For this reason in one day her plagues will come, pestilence and mourning and famine, and she will be burned up with fire; for the Lord God who judges her is strong.

She boasts that she's a queen and not a widow, a boast of her greatest strength, the ability to allure men. The lovers heap riches upon her, hence the queen-reference. Typical of God in judgment, her downfall is sudden and severe when it finally does come. All her transgressions have been tallied and folded into her sentence. John expounds for several more verses.

18:9 "And the kings of the earth, who committed acts of immorality and lived sensuously with her, will weep and lament over her when they see the smoke of her burning,
¹⁰standing at a distance because of the fear of her torment, saying, 'Woe, woe, the great city, Babylon, the strong city! For in one hour your judgment has come.'
¹¹"And the merchants of the earth weep and mourn over her, because no one buys their cargoes any more—
¹²cargoes of gold and silver and precious stones and pearls and fine linen and purple and silk and scarlet, and every kind of citron wood and every article of ivory and every article made from very costly wood and bronze and iron and marble,
¹³and cinnamon and spice and incense and perfume and frankincense and wine and olive oil and fine flour and wheat and cattle and sheep, and cargoes of horses and chariots and slaves and human lives.
¹⁴"The fruit you long for has gone from you, and all things that were luxurious and splendid have passed away from you and men will no longer find them.
¹⁵"The merchants of these things, who became rich from her, will stand at a distance because of the fear of her torment, weeping and mourning,
¹⁶saying, 'Woe, woe, the great city, she who was clothed in fine linen and purple and scarlet, and adorned with gold and precious stones and pearls;
¹⁷for in one hour such great wealth has been laid waste!' And every shipmaster and every passenger and sailor, and as many as make their living by the sea, stood at a distance,

*Part III: The Visions*

[18]and were crying out as they saw the smoke of her burning, saying, 'What city is like the great city?'
[19]"And they threw dust on their heads and were crying out, weeping and mourning, saying, 'Woe, woe, the great city, in which all who had ships at sea became rich by her wealth, for in one hour she has been laid waste!'
[20]"Rejoice over her, O heaven, and you saints and apostles and prophets, because God has pronounced judgment for you against her."
[21] Then a strong angel took up a stone like a great millstone and threw it into the sea, saying, "So will Babylon, the great city, be thrown down with violence, and will not be found any longer.
[22]"And the sound of harpists and musicians and flute-players and trumpeters will not be heard in you any longer; and no craftsman of any craft will be found in you any longer; and the sound of a mill will not be heard in you any longer;
[23]and the light of a lamp will not shine in you any longer; and the voice of the bridegroom and bride will not be heard in you any longer; for your merchants were the great men of the earth, because all the nations were deceived by your sorcery.
[24]"And in her was found the blood of prophets and of saints and of all who have been slain on the earth."

Prophesying the fallout from the harlot's demise, John shifts words when referring to the woman, using the alternate names "city" or "great city", repeated in 18:10 (2 times), 18:16 (2 times), 18:18, and 18:19. He also details the wealth lost as a result of her destruction, not only her wealth but also the wealth of those who had profited from her. Her destruction is viewed from a spectator's perspective. Just as one watches the spectacular sight of a building being leveled by the detonation of carefully placed explosives, so is the scene of her destruction by those who are fortunate enough to witness it but not partake of it. The impression is of a city, the collection of those whose hearts are given to the woman, going up in flames, and of merchants who've lost their fortunes.

The suddenness of her end and the finality of it are remarkable, so much so that it should be easy to match the woman to her earthly counterpart. The end of paganism and idolatry was swift and final. Paganism was eradicated quickly in the Roman Empire, and as missionaries spread out beyond its borders, so with them did the demise of paganism. And it has never been reinstated. Though intertwined in most aspects of ancient society, those aspects were

*Part III: The Visions*

revamped with the insertion of Christianity. So the harlot could symbolize pagan, idolatrous worship.

But from a larger perspective, she's the archetype of any false religion or ungodly philosophy that has dominated or will dominate mankind. Each has a quick end. Modern liberalism is an example. Concerning any philosophy that acquires a grip over the hearts and minds of men and women, one might argue that it's God's judgment to vanish overnight. Just as years ago devout Christians who were repressed by the then-corrupt leadership of the Roman Catholic Church claimed that the Revelation-whore is the Catholic Church, so one expects nowadays to hear the same claims for Islam instead of Catholicism. The woman doesn't symbolize any single religion or philosophy, but all of them, and at phases in their evolution.

All of heaven is elated over her end. Even the end of the beast or the false prophet is not accompanied by such rejoicing.

> 19:1 After these things I heard something like a loud voice of a great multitude in heaven, saying, "Hallelujah! Salvation and glory and power belong to our God;
> ²BECAUSE HIS JUDGMENTS ARE TRUE AND RIGHTEOUS; for He has judged the great harlot who was corrupting the earth with her immorality, and HE HAS AVENGED THE BLOOD OF HIS BOND-SERVANTS ON HER."
> ³And a second time they said, "Hallelujah! HER SMOKE RISES UP FOREVER AND EVER."

Just as Revelation was a comfort to the early Christians, assuring them that the city of paganism will meet its end, the brethren in this century can take comfort that God will judge all false religion and philosophy in the same way. Christians can rest assured knowing that the Left's foolish philosophies will meet the same fate as the whore: a sudden end with no hope of resurrection. Having been reminded in 19:2, it's ultimately because of the justice of God that judgment must strike down the great harlot.

## 26. Long-Awaited Endings (19:4–19:21)

John lists the marriage supper of the Lamb, the end of the beast, and the triumphant return of Jesus in rapid succession, as though the events happen within a short time (earth-time that is). One

*Part III: The Visions*

cannot assume that this is the case, as the Bible starting in Genesis chronicles events irrespective of the true duration of the epoch. In other words, the first chapter of Genesis covers many millenia, whereas the latter half of John's Gospel covers but two weeks of Jesus' life.

> 19:4 And the twenty-four elders and the four living creatures fell down and worshiped God who sits on the throne saying, "Amen Hallelujah!"
> 
> ⁵And a voice came from the throne, saying, "Give praise to our God, all you His bond-servants, you who fear Him, the small and the great."
> 
> ⁶Then I heard something like the voice of a great multitude and like the sound of many waters and like the sound of mighty peals of thunder, saying, "Hallelujah! For the Lord our God, the Almighty, reigns.

Those gathered around the throne of God are concerned with what happens on earth, and respond accordingly. Just as the king's courtiers cheer the advancements of the king's interests, those in God's court do the same.

One of the most anticipated events of the twentieth Century was the long-awaited wedding of Prince Charles. In this way—but greater—the marriage supper of the Lamb has been anticipated for ages. Heaven's not a dull place, and an event this momentous will not pass by quietly.

> 19:7 "Let us rejoice and be glad and give the glory to Him, for the marriage of the Lamb has come and His bride has made herself ready."
> 
> ⁸It was given to her to clothe herself in fine linen, bright and clean; for the fine linen is the righteous acts of the saints.
> 
> ⁹Then he said to me, "Write, 'Blessed are those who are invited to the marriage supper of the Lamb.'" And he said to me, "These are true words of God."

In biblical times ceremonial garments were made of fine linen and were reserved for special occasions. These in 19:5 are "bright and clean", symbolic of purity. And they are given to the bride. In the Bible when clothes are given from God to man, as in 3:18 and Gen. 3:21, it's symbolic of God conferring righteousness on the recipient. But in 19:8 these garments of fine linen, though given by God, are the "righteous acts of the saints". This is another example

*Part III: The Visions*

of God's sovereignty vs. man's free will. God bestows righteousness. This corresponds to the "was given" in 19:8. But man is expected to walk in righteousness, corresponding to the "righteous acts of the saints" in 19:8. God does not bestow righteousness on those who do no not have righteous acts. However, the righteous acts of man are not a means of earning God's righteousness. The balance between sovereignty and free will is again expressed in 19:9. "Blessed are those who are invited to the marriage supper" implies that the invitation is the exercise of God's will. It is. But God invites only those who've softened their hearts towards his Son.

In Revelation Jesus is portrayed as both the Lamb and the King of Kings, the occurrences even in close proximity to one another. The two are the antithesis of each other, but it's as the former that Jesus appears in the marriage supper of the Lamb. Like a story book, one expects the King of Kings, the strong, triumphant conqueror, to come and claim his bride—but along comes the meek Lamb instead. It was through love that the Lamb Jesus cleansed his bride, preparing her for the day of matrimony, so it's fitting he appear as such to claim her.

After this, the voice in the vision speaks again. One expects the same being to have been speaking to John throughout the visions, and one surmises that John has never seen the one speaking to him, but has only heard his voice. Having known Jesus personally, John should easily recognize him, but the Jesus that John knew was the Son of man absent his resurrected glory, the brilliance of which overshadows his earthly countenance. In other words, the Jesus whom John knew on earth was the Son of God who walked in perfect love and holiness, but the Jesus in heaven is enshrined in so much splendor of glory that this radiance dominates his appearance, at times making it difficult to correlate the heavenly person and the earthly. The voice comes from one close to the presence of God, and has the sound of a trumpet or the sound of many waters. It has such majesty that John believes it must be the glorified Christ speaking to him. John makes the mistake of worshipping him.

> 19:10 Then I fell at his feet to worship him. But he said to me, "Do not do that; I am a fellow servant of yours and your brethren who hold the testimony of Jesus; worship God. For the testimony of Jesus is the spirit of prophecy."

\*

The last phrase in 19:10 is one of the most important guidelines the Bible gives concerning prophecy. Christians, through the gift of

*Part III: The Visions*

prophecy (for one), have the ability to prophesy. Prophetic utterances must be judged, as Paul instructed the Corinthians:

> 1 Cor. 14:29 Let two or three prophets speak, and let the others pass judgment.

Prophecies should not be received without being critically examined. Paul instructs the Corinthians to allow a few prophets to speak. What he means by, "Let two or three prophets speak", is, *let a handful at a time speak*. The words "two or three" are an idiom—the same idiom used when Jesus said, "where two or three have gathered" (Matt. 18:20); he meant *where a handful are gathered*. Jesus didn't mean exactly two or three but approximately two or three. The first means of judging a prophecy is to verify that it doesn't contradict any of the teachings of the Bible. In the early days of the Charismatic movement, some pockets of followers became more developed in prayer and yielding to the Holy Spirit than in their understanding of the Word of God. As a result, in their prayer meetings some so-called prophecies were received that were unscriptural. This invariably resulted in one problem or another, and has damaged the reputation of the movement as a whole. But 19:10 provides the means of judging a prophecy: any prophecy must exalt the testimony of Jesus. Put another way, the spirit of prophecy and the testimony of Jesus are equivalent, therefore one expects to hear in a prophecy something that testifies of Jesus, his works, who he is. A true Holy Spirit-inspired prophecy will exalt Jesus—and no other man.

\*

Any preacher worth his salt has strutted the podium, preaching out of the following passage:

> 19:11 And I saw heaven opened, and behold, a white horse, and He who sat on it is called Faithful and True, and in righteousness He judges and wages war.
> [12] His eyes are a flame of fire, and on His head are many diadems; and He has a name written on Him which no one knows except Himself.
> [13] He is clothed with a robe dipped in blood, and His name is called The Word of God.
> [14] And the armies which are in heaven, clothed in fine linen, white and clean, were following Him on white horses.
> [15] From His mouth comes a sharp sword, so that with it He may strike down the nations, and He will rule them with a

*Part III: The Visions*

> rod of iron; and He treads the wine press of the fierce wrath of God, the Almighty.
> [16]And on His robe and on His thigh He has a name written, "KING OF KINGS, AND LORD OF LORDS."

One of the great metaphors of the Bible, "he treads the wine press of the fierce wrath of God the Almighty", repeated from 14:19. This is Jesus coming the second time. The first was to pay for the sins of mankind. But his Second Coming will not be to solve the sin problem (Heb. 9:28). He comes a second time to wage war and destroy those who are opposed to him—not appearing as the Lamb of God but as a conquering warrior. This makes Revelation different than most books of the NT, because the other books (for the most part) portray him as the Lamb, not the warrior. But he's both, incomplete without either. Hence, Revelation's a crucial part of the NT, since it magnifies him in this latter guise.

> 19:17 Then I saw an angel standing in the sun, and he cried out with a loud voice, saying to all the birds which fly in midheaven, "Come, assemble for the great supper of God, [18]so that you may eat the flesh of kings and the flesh of commanders and the flesh of mighty men and the flesh of horses and of those who sit on them and the flesh of all men, both free men and slaves, and small and great."

The word "midheaven" is used three times in Revelation, and it means *very high in the sky*. This is where vultures, eagles, and other unclean birds soar in search of a carcass. Not only will the Lord of Hosts slaughter his foes, but they'll suffer the further ignominy of their unburied corpses delivered to the foul birds. Since this defilement is more repugnant to one from the Near East than to us, the Western ear is not attuned to the hideousness of it.

The mention in 19:18 of horses and slaves makes one wonder how this could be fulfilled in modern times. On the other hand, where can one find enough vultures to eat all this flesh before it decomposes? Is this vision figurative, and not to be taken literally? But one thing's certain: the hardness of man's heart is complete. Those who will have survived all the plagues God unleashes on them, knowing it to be the wrath of God—these survivors are still unrepentant. In the folly of their deception, they gather for the return of Jesus, thinking they can overpower him upon entry.

*Part III: The Visions*

19:19 And I saw the beast and the kings of the earth and their armies assembled to make war against Him who sat on the horse and against His army.
[20]And the beast was seized, and with him the false prophet who performed the signs in his presence, by which he deceived those who had received the mark of the beast and those who worshiped his image; these two were thrown alive into the lake of fire which burns with brimstone.
[21]And the rest were killed with the sword which came from the mouth of Him who sat on the horse, and all the birds were filled with their flesh.

## 27. First, the Abyss, then the Lake of Fire (20:1–20:15)

The abyss, that spiritual toxic-waste dump, incarcerating filthy creatures lest they defile the earth, appears one last time. It's not necessarily a place of torment, like the Lake of Fire. But it has a lid over it, and is kept locked, should anything seep out.

> 20:1 Then I saw an angel coming down from heaven, holding the key of the abyss and a great chain in his hand.
> [2]And he laid hold of the dragon, the serpent of old, who is the devil and Satan, and bound him for a thousand years;
> [3]and he threw him into the abyss, and shut it and sealed it over him, so that he would not deceive the nations any longer, until the thousand years were completed; after these things he must be released for a short time.

In 20:2 John lists Satan's aliases, each of his defining characteristics embedded in one of the names. As the *dragon* he's the destroyer, the one roaming the earth looking to kill, steal, and destroy. As the *serpent* he's the cunning deceiver, the one who plants lies in the minds of men, the father of deception, deceit, and all false religion and philosophies. As the *devil*, the Greek word *diabolos*, he's the slanderer, the malicious gossip (according to the UBS *Greek NT*), the accuser of the brethren. And as *Satan*, he's the anointed cherub Lucifer who conceived sin in his heart and rebelled against God.

Like all spiritual beings, once created Satan cannot be destroyed, so he must be bound instead. And how easily done this is,

*Part III: The Visions*

as it only takes one angel with a chain to bind him up and cast him into the pit. The only mystery is why the Lord's disciples in this age are engaged in protracted wars against him and his cohorts. Jesus by his death and resurrection was given authority over all things in heaven and earth. Why now the constant struggles? It's because God allows it to be so. The work of salvation is progressive, and isn't complete until the end of Revelation. In this dispensation Satan is allowed to roam the earth, and his legions are at war against the Faithful. But though God allows the devil to test the faith of Christians and expects believers to persevere through each trial, the outcome is a foregone conclusion, as the Father has left promises in his Word, and has given the Holy Spirit as a helper.

But Satan is to be held for a thousand years, the millennial rule of Christ. Jesus will have absolute rule in the millennia, and won't allow the rogue creature to even attempt to perturb it. In addition, in 20:4 there are "thrones" created, not just a single throne for Jesus. He's accompanied in his reign by those who were most faithful to him on earth, as measured by a believer's defiance in the face of opposition by the world. These share in the regal responsibilities, and according to 20:6 are priests, which in this context means they're attendants to Jesus' holy presence.

> 20:4 Then I saw thrones, and they sat on them, and judgment was given to them. And I saw the souls of those who had been beheaded because of their testimony of Jesus and because of the word of God, and those who had not worshiped the beast or his image, and had not received the mark on their forehead and on their hand; and they came to life and reigned with Christ for a thousand years.

The word "beheaded" in 20:4 refers to the method that the Romans used for executing their own citizens (Paul for example), in this case Roman persecution of Christians. The theories that many of the visions and prophecies of Revelation have come to pass are not without evidence.

> 20:5 The rest of the dead did not come to life until the thousand years were completed. This is the first resurrection. ⁶Blessed and holy is the one who has a part in the first resurrection; over these the second death has no power, but they will be priests of God and of Christ and will reign with Him for a thousand years.

## Part III: The Visions

There's some confusion when the Bible speaks of resurrection, as it has multiple meanings. The dispute between the Pharisees and Sadducees over the doctrine of the resurrection of the dead is actually a dispute concerning life after death. One does not cease to exist after he or she dies; instead, his or her body is resurrected. Therefore all are resurrected, both the godly and the wicked, but what they're resurrected to differs. The doctrine of the "resurrection of the dead and eternal judgment" is one of the five elementary doctrines ("teaching" in Heb. 6:1 implies *doctrines*) listed in Hebrews:

> Heb. 6:1 Therefore leaving the elementary teaching about the Christ, let us press on to maturity, not laying again a foundation of repentance from dead works and of faith toward God,
> ²of instruction about washings and laying on of hands, and the resurrection of the dead and eternal judgment.

What happens to people after they die, where they go, what state they'll be in, and how they'll be judged are foundational Christian doctrines. Revelation 20 is a main piece of the puzzle. The first resurrection is a resurrection to glory, whereas the second resurrection is reserved for those who never received Christ. The second resurrection results in the Second Death—not a physical death but a final condemnation.

There'll be survivors of the judgments, so that during the millennium there'll be ordinary human beings dwelling on the earth, and their abilities to choose good or evil will be left intact. But since Satan will have been bound, there'll be no source of temptation for them. And with Christ's benevolent yet firm rule over mankind, there can be no opportunity for sin. But after the thousand years is complete, Satan will be released from the abyss, unrepentant, and will continue in his old ways. God's justice extends to this once-great cherub one more opportunity to repent.

> 20:7 When the thousand years are completed, Satan will be released from his prison,
> ⁸and will come out to deceive the nations which are in the four corners of the earth, Gog and Magog, to gather them together for the war; the number of them is like the sand of the seashore.
> ⁹And they came up on the broad plain of the earth and surrounded the camp of the saints and the beloved city, and fire came down from heaven and devoured them.

*Part III: The Visions*

But Satan can never repent and be restored to the Father because his nature is intransigent. He's able to corrupt even those who are firsthand witnesses to the reign of Christ, something to be noted about human nature and man's free will.

\*

These nations come from the four corners of the earth, i.e. the remotest parts, and John refers to them as Gog and Magog, the name taken from Ezekiel. Magog is listed in Gen. 10:2 as a son of Japheth the son of Noah. Gen. 10:5 says that "From these the coastlands of the nations were separated into their lands, every one according to his language, according to their families, into their nations." Because *Gog and Magog* rhyme, and because the only thing Genesis says about Magog is that he settled long ago in a some unknown, remote land, in Ezekiel *Gog and Magog* had come to mean some far-away nation, in the same way that we say *Timbuktu* or *all the way to Timbuktu*. Even if Magog's location were known, barbarian tribes have migrated over the years. (Not to mention that 20:7 is post-millennium.) What follows is the original reference in Ezekiel to Gog and Magog. The prophecy over them extends into the thirty-ninth chapter.

> Ezek. 38:2 "Son of man, set your face toward Gog of the land of Magog, the prince of Rosh, Meshech and Tubal, and prophesy against him
> ³and say, 'Thus says the Lord GOD, "Behold, I am against you, O Gog, prince of Rosh, Meshech and Tubal.

Some Bible prophecy experts have claimed that Gog and Magog is Russia, or more correctly the Soviet Union, as this claim has its roots in the Cold War. They said that, at the commencement of the tribulation, Russia will launch a preemptive strike against Israel, and the Russian army will be destroyed. They say that the prophecy concerns a nation that comes out of the north—Moscow is due north of Israel—and that the Russians are descendants of Gog and Magog. So popular was this belief in the United States, and so universally received across denominational barriers, that in the 1970s and early 1980s Christians were watching for indications of the Soviet preparation for the long-prophesied invasion, and hence the tribulation. Nowadays such a theory is nonsense, but impervious to these facts, some Christians have held steadfast (Christians in the United States, not Russian Christians). The then-superior forces of the 1970s Warsaw Pact Soviet alliance rapidly became obsolete during the 1980s, followed by the breakup of the Soviet Union. A lesson

*Part III: The Visions*

to be learned from this episode is that Christians must be on the guard to recognize when patriotic fervor spills over into theology.

\*

The twentieth chapter has a few key doctrinal passages. The next anticipates the judgment of the damned, the great White Throne judgment. This is in contrast to the judgment of believers in 2 Cor. 5:10, the judgment seat of Christ. God the Father presides over the judgment of the damned, whereas Jesus presides over the judgment of Christians.

> 20:10 And the devil who deceived them was thrown into the lake of fire and brimstone, where the beast and the false prophet are also; and they will be tormented day and night forever and ever.
> [11]Then I saw a great white throne and Him who sat upon it, from whose presence earth and heaven fled away, and no place was found for them.
> [12]And I saw the dead, the great and the small, standing before the throne, and books were opened; and another book was opened, which is the book of life; and the dead were judged from the things which were written in the books, according to their deeds.
> [13]And the sea gave up the dead which were in it, and death and Hades gave up the dead which were in them; and they were judged, every one of them according to their deeds.
> [14]Then death and Hades were thrown into the lake of fire. This is the second death, the lake of fire.
> [15]And if anyone's name was not found written in the book of life, he was thrown into the lake of fire.

Notice how 20:12 describes two sets of books. The first is a collection of books. Based on the judgment in 20:13, one deduces that these are the Books of Works. The second is a single book, the Book of Life. Those who are judged from the first set, the Books of Works, are all condemned. Man has always asserted that he can—and should—stand before God in judgment and be judged on the basis of his works. This is a strategy of failure. According to the above passage, man, when judged by his works, will be cast into the Lake of Fire. Man's works may seem adequate, even impressive, from a human perspective, but they fail to live up to the stringent standard that the holiness of God demands. God's holiness so far eclipses even the best of man's works that there must always be a gap between the works of man, who's fallen, and God, who's holy.

*Part III: The Visions*

When one substitutes the works of the Son for his own, only then can he bypass the White Throne judgment. His works are then presented before the judgment seat of Christ, but not for the purpose of determining if his name appears in the Book of Life or not.

Ending the passage, into the Lake of Fire goes not a creature but death and Hades themselves. As there's no escaping the Lake for any unclean creature, it's fitting that death and Hades be tossed in as well. This is the end of aging, of dying, of the sorrows that have accompanied man since that Pandora's Box was opened in the Garden.

## 28. The New Replaces the Old (21:1–22:5)

Exemplified by the anticipation over the new Jerusalem, there's an inherent pessimism in Christianity that's absent from humanism. The corruption of this life can't be straightened out by man's own doing, but requires God to bring a new Jerusalem down to earth. The NT instructs Christians how to live in a fallen world and specifies what a believer's moral responsibilities are. Christianity is a self-help religion—it teaches one to change himself or herself; humanism strives to change the world instead of oneself. Christianity works from the inside out; humanism attempts to work from the outside in. Humanistic philosophy attempts to change human nature but fails miserably instead. Only when the old passes away will the outside world be perfected. This long awaited day is described in Revelation 21:

> 21:1 Then I saw a new heaven and a new earth; for the first heaven and the first earth passed away, and there is no longer any sea.

According to Metzger, the word "new" in 21:1 does not mean "another" but a "radically different" kind of. Metzger later notes that throughout the Bible the sea "represents restlessness and insubordination (see Job 38:8-11; Ps. 89:9; Isa. 57:20)", hence its removal. To further elaborate on 21:1, in this context the word "heaven" should (again) be translated *sky* or *atmosphere*. This could extend to outer space—there's no telling how much is being replaced.

> 21:2 And I saw the holy city, new Jerusalem, coming down out of heaven from God, made ready as a bride adorned for her husband.

## Part III: The Visions

> ³And I heard a loud voice from the throne, saying, "Behold, the tabernacle of God is among men, and He will dwell among them, and they shall be His people, and God Himself will be among them,
> ⁴and He will wipe away every tear from their eyes; and there will no longer be any death; there will no longer be any mourning, or crying, or pain; the first things have passed away.
> ⁵And He who sits on the throne said, "Behold, I am making all things new." And He said, "Write, for these words are faithful and true."

The Father makes all things new in the lives of Christians. Just as the new Jerusalem must come from above, so change comes down from the Father by the implanted Word of God activated by the Holy Spirit. God is repairing broken families, comforting hearts, building moral fortitude.

Finally, after Jesus says "It is done", he proclaims a universal promise to the Church:

> 21:6 Then He said to me, "It is done. I am the Alpha and the Omega, the beginning and the end. I will give to the one who thirsts from the spring of the water of life without cost.

Jesus' mission is to provide water to those who thirst, spiritually speaking. God is pleased by those who have a spiritual hunger and spiritual thirst for him, and will visit them in spite of their faults. Jacob was chosen over Esau because he hungered after the birthright, and Esau did not. Even after David was dead, God delighted over him, his promises to him repeated and reaffirmed throughout the ages. Jesus heeded the cries of Blind Bartimaeus (Mark 10:46-52), calling him out of the crowd; likewise, the woman with the issue of blood (Mark 5:25-34) got Jesus' attention in spite of the crowd. Cornelius (Acts 10) became the first Gentile to receive Christ—this because of his many prayers and alms. Man likes those who are clean on the outside, who are amiable, sociable, or who have a charismatic personality. God likes those who are hungry.

A final encouragement to overcome, likewise accompanied with a promise to those who obey:

> 21:7 "He who overcomes will inherit these things, and I will be his God and he will be My son.

*Part III: The Visions*

⁸"But for the cowardly and unbelieving and abominable and murderers and immoral persons and sorcerers and idolaters and all liars, their part will be in the lake that burns with fire and brimstone, which is the second death."

Verse 21:8 insinuates that the opposite of overcoming is slinking into sin. The binary categories of overcomer and sinner are specified. No third category is listed. But the contrast is not between those who profess to be Christians and those who don't, but is between the actions of the one group vs. the other. It would do Christians well to heed this distinction; Jesus is not interested in what one professes but in what he does.

> 21:9 Then one of the seven angels who had the seven bowls full of the seven last plagues came and spoke with me, saying, "Come here, I will show you the bride, the wife of the Lamb." ¹⁰And he carried me away in the Spirit to a great and high mountain, and showed me the holy city, Jerusalem, coming down out of heaven from God,

What's implied in 21:9-10, strange at first, is that the bride is the new Jerusalem. But throughout the Bible, the Jerusalem from above is symbolical of more than one thing. For example, Paul in Galatians compares it to the new covenant:

> Gal. 4:24 This is allegorically speaking, for these women are two covenants: one proceeding from Mount Sinai bearing children who are to be slaves; she is Hagar.
> ²⁵Now this Hagar is Mount Sinai in Arabia and corresponds to the present Jerusalem, for she is in slavery with her children.
> ²⁶But the Jerusalem above is free; she is our mother.

In both 21:10 and Gal. 4:26, the new Jerusalem comes from above, or comes down to the earth. This means that it's of a purity that can never be achieved by human hands but can only come from God. Since the corruption of man precludes his building the new Jerusalem by his own hands, the only alternative is that it come down from heaven. The gap between God and man can only be closed by God's doing, not man's.

Sounding like the fourth chapter's description of heaven, John can only describe the beauty of the city in terms of gems and other precious stones and metals. The description of the city draws on OT

*Part III: The Visions*

parallels. The gems remind one of the hoshen, the breastplate that the High Priest wore (Exod. 28:29). The number twelve appears repeatedly, even 144 (12×12) cubits is used in 21:17. As the temple is measured in 11:1, the city is measured as well, symbolizing its perfection. The dimensions are noted in 21:15: 12,000 stadia (2410 km, 1500 miles) cubed. It's difficult to take this literally, if for no other reason than the fact that the city would be 2410 km (1500 miles) high. But the remark in 21:17, "...human measurements, which are also angelic measurements", makes one wonder if Revelation is insisting that these are literal measurements, and not symbolic in any way. Like the Most Holy Place, the symmetry of the city is also cubic. When in 21:25 John says there'll be no more night, (night throughout the Bible symbolic of evil and the day of temptation), one cannot conceive that the earth will stop spinning on its axis. Modern man in his scientific and technical glory can't imagine how verses such as these will be fulfilled. The increase in mankind's scientific knowledge-base only compounds the mystery surrounding passages such as these.

> 21:10 And he carried me away in the Spirit to a great and high mountain, and showed me the holy city, Jerusalem, coming down out of heaven from God,
> ¹¹having the glory of God. Her brilliance was like a very costly stone, as a stone of crystal-clear jasper.
> ¹²It had a great and high wall, with twelve gates, and at the gates twelve angels; and names were written on them, which are the names of the twelve tribes of the sons of Israel.
> ¹³There were three gates on the east and three gates on the north and three gates on the south and three gates on the west.
> ¹⁴And the wall of the city had twelve foundation stones, and on them were the twelve names of the twelve apostles of the Lamb.
> ¹⁵The one who spoke with me had a gold measuring rod to measure the city, and its gates and its wall.
> ¹⁶The city is laid out as a square, and its length is as great as the width; and he measured the city with the rod, fifteen hundred miles; its length and width and height are equal.
> ¹⁷And he measured its wall, seventy-two yards, according to human measurements, which are also angelic measurements.
> ¹⁸The material of the wall was jasper; and the city was pure gold, like clear glass.

## Part III: The Visions

[19]The foundation stones of the city wall were adorned with every kind of precious stone. The first foundation stone was jasper; the second, sapphire; the third, chalcedony; the fourth, emerald;

[20]the fifth, sardonyx; the sixth, sardius; the seventh, chrysolite; the eighth, beryl; the ninth, topaz; the tenth, chrysoprase; the eleventh, jacinth; the twelfth, amethyst.

[21] And the twelve gates were twelve pearls; each one of the gates was a single pearl. And the street of the city was pure gold, like transparent glass.

[22]I saw no temple in it, for the Lord God the Almighty and the Lamb are its temple.

[23]And the city has no need of the sun or of the moon to shine on it, for the glory of God has illumined it, and its lamp is the Lamb.

[24]The nations will walk by its light, and the kings of the earth will bring their glory into it.

[25]In the daytime (for there will be no night there) its gates will never be closed;

[26]and they will bring the glory and the honor of the nations into it;

[27]and nothing unclean, and no one who practices abomination and lying, shall ever come into it, but only those whose names are written in the Lamb's book of life.

The Tree of Life first appeared in the Garden of Eden. Adam and Eve were expelled from the Garden, and a cherub was posted to prevent them from reentering it (Gen. 3:24). The Bible is the history of mankind's journey back to the Tree of Life, the Tree finally reappearing in the second to the last chapter of the Bible. All this to undo the consequences of the original sin. The curse, first instated in Gen. 3:16-19, then codified in Deuteronomy (starting at Deut. 28:15), is finally lifted. It took much maneuvering by the Father to restore mankind's access to the Tree, and to remove the curse, but that has always been his will. A lot of poor theology is built on the premise that the curse is not a curse but is God's plan. A prime example is the assertion that from time to time that it's God's will for Christians to suffer sickness and disease. Sickness and disease are a part of the curse, and it has always been God's goal to cancel the curse, sickness included. But the reality is that Christians nevertheless are afflicted by it. The curse ends in 22:3.

*Part III: The Visions*

> 22:1 Then he showed me a river of the water of life, clear as crystal, coming from the throne of God and of the Lamb, ²in the middle of its street. On either side of the river was the tree of life, bearing twelve kinds of fruit, yielding its fruit every month; and the leaves of the tree were for the healing of the nations.
> ³There will no longer be any curse; and the throne of God and of the Lamb will be in it, and His bond-servants will serve Him;
> ⁴they will see His face, and His name will be on their foreheads.
> ⁵And there will no longer be any night; and they will not have need of the light of a lamp nor the light of the sun, because the Lord God will illumine them; and they will reign forever and ever.

The leaves from the Tree of Life (22:2) are for the healing of the nations. In this present age these leaves can be brought down to earth through the intercession of the Faithful who cry out to God with a pure heart. These leaves are the times of refreshing which come from the presence of the Lord (Acts 3:19). The leaves will heal ethnic and racial strife, or a citizenry oppressed by wickedness, or will end starvation, to name a few.

## 29. The Final Message (22:6–22:21)

With a message to the churches, Revelation ends in the same way it begins.

> 22:6 And he said to me, "These words are faithful and true"; and the Lord, the God of the spirits of the prophets, sent His angel to show to His bond-servants the things which must soon take place.

Either most of the prophecies of Revelation were for John's time ("the things which must soon take place"), or "soon" means *many centuries*. Said twice within a few verses, the broader message for all ages is this: Jesus is coming quickly.

> 22:7 "And behold, I am coming quickly. Blessed is he who heeds the words of the prophecy of this book."

*Part III: The Visions*

⁸I, John, am the one who heard and saw these things. And when I heard and saw, I fell down to worship at the feet of the angel who showed me these things.
⁹But he said to me, "Do not do that I am a fellow servant of yours and of your brethren the prophets and of those who heed the words of this book. Worship God."
¹⁰And he said to me, "Do not seal up the words of the prophecy of this book, for the time is near.

Based on the previous verse, it seems that John had finished writing Revelation by the time of these last words, confirming the theory that the visions occurred over several days, allowing pauses long enough for John to write.

Predestined judgment explains 22:11—it's like a football game where the score is such that both teams let the last few seconds of the clock run out in a game that's already been decided. The conclusion is sealed.

22:11 "Let the one who does wrong, still do wrong; and the one who is filthy, still be filthy; and let the one who is righteous, still practice righteousness; and the one who is holy, still keep himself holy."

One last time, like the messages to the churches, Jesus reaffirms who he is, encourages believers to do right, and reminds them of the rewards. On the other hand, sinners are compared to dogs (to Jews, dogs were dirty animals), and they are "outside" (22:15) the city, where the trash is heaped—incidentally, the same place Jesus was crucified. The grace extended to sinners comes to an end. They become refuse to be discarded.

As heretics in those days had begun to propagate modified versions of the NT epistles, John injects a stern warning in an attempt to dissuade them from doing this to his book, just as Paul for this reason wrote at least some of his epistles with his own hand, rather than using a scribe, so that the recipients would know that the scroll was authentic, as they would recognize his handwriting (Gal. 6:11).

22:12 "Behold, I am coming quickly, and My reward is with Me, to render to every man according to what he has done.
¹³"I am the Alpha and the Omega, the first and the last, the beginning and the end."

## Part III: The Visions

¹⁴Blessed are those who wash their robes, so that they may have the right to the tree of life, and may enter by the gates into the city.

¹⁵Outside are the dogs and the sorcerers and the immoral persons and the murderers and the idolaters, and everyone who loves and practices lying.

¹⁶"I, Jesus, have sent My angel to testify to you these things for the churches. I am the root and the descendant of David, the bright morning star."

¹⁷The Spirit and the bride say, "Come". And let the one who hears say, "Come". And let the one who is thirsty come; let the one who wishes take the water of life without cost.

¹⁸I testify to everyone who hears the words of the prophecy of this book: if anyone adds to them, God will add to him the plagues which are written in this book;

¹⁹and if anyone takes away from the words of the book of this prophecy, God will take away his part from the tree of life and from the holy city, which are written in this book.

²⁰He who testifies to these things says, "Yes, I am coming quickly". Amen. Come, Lord Jesus.

²¹The grace of the Lord Jesus be with all. Amen.

The words with which Revelation ends, and hence the entire Bible, take the breath away in their sobriety. They are nourishment to those afflicted, a chastisement to the disobedient, and a promise of the great hope of all Christianity, his soon coming.

# Part IV

# Epilogue

*Part IV: Epilogue*

In spite of the fog of understanding that Revelation is mired in, the themes are clear. For those who do right, Revelation is an encouragement; for those who do wrong, it's a warning. There's a reward for those who persevere in doing good; there's a day of reckoning for those who do evil. There're unseen forces in the parallel spirit-world that contend for the hearts and minds of those who dwell on the earth. All this leads up to the Second Coming of Christ, when the unseen will be replaced with the seen.

*

The hour is late. The Church in the United States is falling into a state of slumber. As the older generation dies off, the younger pales in comparison. The pews on which sat congregants for mid-week prayer meetings are empty. The demonstration of the power of the Spirit is being replaced by audio-visual stimulation. And as the Church goes, so does the country. Inevitably, this will result in the loss of freedom and prosperity—unless Christians repent and do the works of old.

But to the Faithful, the word is this: be vigilant and persevere until the end. To the overcomer, the one who's watchful as though he or she be taken by a thief in the night, rewards will be granted.

**Back Sections**

# Appendix A:
# The Third Horseman's Cost of Living Increase

> 6:5b "A quart of wheat for a denarius, and three quarts of barley for a denarius; and do not damage the oil and the wine."

This appendix estimates the cost of living imposed by the prices specified in 6:5b. Consider that there're approximately 200 calories per cup of slightly refined barley (called pearled barley; of course, the ancient's barley was a different strain than the modern one). A quart (a bit less than a liter) is 4 cups; 3 quarts of barley is therefore 2400 calories, which is a bit less than the minimum daily caloric intake needed by the average man. Assuming in John's time that every working man (there's more than one wage-earner per family) supports himself plus ½ of another person (reduced to ½, because the other is probably a child, or elderly relative, either requiring less nourishment than the average man, used as the standard), then this man would need a minimum of 3500 calories of sustenance per day. Even if he were to work 7 days a week, earning a denarius a day, at the inflated rate for barley specified by 6:5 he would only be able to purchase 69% of his family's caloric needs (and would live on barley soup!) In addition, this means he would have to spend his spare time scavenging for food, he and his children and infirm dependents. The weaker ones would stand a good chance of dying. There would be no extra money for clothing or other necessities. The price of barley in 6:5 signifies famine conditions, but not starvation, like the conditions of a city under siege.

Now, as a point of comparison, consider that Ruth collected an ephah of barley in a day's gleaning in Boaz's field (Ruth 2:17). An ephah is the old measure for a bushel (crudely equivalent), which is 32 quarts. Boaz, of course, directed her so that she would gather an above-average amount (Ruth 2:15-17). So she must've gleaned 2 or perhaps 3 times what she would've otherwise. This means an average day's gleaning (i.e. reduced by a factor of 2 or 3) would yield 10 to 15 quarts of barley. Since only the poor Israelites gleaned (the Law of Moses commanded farmers to leave some extra for the poor to glean [Lev. 19:9,10]), a person of not quite as humble circumstances faired at least as well—but not much better. Therefore, the lowliest working man's daily production would buy him 15 or 20 quarts of barley. Assuming equivalent productivity throughout ancient history, correlated to data from the Book of Ruth, the cherub commands the horseman to inflate the price of barley by a factor of 5 times over normal market conditions.

In estimating daily food prices and per-capita consumption in biblical times, Jesus feeding the 5000 is another supporting reference that provides quantitative data. John 6:9 enumerates the contents of a boy's lunch: 2 fish and 5 loaves of barley bread. The loaves must've been small, for he couldn't carry 5 large ones. The assumption is made that 1 cup of barley produces 1 small loaf of bread (the other ingredients in the bread are ignored for simplicity). Assume the 2 fish weighed 1 lb. apiece (0.90 kg total), and that the fish had been gutted and cleaned, yielding a net combined weight of 1 lb (0.45 kg). Based on an average of 125 calories per 100 grams, there were 550 calories in the fish. Each loaf would be 200 calories, so the lunch would have a grand total of 1550 calories. That's more than enough for a single meal. More likely it was a day's worth of food, enough to sustain him for the duration of Jesus' sermon, plus the trip from home and back, which might've been a good distance. In other words, this is probably what the boy typically ate in a day. The market value of the 2 fish was probably as much, if not higher, than the 5 loaves. Assume that the cost of 2 fish is equivalent to 6 loaves of barley. Adding the 6 to the 5 gives 11, and this would equal 2.75 quarts of barley. It's not unusual for people in developing countries to spend 75% of their income on food, therefore it's not unreasonable to assume that this was the case in ancient times. Again, using the same assumption as the previous example, a man must earn enough to support 1.5 people. So 75% of his wages go to feed 1.5 people. The boy counts for ½ a person (1/3 of the man's support), in this case, so 25% percent (1/3 of 75%) of the man's daily wages goes to feeding the boy (assuming the man works 7 days a week). Therefore 100% of the man's wages would be able to purchase 2.75 × 4 = 11 quarts of barley. Adjust this up to 13 (he doesn't earn money on the Sabbath but he still must pay for food), and a single day's worth of work (1 denarius) will earn the man 13 quarts of barley. This seems a conservative estimate, but nevertheless, the relative cost of barley for the father of this boy who had the 2 fish and 5 loaves is 4.3 times cheaper than the price established by the horseman.

These estimates, crude as they are, point to a 5-to-1 increase in the price of barley. People in modern, developed nations spend much less of a percentage of their income on food as do those in developing countries, and equivalently those in ancient times. A 5 times increase in the price of food, while painful, wouldn't sting as badly to those in industrialized nations. But a 5× across-the-board increase in goods and services would.

The horseman also sets the price of wheat. Its price is set at 3 times that of barley per quart. In modern times, flour is more commonly made out of wheat than barley, so the data is more comprehensible. Keep in mind that modern strains of wheat are different than ancient ones. Nevertheless, a cup of flour nowadays contains around 500-600 calories. Typically, one third of the wheat's weight is lost when converting it to flour. A standard bushel of wheat weighs 60 lbs (27 kg), and a bushel is 32 quarts. Since a cup of flour weighs around 4 ounces, and a quart of wheat weighs 1.88 pounds, a quart of wheat produces 1.24 pounds of flour, which is about 5 cups of flour. So 5 cups of flour, which comes from 1 quart of wheat, is 2500-3000 calories. This is not too far from the 2400 calories estimated for the barley, which, considering the crudeness of the estimates here, is somewhat coincidental in its accuracy. Therefore, the calories in a quart of wheat are roughly the same as for a quart of barley, meaning that the cost of wheat per calorie is 3 times greater than the cost of barley per calorie. If the cost of living dictated by the prices in 6:5 were computed based on the cost of wheat set therein, then a 3× factor would have to be multiplied by 5×. But it's assumed that the wheat prices are skewed, so they don't affect minimal sustenance calculations (in other words, folks would just buy barley and forgo wheat).

## Appendix B:
## Practical Difficulties of 6:13

> 6:13 and the stars of the sky fell to the earth, as a fig tree casts its unripe figs when shaken by a great wind.

Interpreting literally what John says about the stars falling to the earth, and, applying scientific analysis, does that mean that all the stars in the universe suddenly move in wild directions? More likely the stars disappear entirely, but without anyone actually seeing them shoot across the sky like a comet. The Greek tense for "fell" suggests this. To believe that the stars would actually drop to beneath the horizon in a few seconds, to display a falling motion to those watching from the earth, is precluded by the geometric challenges it imposes. The closest start is about 4 light-years away. For it to appear from earth to move across the horizon would necessitate that it travel at least that distance in a few seconds. The star would have to travel at over 100 million times the speed of light. This, of course, violates a few laws of physics right from the start, but signs and wonders by nature don't honor the laws of physics in the first place. From these facts one concludes that no one will actually see the stars falling, as John's analogy to the fig tree in 6:13 states, but they'll be there one moment and gone the next. How this is accomplished is a mystery. It could be a thick asteroid belt that wraps itself around the galaxy, obscuring the sight of anything beyond it. But no one will actually see them fall like Johns suggests—instead they'll just disappear all of a sudden.

Similar to the dilemma that the star's falling in 6:13 poses is the star that the Magi followed to discover the Christ child. That could not have been a star in the ordinary sense of the word. Some have said that God caused a supernova, and this was the star that lead the Magi to Jesus. Not true. First, Herod and his cohorts would've seen it, and would not have needed to inquire of the Magi where to find the Christ child (Matt. 2:1-12). The star was only visible to a select few, those who were pure of heart. But this is not the only issue: had the star been several light-years away, like stars normally are, like any other star it would've appeared to be at a fixed location, after taking into consideration the rotation of the earth on its axis and its revolving around the sun. To illustrate this, consider the North Star. Unlike other stars, it's not affected by the rotation of the earth. But it's always north, no matter where one is in the northern hemisphere; otherwise, it could not be used at night in lieu of a compass. The star that lead the Magi to Jesus guided them through city streets, so it must not have been that far away, relatively speaking. Matt. 2:9 says the star, "came and stood over the place where the Child was". More realistically it was hovering at the same height as a hot weather balloon, or even lower.

## Appendix C:
## The 144 Thousand from the Twelve Tribes

This appendix explores the implications of a literal interpretation of 7:4-8, which lists twelve tribes from which the 144 thousand are drawn. To understand this, one must recount some of the history of Israel. By Moses' time the tribe of Joseph had split into two, one named after each son of Joseph, namely the half tribes of Ephraim and Manasseh (Gen. 48:4-6). The inheritance in the Book of Joshua divides the land into twelve portions giving Ephraim and Manasseh equal portions in place of Joseph, with Levi dispersed among the tribes. The encampment of the tribes around the Tabernacle, specified in Num. 2, allocates slots for Ephraim and Manasseh, but not Joseph. In this encampment the tribes are partitioned into four divisions, each taking a point on the compass, one tribe dominating each point. The tribe of Ephraim is the dominant tribe on the western side of the Tabernacle; Manasseh is listed under Ephraim's banner. Jacob blessed Ephraim above Manasseh (Gen. 48:17-22). Several times Isaiah refers to the combined Northern Kingdom as Ephraim.

To see Manasseh along with Joseph listed in the seventh chapter of Revelation as one of the twelve tribes but with Ephraim omitted is unexpected. Furthermore, by the time Revelation was written, Moses and Jacob were as distant in time to John as the Middle Ages are to the twenty-first century. Much had transpired in the interim. Judah, the Southern Kingdom, had absorbed Simeon, which had been an enclave within Judea. Benjamin sided with Judah during the split between North and South; the kingdom of Judah thus consisted of four tribes: Judah, Simeon, Benjamin, and Levi. Of the tribes listed in Joshua's inheritance, when Israel was divided the remainder went with Samaria, the Northern Kingdom. Eventually the Assyrians conquered Samaria and took them into exile, never to return to the Promised Land. Some stragglers remained in the land, and by Jesus' time they were known as the *Samaritans*, following a corrupted form of Judaism. The northern tribes hence became known as the *Ten Lost Tribes of Israel*, ceasing to exist as a nation, having been absorbed and scattered. Taken captive by the Babylonians, Judah later returned to the land of Israel and reconstituted the nation. Hence, by the time of Christ only four of the original twelve could be traced back through the ages. Individuals descendent from three of the four (Judah, Levi, and Benjamin, but not Simeon) are mentioned in the NT. These formed the greater part of the Jewish diaspora, which started before the time of Christ's birth. By the writing of Revelation, there were Jews all over the Roman Empire, as noted in Acts and in the Epistles. There were likely more Jews outside Israel than in Israel by this time. They were almost entirely descended from the Southern Kingdom. Paul, a Benjaminite (Rom. 11:1; Phil. 3:5), was one such.

So by the time of John and Paul, only three of the original twelve tribes remained. With the passing of two millennia, tribal identity is confined to Jewish tradition which recognizes a few as descendent from Levi. The modern-day Jew has only a sliver of Hebrew blood still in him. Most Jews are of European descent, and therefore have Caucasian features. This agrees with the following simple mathematical analysis. Assume that there has been 2000 (rounded up) years from John to today, and that each generation is 25 years. This gives 40 generations. Looking at the race as a whole, if each generation suffers a 10% influx of non-Hebrew blood due to intermarriage, illegitimacy, or rape, then in the course of 40 generations the Jewish gene-pool would be comprised of a mere 1.48% (0.90 to the 40$^{th}$ power) Hebrew blood, the remainder being Gentile. A crude model, but the point is nevertheless demonstrated: the contemporary Jewish stock, especially those of European descent, have virtually no Hebrew blood in them. And this ignores the tribal dilution prior to the first century A.D.. And the little remaining is comprised mostly from three tribes, not twelve. How the 144,000 are gathered, 12,000 per tribe, is a mystery.

On the other hand, in order to fill the quota here in Revelation, in which three-fourths are non-Judean (i.e. descendant from the Southern Kingdom), it's not unreasonable to presume that at least some of the progeny of the Ten Lost Tribes contribute. Only God can trace their descendents, they having intermingled with other populations far and wide. But if 7:4-8 is to be taken literally, God would have to sort this out. Since this part of Revelation has not been fulfilled yet, this begs the question: how will God fill the quota of 12,000 per tribe? The commentators say that there are 144,000 Jews who become Christians, but that skirts the issue. There must be a logical method to determine if one of the chosen is, say, of the tribe is Issachar, in spite of the tribe's assimilation into the Assyrian Empire over 2,000 years ago. What method will God use? Father-to-son tracked over untold centuries? It's unlikely that present-day descendents of Issachar—difficult as that is to fathom—consider themselves Jews.

Maintaining the assumption that all the 144,000 will be converted Jews, how then are these Jews sorted by tribe? If a contemporary Jew has even a drop of ancestry from one tribe—and the chances are good that he would—does that make him eligible to be categorized as an offspring of that tribe, in spite of having a greater ancestry from another tribe? Revelation doesn't say the 144,000 are Jews, but it says that they're from the twelve tribes. In the light of the difficulty of ascertaining tribal identity, the constraint that they all be Jewish is not necessarily true. In any event 7:4-8 presents several questions, if one is to take it literally.

## Appendix D:
## Electronic Banking System Technology

The purpose of this appendix is to refute the claims made by many an end-times book that it was possible to build a mark-of-the-beast financial system (all-electronic financial transactions) in the 1980s, and even later. This appendix examines an isolated portion of the technology required by such a system.

What's necessary to build an all-electronic financial system? At a minimum, a worldwide network on the same scale as the Internet. It wouldn't have to carry as much traffic or be connected to as many subscribers, but the problems in scale are approximate. To implement a worldwide financial network with a minimum of technology, first it would have to be limited to traffic for financial transactions only, as the bandwidth could not be squandered on non-essential applications. By making this assumption, however, one is throwing out one of the basic design criteria of a practical system: cost feasibility. Other criteria that a bare-bones system jettison are reliability, security, and maintainability; without these any system would be intolerable. But a crazed government might foist a minimal system on the public.

A modern data network is comprised of routers, trunks, and access connections. Built in the 1980s the early routers used microprocessors to forward packets. The first Cisco router ran on a Motorola 68010 and was capable of 200 packets per second (pps). In a well-planned and designed network, this might've been increased to 1000 pps—but no more. It wasn't until the widespread introduction of label-switched routers (ATM), that this rate could be sped up (apart from the CPU speed increases). But herein lies another barrier: it wasn't until the late '80s and into the '90s that researchers devised the algorithms to solve many of the networking problems that were barriers to designing a large network. Label switching is just one of them. Sophisticated routing protocols are necessary to make the Internet operate. More on that later.

A modern Internet core router can switch more than 50,000,000 pps, and is smaller than a refrigerator. Scaling down the present-day Internet by 10-to-1 (the reduction by an order of magnitude reflects the exclusion of non-financial traffic on current Internet traffic), assume that a minimum 5,000,000 pps router is needed. This is a 5,000:1 increase in capacity from the mid 1980s router. Such an increase means that a router built in the 1980s to handle this volume of traffic would occupy an office building. As a modern network switching office contains many routers in a single room, the 1980s equivalent would be housed in a large warehouse. The electricity to power these machines is a fraction of the electricity to run the air conditioners to cool them. Furthermore, the complexity increases exponentially with size. When that many disparate components are aggregated into a single node, then the chances of a single failure increase. Plus, the traffic has to be distributed evenly among all the individual routers. There must be a means of taking routers in and out of service without disrupting traffic. All these problems are tackled in modern networks, but only because a tremendous amount of engineering is applied. Operating less-powerful equipment necessitates massive parallel processing. As the number of parallel routers increases, so too does the complexity of the software to manage these routers. A router must not only forward packets, but it must process control information.

Besides forwarding traffic, routers must maintain a routing table, a list of destinations to send traffic to. The Internet has (as of this writing) approximately ½ million destinations (*routes*). Each packet sent into an Internet core router can be sent to one of these ½ million routes. A router must examine each packet and decide where it goes. The routing problem was never tackled with the 1980s routers—they were never used on such large networks. The assumption that a bunch of small routers could be combined into one large router is erroneous from the get-go. The ½ million routes on the Internet are constantly changing, and the routers must keep up with the changes. Apart from the actual traffic, that's a chore in and of itself. This requires sophisticated algorithms embedded in routing protocols. Running these routing protocols on a live network consumes a lot of CPU power. Because a 1980s machine both forwards packets and updates the routing table using the same CPU, the pps rate would plummet; just ganging computers together wouldn't work with '80s technology.

Computer processing power is just one advance in technology over the years. Another is the invention of Application Specific Integrated Circuits (ASICs) and Field Programmable Gate Arrays (FPGAs). These are the engines that large, modern routers use to forward packets—not microprocessors. ASICs and FPGAs customized for the networking industry have caused quantum leaps in router pps rates and routing table capacity, more so than the increase in CPU power. Also thrown into the fray is a specialized memory chip called a Ternary Column Access Memory (TCAM). The Internet routing table is loaded into these specialized memories, and they do very fast routing destination look-ups, replacing label-switched systems. Comparing the Cisco 7200 to the Cisco 6500, the first a microprocessor based forwarding product, the second an ASIC-based product, both made in the same time period, the leap in routing capability from microprocessor to ASICs is an approximate 25-to-1 increase. This is why Internet routers weren't feasible until the '90s.

There are more things to consider when building a large network. Since the '80s, trunks (cables over which traffic flows) have been upgraded to fiber optics. The equivalent amount of cable that would have had to have been laid in the '80s—though huge—is not considered. The problems of bundling these cables together, then bundling them into routers, is also neglected—though it would also be in and of itself a massive problem.

To design and install a national network like the Internet in the '80s would be a project doomed to cost overruns, schedule overruns, etc. It would've taken years of planning, of close collaboration, and an army of engineers, including specialists that didn't exist in those numbers nor had the education and experience necessary to fill the positions. They would not have the benefit of modern software tools, analysis tools, simulation tools, email, word processors, or other things taken for granted in today's design environment. This would multiply the number of hours necessary to do the same task as today, and make collaborating on a grand scale much more difficult.

The computing industry, of which networking is one component, evolved through ideas contributed by many sources. Though there has emerged industry-wide standardization of operating systems, programming languages, protocols, etc., there's been little restriction on who can contribute to and influence the direction of networking technology. This vibrant atmosphere of research guided by experience has made manageable the complexities of large networks and interconnected computer systems. The protocols in current use on the Internet evolved through the lessons learned from previous generations of protocols. These didn't mature until the early to mid '90s. Without such innovations it would've been difficult in some cases, impossible in others, to fulfill all the requirements of a large-scale network. Absent well-designed standards and computing solutions, computing power and network bandwidth are not sufficient to build a viable network.

And this is just designing the network for the mark-of-the-beast-system. This doesn't include the computing, application, or access infrastructure needed in the banking industry, or the hardware required by every retailer in the country. Similar arguments can be made for these systems. The point of this essay is to prove that, in spite of countless books written over the years, replacing cash transactions with electronic ones was, from a technological point of view, not only difficult but impossible.

## Notes

1 Unless otherwise noted all quotations are from the NASB.

2 Quotations from the book of Revelation itself appear simply as chapter and verse number, omitting the book name.

3 Quotations from books are given by author name, not title name. See *References* for title names.

4 Scripture appearing in double-quotation marks is a verbatim extract from a verse, usually recent; italics used otherwise.

## Abbreviations

| | |
|---|---|
| *KJV* | King James Version |
| *NASB* | New American Standard Bible |
| *NT* | New Testament |
| *OT* | Old Testament |
| *UBS* | United Bible Society |

## References

Bullinger, E.W. *The Companion Bible*. Original publication 1923.
Bury, J.B. *The Invasion of Europe by the Barbarians*. W. W. Norton & Compay, 2000.
*The Children's Bible*. Joseph A. Grispino, Joseph A., Terrien, Samuel, Wice, David H. Wice, editors. Golden Press, 1965.
Gibbons, Edward, Womersley, David P. *The History of the Decline and Fall of the Roman Empire*.
Grosvenor, Mary, Zerwick, Max. *A Grammatical Analysis of the Greek New Testament*. 5th Revised Edition. Editrice Pontificio Isitituto Biblico, 1996.
Johnson, Paul. *A History of Christianity*. Touchstone, 1995.
Lewis, C.S. *The Lion, the Witch, and the Wardrobe*. HarperCollins, 1994.
Metzger, Bruce. *Breaking the Code: Understanding the Book of Revelation*. Abingdon Press, 1993.
Summers, Ray. *Worthy is the Lamb*. Broadman Press, 1951.
UBS. *The Greek New Testament*. 3rd Edition. Biblia-Druck GmbH, 1983.
Wuest, Kenneth. *Word Studies in the Greek New Testament*. Wm. B. Eerdmans Publishing, 1980.

# Scripture Index

*number-number* refers to chapter number (*part-chapter*)

| | | | |
|---|---|---|---|
| 3-17 | Gen. 1:16 | 3-7 | Exod. 29:18 |
| 2-2 | Gen. 3:15 | 3-11 | Exod. 30 |
| 3-28 | Gen. 3:16-19 | 2-9 | Exod. 32:1 |
| 1-5 | Gen. 3:24 | 2-9 | Exod. 32:9 |
| 3-26 | Gen. 3:21 | 1-7 | Exod. 34:15 |
| 3-28 | Gen. 3:24 | 3-7 | Lev. 6:12 |
| 2-5 | Gen. 4:10 | 3-11 | Lev. 6:13 |
| 3-7 | Gen. 4:10 | 2-7 | Lev. 10:1 |
| 2-2 | Gen. 6:1 | 3-18 | Lev. 11 |
| 3-15 | Gen. 6:14-16 | 3-18 | Lev. 11:13 |
| 1-9 | Gen. 6:4 | 3-18 | Lev. 11:16 |
| 3-7 | Gen. 8:20 | 3-25 | Lev. 11:13 |
| 3-19 | Gen. 9:1 | App-A | Lev. 19:9,10 |
| 1-7 | Gen. 9:20-27 | App-C | Num. 2 |
| 3-19 | Gen. 10:10 | 2-7 | Num. 4:15,7 |
| 3-27 | Gen. 10:2 | 1-7 | Num. 25 |
| 3-27 | Gen. 10:5 | 1-7 | Num. 25:2 |
| 3-19 | Gen. 10:8,9 | 3-9 | Deut. 6:8 |
| 3-19 | Gen. 11:1 | 3-9 | Deut. 11:18 |
| 3-19 | Gen. 11:4 | 3-21 | Deut. 22:13-29 |
| 3-19 | Gen. 11:6 | 3-10 | Deut. 28 |
| 3-19 | Gen. 11:7 | 3-17 | Deut. 28:1 |
| 2-9 | Gen. 18:16 | 3-28 | Deut. 28:15 |
| 1-7 | Gen. 19:37 | App-A | Ruth 2:17 |
| 3-7 | Gen. 22:9 | App-A | Ruth 2:15-17 |
| 3-17 | Gen. 37:9 | 2-7 | 2 Sam. 6:6 |
| App-C | Gen. 48:17-22 | 2-7 | 1 Chron. 15:1 |
| App-C | Gen. 48:4-6 | 3-22 | 2 Chron. 5:13 |
| 2-3 | Exod. 7:13 | 2-9 | 2 Chron. 20:7 |
| 2-3 | Exod. 7:22 | 2-4 | Job 1:10 |
| 2-3 | Exod. 8:19 | 2-4 | Job 1:4,5 |
| 2-3 | Exod. 9:12 | 2-4 | Job 1:9 |
| 3-9 | Exod. 13:9,16 | 2-4 | Job 2:9 |
| 1-12 | Exod. 18 | 3-28 | Job 38:8-11 |
| 2-10 | Exod. 19 | 3-6 | Ps. 22 |
| 1-2 | Exod. 19:16 | 3-6 | Ps. 22:12 |
| 3-18 | Exod. 19:4 | 3-1 | Ps. 33:3,40 |
| 2-5 | Exod. 20:5 | 3-1 | Ps. 40:3 |
| 3-21 | Exod. 23:17 | 3-21 | Ps. 75:8 |
| 3-15 | Exod. 25:8 | 3-28 | Ps. 89:9 |
| 3-28 | Exod. 28:29 | 3-21 | Prov. 9:2,5 |
| 3-9 | Exod. 28:38 | 1-6 | Prov. 10:15 |

| | | | |
|---|---|---|---|
| 3-10 | Prov. 14:11 | 3-23 | Matt. 12:43 |
| 3-3 | Prov. 22:13 | 2-6 | Matt. 13:47 |
| 3-13 | Isa. 1:16,17 | 3-26 | Matt. 18:20 |
| 1-12 | Isa. 1:2 | 3-21 | Matt. 20:22,23 |
| 2-3 | Isa. 6:8 | 2-2 | Matt. 24 |
| 2-9 | Isa. 38:1 | 3-15 | Matt. 24:15-26 |
| 3-18 | Isa. 40:31 | 3-18 | Matt. 24:28 |
| 2-9 | Isa. 41:8 | 2-2 | Matt. 24:37 |
| 1-3 | Isa. 52:7 | 2-6 | Matt. 25:32 |
| 3-28 | Isa. 57:20 | 2-6 | Matt. 25:34 |
| 1-12 | Ezek. 1:4 | 2-6 | Matt. 25:32,25 |
| 3-14 | Ezek. 3:1 | 2-5 | Matt. 27:25 |
| 3-9 | Ezek. 3:8-9,9 | 3-6 | Mark 1:12 |
| 3-9 | Ezek. 9:4 | 3-6 | Mark 1:13 |
| 3-27 | Ezek. 38:2 | 3-25 | Mark 1:23 |
| 3-15 | Ezek. 39 | 2-8 | Mark 3:28-30 |
| 3-15 | Ezek. 40 | 2-3 | Mark 4:12 |
| 3-15 | Ezek. 40:3 | 2-3 | Mark 4:10 |
| 3-15 | Ezek. 43:4 | 3-28 | Mark 5:25-34 |
| 3-23 | Dan. 2:31 | 3-28 | Mark 10:46-52 |
| 3-9 | Dan. 7:2 | 2-5 | Mark 11 |
| 3-19 | Dan. 7:2 | 3-8 | Mark 11:23 |
| 3-15 | Dan. 9:27,11 | 3-15 | Mark 13:14 |
| 3-18 | Dan. 12:1 | 3-15 | Mark 15:38 |
| 3-8 | Hos. 10:8 | 2-2 | Mark 16:16 |
| 3-8 | Joel 2 | 3-14 | Luke 1:19 |
| 3-8 | Joel 2:31 | 3-18 | Luke 10 |
| 3-8 | Joel 2:31 | 2-10 | Luke 10:12 |
| 3-15 | Mic. 7:19 | 3-12 | Luke 10:18 |
| 3-1 | Zech. 1:18 | 3-18 | Luke 10:17 |
| App-B | Matt. 2:1-12 | 2-5 | Luke 11:47 |
| App-B | Matt. 2:9 | 2-5 | Luke 11:50 |
| 3-4 | Matt. 5:11 | 3-18 | Luke 13:16 |
| 3-7 | Matt. 5:10 | 1-8 | Luke 16:8 |
| 1-1 | Matt. 5:31,32 | 2-2 | Luke 17 |
| 2-10 | Matt. 5:38 | 2-5 | Luke 20:9-18 |
| 2-10 | Matt. 5:38-44 | 3-15 | Luke 21:24 |
| 3-9 | Matt. 6:22 | 2-10 | John 1:16 |
| 3-10 | Matt. 6:30-34 | 3-5 | John 2 |
| 2-8 | Matt. 8 | 2-3 | John 6:44 |
| 2-8 | Matt. 9 | App-A | John 6:9 |
| 2-10 | Matt. 9:15 | 1-2 | John 21:18-23 |
| 2-8 | Matt. 9:36 | 1-12 | Acts 1:11 |
| 2-8 | Matt. 10 | 3-2 | Acts 1:8 |
| 2-8 | Matt. 10:1 | 1-9 | Acts 2 |
| 2-8 | Matt. 10:14,15 | 2-3 | Acts 2:21 |
| 3-18 | Matt. 12:26 | 3-28 | Acts 3:19 |
| 2-8 | Matt. 12:31,32 | 2-7 | Acts 5 |

| | | | |
|---|---|---|---|
| 1-7 | Acts 6:5 | 3-26 | 1 Cor. 14:29 |
| 3-28 | Acts 10 | 1-2 | 1 Cor. 14:8 |
| 1-12 | Acts 10:10 | 3-6 | 1 Cor. 15:32 |
| 2-10 | Acts 12:20-25 | 1-10 | 1 Cor. 16:9 |
| 1-8 | Acts 15:30-33 | 1-10 | 2 Cor. 2:12 |
| 3-25 | Acts 19 | 2-10 | 2 Cor. 3:6 |
| 2-10 | Acts 23 | 3-14 | 2 Cor. 3:7 |
| 1-10 | Acts 23:12 | 1-9 | 2 Cor. 4:13 |
| 2-4 | Rom. 1 | 2-27 | 2 Cor. 5:10 |
| 2-4 | Rom. 1:18 | 3-15 | 2 Cor. 6:16 |
| 1-10 | Rom. 2:28,29 | 1-10 | 2 Cor. 12:7 |
| 1-8 | Rom. 3:5 | 1-2 | Gal. 1:15 |
| 2-2 | Rom. 6:4 | 1-4 | Gal. 1:2 |
| 1-5 | Rom. 8 | 1-8 | Gal. 1:8,9 |
| 1-8 | Rom. 8:27 | 2-10 | Gal. 4:21-31 |
| 3-1 | Rom. 8:26 | 3-28 | Gal. 4:24 |
| 3-1 | Rom. 8:27 | 3-28 | Gal. 4:26 |
| 3-16 | Rom. 8:36 | 3-17 | Gal. 4:4 |
| 2-3 | Rom. 9:10 | 2-2 | Gal. 5:2 |
| 2-3 | Rom. 9:13 | 3-29 | Gal. 6:11 |
| 1-3 | Rom. 10:15 | 3-23 | Eph. 1:19 |
| 3-1 | Rom. 10:6 | 2-3 | Eph. 1:5 |
| 3-12 | Rom. 10:7 | 1-8 | Eph. 4 |
| App-C | Rom. 11:1 | 1-9 | Eph. 5:14 |
| 2-10 | Rom. 12:19 | 3-1 | Eph. 5:19 |
| 3-1 | 1 Cor. 1:2 | 3-1 | Eph. 5:2 |
| 3-1 | 1 Cor. 2:10 | 3-7 | Eph. 5:2 |
| 3-1 | 1 Cor. 2:9 | 1-3 | Eph. 6 |
| 1-8 | 1 Cor. 5 | 3-17 | Eph. 6 |
| 2-10 | 1 Cor. 5:4,5 | 3-3 | Eph. 6:16 |
| 1-8 | 1 Cor. 5:5,11 | App-C | Phil. 3:5 |
| 3-15 | 1 Cor. 6:19 | 3-7 | Phil. 4:18 |
| 3-1 | 1 Cor. 6:2 | 3-10 | Phil. 4:19 |
| 3-12 | 1 Cor. 6:9 | 3-23 | Col. 1:26,27 |
| 1-1 | 1 Cor. 7 | 1-10 | Col. 4:3 |
| 1-5 | 1 Cor. 7 | 2-10 | 1 Thess. 4:6 |
| 3-21 | 1 Cor. 7:34 | 1-2 | 1 Thess. 5 |
| 1-7 | 1 Cor. 8 | 3-12 | 1 Thess. 5:9 |
| 3-10 | 1 Cor. 9:7 | 2-10 | 2 Thess. 1:6 |
| 2-10 | 1 Cor. 10:1-11 | 2-10 | 1 Tim. 2:4 |
| 1-7 | 1 Cor. 10:8 | 1-3 | 1 Tim. 2:5 |
| 2-10 | 1 Cor. 11:29-32 | 1-9 | 2 Tim. 1:7 |
| 1-2 | 1 Cor. 12 | 2-10 | 2 Tim. 4:14 |
| 1-8 | 1 Cor. 12 | 1-3 | Heb. 4:12 |
| 3-18 | 1 Cor. 12:10 | 3-27 | Heb. 6:1 |
| 1-12 | 1 Cor. 12:2 | 1-7 | Heb. 6:4-8 |
| 1-12 | 1 Cor. 12:2,3 | 2-7 | Heb. 7:25 |
| 1-2 | 1 Cor. 12:3 | 3-7 | Heb. 8:4,5 |

| | | | |
|---|---|---|---|
| 1-2 | Heb. 9:28 | 3-7 | 1 Pet. 4:12 |
| 2-5 | Heb. 9:22 | 3-7 | 1 Pet. 4:14 |
| 3-7 | Heb. 9:24 | 3-7 | 1 Pet. 4:15 |
| 3-26 | Heb. 9:28 | 2-10 | 1 Pet. 4:4 |
| 2-2 | Heb. 11 | 2-10 | 1 Pet. 5:18 |
| 2-5 | Heb. 11:4 | 2-2 | 2 Pet. 2:4 |
| 2-2 | Heb. 11:7 | 2-10 | 2 Pet. 2:9 |
| 1-8 | Heb. 12:16 | 1-1 | 1 John 1:10 |
| 2-3 | Heb. 12:16 | 1-1 | 1 John 1:8-10 |
| 2-10 | Heb. 12:18 | 2-5 | 1 John 3:12 |
| 2-5 | Heb. 12:24 | 1-1 | 1 John 3:4-9 |
| 3-7 | Heb. 13:11-13 | 1-1 | 1 John 3:6 |
| 3-13 | James 2:17 | 3-1 | 1 John 5:14 |
| 2-4 | James 5:11 | 3-25 | 1 John 5:21 |
| 3-4 | 1 Pet. 1:4 | 2-2 | Jude 6 |
| 3-1 | 1 Pet. 2:9 | 1-7 | Jude 11 |
| 2-2 | 1 Pet. 3:18 | 2-5 | Jude 11 |
| 2-10 | 1 Pet. 3:8 | 2-2 | Jude 14 |
| 3-7 | 1 Pet. 4:1 | | |

# Index

144,000, 142, 168, 178, 180, 224, 226
666, 173, 174
Aaron, 86, 87, 90
Abel, 79, 80, 97, 124
Abomination of Desolation, 153
Abraham, 23, 90, 91, 123, 131, 135, 163
abyss, 140, 141, 143, 156, 172, 193, 194, 205, 207
Achan, 87
active judgment, 68, 76, 92, 137
afterlife, 13
Ahab, 29
altar, 62, 79, 122, 123, 124, 137, 138, 144, 153, 184, 186
Anabaptist, 56
angel, angels, 11, 14, 15, 18, 101, 105, 132, 137, 140, 143, 144, 147, 148, 149, 154, 158, 181, 182, 183, 184, 186, 187, 188, 190, 193, 196, 197, 199, 204, 205, 206, 215, 216, 217
Antioch, 10, 26
Antipas, 22, 95
apocalypse, 5
Apostles, 27, 48
archers, 113, 114
Artemis, 121, 196
associative judgment, 78
B-2, 164
Baal, 23, 24, 29, 30
Babel, 43, 172, 191
Balaam, 22, 23, 24, 26, 27, 29
Baptism in the Holy Spirit, 111, 112
barley, 119, 120, 221, 222, 223
beast, the, 122, 156, 160, 168, 169, 170, 171, 172, 173, 178, 182, 183, 185, 186, 187, 189, 193, 194, 195, 196, 200, 205, 206, 209
beasts, 50, 114, 120, 121, 122, 169, 170

Belshazzar, 37
Benjaminite, 225
binary judgment, 82, 84
bishop, 14, 15, 22
Boeing, 175
Book of Life, 38, 209
Brazen Altar, 124
brimstone, 145, 182, 205, 209, 212
bronze, 11, 12, 113, 151, 191, 192, 198
Bullinger, E.W., 50, 55, 85, 172
Bury, J.B., 117
Cain, 23, 79, 80, 82
Canaan, 23, 24
Charismatic movement, 112, 203
Charles Lindbergh, 174
cherubim, 18, 49, 50, 112, 119, 120, 122, 205, 207, 214, 221
Children's Bible, The, 121, 231
China, 118, 187
communion, 86, 109, 122
crown, 20, 42, 112, 114, 115, 143, 158, 160, 183
Dagon, 84
Daniel, 4, 7, 104, 135, 149, 153, 155, 162, 167, 169, 170, 191
Dante's *Inferno*, 102
David, 2, 22, 59, 70, 71, 84, 85, 91, 103, 106, 121, 211, 217, 231
delegate judgment, 89
demon, 22, 41, 46, 47, 140, 144, 145, 160, 162, 163, 164, 187, 189, 196
Didache, 15, 30
dragon, 159, 160, 161, 162, 163, 164, 165, 166, 167, 168, 169, 171, 178, 187, 189, 205
eagle, 50, 167, 169
earth-time, 101, 102, 129, 145, 155, 162, 196, 200
Egypt, 31, 61, 65, 69, 77, 88, 128, 129, 157, 173, 185, 193
Einstein, 101

elder, 15, 103, 134
Elijah, 156
Enoch, 53, 54, 58
environmentalism, 34
Ephesus, 8, 9, 10, 14, 16, 17, 18, 30, 38, 121, 161
Ephraim, 224, 225
Esau, 30, 63, 64, 211
Euphrates, 144, 187
Europe, 116, 117, 118, 192, 231
Exodus, 61, 77, 80, 151
Ezekiel, 4, 10, 11, 49, 50, 132, 149, 150, 151, 152, 153, 208
F-117, 164
forehead, 132, 133, 141, 142, 173, 174, 178, 179, 182, 190, 206, 215
fornication, 24, 26, 27, 30, 63, 146, 180, 182, 190, 191
free will, 40, 61, 62, 64, 68, 69, 91, 127, 202, 208
Gabriel, 147
Garden of Eden, 18, 214
Genesis, 4, 18, 30, 38, 43, 53, 58, 80, 144, 172, 191, 201
Gentile, 31, 126
Gibbon, Edward, 95
Gnosticism, 16
God's sovereignty, 63, 64, 65, 107, 127, 195, 202
Gog and Magog, 207, 208
gold, 11, 15, 44, 90, 105, 116, 137, 143, 144, 145, 183, 185, 189, 191, 192, 193, 198, 213, 214
Govnet, 177
Great City, 43, 157
Great Tribulation, 133, 135, 136
Greek words
  agape, 39
  angelos, 14
  aphiami, 17
  apokalupsis, 5
  diabolos, 165, 205
  eidoluthuta, 24, 25, 30
  en pneumati, 8
  iaspis, 47
  kata, 100

kronos, 31
mā klaie, 103, 104
machaira, 12
mustarion, 190
peirazo, 16
phila, 39
porneia, 182
rhomphaia, 12, 13, 21
sard, 47
stephanos, 20, 42, 160
Hades, 13, 92, 120, 122, 209, 210
heavens, the, 45, 46, 102, 124, 129, 130, 139, 156, 159, 163, 172, 204, 210, 223
heaven-time, 101, 102, 129, 145, 155, 162
hell, 13, 46, 54, 55, 91, 93, 102, 116, 140, 144, 147, 165
Herod, 92, 129, 224
holiness, 9, 11, 18, 48, 50, 85, 86, 87, 98, 110, 148, 158, 180, 202, 209
Holy of Holies, 123, 154
homosexuality, 75, 76
horns, 104, 105, 144, 159, 160, 168, 169, 170, 171, 189, 193, 194, 195
hoshen, 213
Huguenots, 73
hyperbole, 142
in the Spirit, 8, 9, 46, 97, 110, 111, 162, 180, 189, 212
incense, 87, 105, 110, 137, 138, 198
India, 118, 188
Internet, 177, 227, 228, 229
iron, 11, 12, 113, 143, 146, 161, 169, 191, 192, 193, 198, 204
Isaiah, 66, 67, 68, 91, 225
Israel, 9, 22, 23, 24, 25, 27, 30, 31, 37, 48, 68, 69, 70, 71, 73, 77, 78, 84, 85, 87, 90, 92, 95, 97, 98, 105, 111, 124, 126, 133, 135, 142, 147, 149, 151, 152, 155, 159, 160, 161, 162, 164, 166, 168, 170, 180, 208, 213, 221, 224, 225

237

Jacob, 30, 63, 65, 88, 133, 159, 211, 225
James, 72, 147, 230
jasper, 47, 213, 214
Jehovah Jireh, 176
Jerusalem, 10, 37, 42, 43, 70, 77, 84, 96, 105, 111, 126, 132, 152, 153, 154, 155, 157, 210, 211, 212
Jethro, 47
Jewish apocryphal literature, 26
Jezebel, 29, 30, 32, 35
Job, 72, 210
Joel, 128, 129
Johnson, Paul, 95
Joseph, 88, 133, 224, 225, 231
Josephus, 172
Jude, 23, 53, 54, 58, 59
Judgment Seat of Christ, 209
Korah, 23
Lake of Fire, 21, 205, 209, 210
lampstand, 14, 15, 17, 156
Laodicea, 19, 38, 39, 43, 44, 45
Law of Moses, 4, 18, 41, 56, 57, 85, 87, 94, 95, 97, 110, 124, 136, 151, 180, 181, 196, 221
Law of Sin and of Death, 18
Lewis, C.S., 123
liberal theology, 16, 28, 32
life after death, 13, 92, 93, 120, 193, 207
lighting, 9, 31, 48
*Lion, the Witch, and the Wardrobe, The*, 123, 231
locusts, 141
Magi, 129, 224
Manasseh, 133, 224, 225
Marriage Supper of the Lamb, 136, 202
martyr, 8, 79, 95, 124, 127
Max & Mary, 22, 43, 45, 46, 134
Maxwell's Equations, 63
Mercy Seat, 124
Mesopotamia, 172, 173
Methuselah, 55
Metzger, Bruce, 9, 112, 143, 210, 231
Michael, 147, 163, 164, 166

Midianites, 23, 24
Moab, 23, 24
*Moby Dick*, 114
moon, 128, 129, 158, 159, 214
Morning Star, 34, 35
Moscow, 208
Moses, 85, 97
Mt. Sinai, 9, 48, 97, 98
Mt. Zion, 42, 97, 178
mythology, 131
Nephilim, 59
Netherlands, 73
new song, 106, 177, 178
New York City, 188
Nicene Creed, 7, 27
Nicolaitans, 22, 26, 27, 35
Nimrod, 172, 173
Noah, 24, 53, 54, 55, 56, 57, 58, 59, 60, 91, 100, 110, 123, 131, 150, 208
North Star, 224
Numbers, 24, 26, 28
olive oil, 119, 198
Parable of the Sower, 45, 66
Parthians, 112, 113, 114
passive judgment, 68, 72, 73, 75, 76
Pax Romana, 115
Pennsylvania, 39
Pentecost, 36, 77, 89, 128
Pentecostal, 46, 112
Pergamum, 21, 22, 26, 27, 28, 29, 30, 35
persecution, 10, 19, 20, 21, 22, 39, 94, 95, 96, 100, 104, 116, 117, 125, 126, 127, 136, 137, 138, 161, 162, 165, 166, 167, 171, 206
Persians, 37, 113, 192
phalanx, 113
Pharaoh, 61, 62, 65, 66, 77, 87, 131
Pharisees, 78, 80, 94, 207
Philadelphia, 39, 41, 43
Pittsburgh, 141
Plague, the, 120
Planck, 63
Potiphar, 88

predestined judgment, 68, 91, 110, 127, 129
priest, 7, 86, 94, 110, 123, 124, 154, 179, 180, 185, 206
prophecy, 15, 21, 34, 38, 41, 43, 47, 54, 55, 60, 64, 71, 90, 92, 98, 102, 109, 112, 115, 118, 121, 122, 126, 127, 128, 129, 153, 155, 156, 161, 175, 202, 203, 208, 215, 216, 217
prophet, 15, 23, 30, 76, 91, 126, 128, 156, 187, 200, 205, 209
Protestants, 73, 95, 196
proxy judgment, 78, 79, 80, 81, 124, 146
Rahab, 41
real-time, 101
Rehoboam, 69, 70, 71
rhomphaia, 28
right hand, 12, 14, 100, 104, 148, 173
Roman Catholic Church, 15, 27, 95, 116, 179, 196, 197, 200
Roman Empire, 9, 10, 12, 13, 15, 20, 58, 78, 113, 115, 116, 117, 118, 124, 170, 179, 192, 193, 194, 196, 197, 199, 200, 206, 225, 231
Russia, 208
Samuel, 84, 85, 231
Sardis, 35, 36, 37, 38, 39
Satan, 19, 22, 26, 33, 41, 46, 72, 109, 121, 140, 148, 159, 160, 161, 162, 163, 164, 165, 166, 171, 172, 177, 195, 205, 206, 207, 208
scroll, 9, 10, 15, 100, 102, 103, 104, 107, 109, 110, 111, 130, 137, 149, 150, 216
seal, 101, 112, 115, 118, 119, 120, 122, 124, 127, 128, 129, 132, 133, 137, 141, 142, 155, 157, 179, 216
Second Coming, 7, 54, 118, 204, 219
Semitic, 3, 4, 84, 93, 132, 142, 147
Sermon on the Mount, 95, 125

seven Spirits of God, 36, 104, 105
Smyrna, 18, 19, 20, 21, 39, 43, 44, 126
Sodom and Gomorrah, 54, 59, 68, 89, 90, 91, 92, 128, 145
Solomon, 69, 71, 106
son of man, 10, 11, 53, 149, 151, 183, 202, 208
Spanish Inquisition, 161
spiritual death, 13, 21, 36
star, 34, 129, 140, 217, 223, 224
stars, 12, 33, 35, 129, 139, 158, 159, 160, 223, 224
steel, 11, 12, 141, 146, 192
Summers, Ray, 14, 148, 189
sun, 13, 128, 129, 130, 132, 135, 147, 158, 159, 186, 204, 214, 215, 224
Sutton, Hilton, 178
sword, 12, 18, 21, 98, 113, 115, 120, 170, 171, 203, 205
Tabernacle, 86, 105, 123, 124, 137, 151, 152, 180, 224
Ten Commandments, 48
tent, 62, 85, 135
Tertullian, 8
*The Grapes of Wrath*, 183
Theory of Special Relativity, 101
thief in the night, 28, 37, 57, 58, 177, 219
Thracians, 12
thunder, 9, 48, 97, 112, 148, 158, 178, 188, 201
thwarted judgment, 90
Thyatira, 29, 30, 32, 33, 34, 35, 65
Tree of Life, 18, 214, 215, 217
tribulation, 15, 19, 114, 115, 134, 135, 136, 155, 208
Trinity, 6, 11, 15, 27, 47, 51, 103, 104, 105, 107, 109, 179, 190
trumpet, 9, 12, 96, 144, 146, 155, 202
Tyre, 30, 92
*UBS Greek New Testament*, 170
Uzzah, 85
virgin, 179, 196
vulture, 167

Western, 3, 4, 45, 78, 84, 112, 147, 167, 204
wheat, 119, 120, 183, 198, 221, 223
Whore of Babylon, 181, 182, 189, 190, 191, 193, 194, 195, 196, 197, 199, 200

wine, 119, 182, 184, 188, 189, 196, 198, 204, 221
Wuest, Kenneth, 161
Zechariah, 4, 79, 104, 149, 152, 153, 156

www.ingramcontent.com/pod-product-compliance
Lightning Source LLC
Chambersburg PA
CBHW061636040426
42446CB00010B/1444